The Language
of Store Planning
& Display

The Language of Store Planning & Display

Martin M. Pegler, ASID & ISP

Fairchild Publications
New York

Franko Agüero, Illustrator
Janet Solgaard, Designer

Standard Book Number: 87005-403-1

Library of Congress Catalog Card Number: 81-69663

Printed in the United States of America

Preface

Once upon a time life was easy and uncomplicated. Lawyers studied law, accountants learned to account and plumbers did plumb. In those halcyon, bygone days, displaymen displayed. Armed with tacker and straight pins, loaded down with crepe paper, felt, and ribbon streamers, he walked into the show window and turned the giant fishbowl into a Valentine candy boxtop filled with frills. So what if the merchandise was drowned and lost in all that frill—it was a pretty sight! But, times have changed. Lawyers do more than just study law, accountants do account and do other things as well and plumbers are now "sanitation engineers." Displaypersons—no longer "displaymen"—are *visual merchandisers*. They are store planners and are immersed in the business of merchandise presentation. The displayperson still uses the tacker and straight pins, but that is only one small facet of the complex business of showing merchandise.

Today's displayperson is no longer a "window trimmer." Many stores are de-emphasizing the display windows and are stressing the point of purchase—the place where the action is—at the counter—on the rack—on the feature table. The white line that has separated "display" from "store planning" for so long, is now a faint, finely dotted line, and passing from one side of the line to the other is not only permitted, but it is encouraged.

The Language of Store Planning & Display is compiled as an aid to a person entering the fields of store planning and/or display, or an aid to someone already established in these fields who is trying to understand the special language spoken within them.

The terms defined in *The Language of Store Planning & Display* are, at the same time, foreign and familiar, broad and specific. They are in English, French, Spanish, and sometimes only a mysterious grouping of capital letters separated by periods, or a nonsensical word that is an acronym for a mouthful of technical terms, or a chemical formulation. They are words spoken and readily understood by carpenters, joiners, wallpainters and scenic artists, architects and interior designers, lighting experts, and sound specialists. It is the working language of buyers and merchants, landscape gardeners and artificial foliage salespeople, building contractors, fashion designers and illustrators, graphic artists and sign printers. The terms found on specification sheets for construction, read in the fashion releases of *Women's Wear Daily* and *Vogue*, heard on the selling floor and around the conference table where promotions are planned and where sales figures are discussed. They are shouted across the store and unearthed from where they are buried in contracts, leases, and order forms. Thus, this language of merchandise presentation, which is store planning plus display, is an amalgam of the jargons of many trades, professions and crafts, all of which are, in one way or another, involved in the designing and producing of merchandise, the wholesale buying of merchandise, the storing, promoting and showing of merchandise, and the eventual selling of merchandise. Since the "housing" has become so important in today's retail scene, and since the "housing" is also the ambiance or selling environment, today's displayperson, also known as store planner or merchandise presenter, has become involved in and indispensable to every aspect of the retail operation.

THE SCOPE OF THE TERMS

The terms defined in this book are taken from the following areas:

1. Joinery and Carpentry
   - A. Hand tools
   - B. Power tools
   - C. Techniques
   - D. Materials
2. Stage Design
   - A. Set construction and painting techniques
   - B. Lighting techniques and devices
   - C. Materials
   - D. Fabrics
3. Lighting
   - A. Electrical terms
   - B. Light sources: fixtures, bulbs, etc.
   - C. Techniques
   - D. Accessories
4. Fixturing
   - A. Merchandisers
   - B. Displayers
   - C. Counter units
   - D. Wall units
   - E. Ledge units
   - F. Free-standing floor units
   - G. Systems
   - H. Construction details
   - I. Materials and finishes
   - J. Accessories
5. Mannequins
   - A. Types
   - B. Measurements
   - C. Construction details
   - D. Materials and finishes
   - E. Accessories
   - F. Non-mannequins: forms, torsos, etc.
6. Graphics and Signage
   - A. Color
   - B. Line and design
   - C. Pigment and media
   - D. Printing techniques and materials
   - E. Graphic art techniques
   - F. Type and typeface styles

Since so many fields and professions are involved, where it is helpful, I have indicated in which field or profession the term is most applicable. As an example, those terms that are relevant to lighting for the store interior and the selling floor will be prefaced with *In store lighting*. When the description is more relevant to stage or display window lighting, the preface will read *In theatrical or window display lighting*. Some terms may have several different applications, or in other cases, the same *word* is used in more than one area. In these instances, each definition is prefaced with the trade or field to which that particular meaning applies.

Some basic information is supplied that was learned long ago and soon thereafter forgotten, because we never thought we would need to use it. For example, under *circle, rectangle, square*, and *triangle* you will find geometric formulas for determining area, perimeter, volume and other theorems, now often needed. A series of charts appears in the back of the book covering the major periods and styles of furniture in France, England, and the United States. These charts give dates, major characteristics of the periods, popular types of furniture, woods, fabrics and colors, and the major art forces in effect at the time.

Many types of displayer and merchandising fixtures are described and illustrated, but these are "generic" descriptions and drawings and are not meant necessarily to represent a specific manufacturer's product. Where trademarks are given, I have specified, when information was available, the owner of the trademark or copyright. Some descriptions are broad rather than specific, because many variations are possible within the framework of the term, and to be specific would be to limit the reader's comprehension.

Changes in the industry are being made all of the time. There are always new developments, new refinements and improvements. The *language* of *store planning* and *display* keeps growing and expanding, becoming more sophisticated and complex. Visual merchandisers must be aware of the whole world, and even outer space. In windows, in cases and on ledges, the display personnel interprets the world we live in—the arts, culture—the daily headlines—trends—fine arts—opera and ballet—books and cartoon strips—the pop, punk and new wave scenes. The displayperson must be aware of everything that is going on, because fashion is a reflection of the world we live in, and everything that is going on in the world.

1981   Martin M. Pegler
                                                                               New York

Acknowledgments

A book does not get "written" by one person. One individual may write down thousands of connected words, but the contents—the concepts—the ideas—are usually contributed by many. These definitions are not necessarily my own. They are colored and shaded with the subtle variations and opinions of others.

The author has culled and compiled these thousands of words and terms from texts, magazines, articles, advertisements, and from conversations with display directors and store carpenters. I have combed through many brochures and booklets in search of the elusive expressions that are part of the *language* of the *store planner* and the *display person*. I have spoken to the manufacturers of the products used in this field, and to the end users of these products always listening for those special words and their special meanings.

There are so many people who "contributed" to this book and there is no way I can thank or credit them in the space allowed. I am grateful to the following for their contribution to this edition: Laurence Fuersich, Retail Reporting; Robert Gordon and Jerry Schoenfeld, Leo Prager, Inc.; Louis Bernstein and Martha Landau, Greneker/Wolf & Vine; Ralph Oestreicher, D.G. Williams, Inc.; Pamela Gramke, *Visual Merchandising* Magazine; Natalie Deutz, Barbizon School of Fashion Merchandising; Marvin Dorfman, National Association of Display Industries.

My special thanks to Hugh T. Christie, chairman and professor of the Display and Exhibit Department at the Fashion Institute of Technology, for carefully editing this edition for accuracy.

Also to some "super astute" displaypeople and very special store planners: James Siegler, Joseph Hoppe, Jean Gazabat, Martha Birmingham, Roxanne Sway, Salvatore Marra, Ron Nelson, Robert Mahoney—and so many more. To Jerry Gerard for his faith, trust and support.

And to the people at Fairchild Publications who recognized the value of this type of book and are aware of the importance of "Merchandise Presentation" and "Display" as an integral part of the ever changing field of fashion merchandising: Ed Gold, Angelo Virgona and Olga Kontzias.

A

ABRASION RESISTANCE The ability of a material to withstand the wear and tear of scraping, rubbing, friction or erosion on the surface. An important factor in selecting the material and finish on fixtures, flooring, wall surfaces, etc.

ABRASIVE Any substance such as emery board, sandpaper and steel wool used to smooth, grind, or even cut out a surface.

ABS A generic term for a strong, *thermoplastic* alloy with the special quality of being able to be chrome plated. It has good heat resistance, is slow burning and has great dimensional stability. Available in sheet form and as molding pellets or molded parts. It can be heat-formed, laminated, fabricated; joined by means of nails, screws, rivets and staples. Used to make inexpensive, chromelike displayers and decorations.

ABSTRACT DESIGN An art expression in which the artistic value resides in the forms and colors rather than in the reproduction or presentation of subject matter. It is the appreciation of line, pattern and color disassociated from theme. It does not imitate or represent directly an external reality.

ABSTRACT MANNEQUIN A highly stylized mannequin (male, female, child), usually without features, wig and/or makeup details; nonethnic, ageless, and finished in a variety of decorative colors, materials or metallics. Though based on human measurements and proportions, the shaping and sculpting is not realistic but strives instead for a decorative, nonobjective effect.

ABSTRACTA SYSTEM Trademark for a connector and tube system. The connectors are precision made of a metal alloy in eight configurations and have a fine tolerance. The tubes are ½″ O.D. heavy gauge steel and are available in special lengths. The connector legs are tapered to permit the joining tube to be centered and to lock tightly when driven in flush to the shoulder. The system is available in polished chrome (plated) and matte black (modified epoxy enamel). Structures can be easily assembled and the interchangeability of components permit modifications in existing units. Used for setting up fixtures, merchandisers and even "walls." Produced by Abstracta Structures, Inc., New York.

AC (ALTERNATING CURRENT) An electric current that reverses its direction of flow, usually at 60 cycles per minute. See *DC.*

ACCESSORY COSTUMER See *costumer* and *draper.*

ACCOMMODATION DESK A centrally located desk or counter to aid and service customers.

ACCORDION PLEATS Narrow and straight folds in fabric or in another material that resemble the continuous in and out folds of an accordion.

A continuous pattern of V-shaped creases similar to a fan.

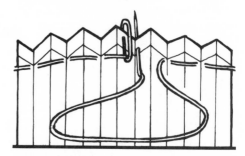

ACCESSORIES Parts that help to create the total look of an outfit or ensemble such as shoes, gloves, hats, bags, scarves, stockings or costume jewelry. Automobile accessories would include tires, seat covers, hubcaps, special horns, hood ornaments and decorative appliqués.

ACCRUED EXPENSES An accounting term for expenses that are yet to be paid. Bills for those expenditures that have not been received or recorded, but will be coming due in the near future. An important consideration in planning and working within a budget.

ACETATE A generic term for fibers, threads, yarns and fabrics made from cellulose acetate. Acetate fabrics drape well and accept dye well, but do not resist abrasion. See *cellulose acetate.*

ACHROMATIC A term referring to black, white and gray. The "colors" that are not really colors.

ACOUSTICAL MATERIALS (TILES) Assorted materials used to (1) enhance the production of sound or reduce the volume of the sound produced; (2) increase insulation; or (3) conceal poor ceilings or walls. Materials are made into tiles and are applied to ceilings or walls. Materials used include pulped wood, compressed styrofoam pellets, asbestos, fiberglas or any combination. Perforated tiles have greater sound absorption qualities.

ACOUSTICS The phenomena of sound and the control of sound. The ability of sound to carry in an area, as well as the ability to baffle or tone down sound.

ACRILAN Acrylic fibers made from acrylonitrile. Acrilan fibers have a soft, wool-like feel, are strong, crease resistant and stable. Used in clothing and carpeting. Trademark of Monsanto Textiles.

ACRYLICS A group of clear plastics that are nontoxic, have optical clarity, and are capable of a high transmission of light. They can carry light, unseen, from one edge to another through straight, bent or curved surfaces or fibers. Available in sheets, fibers, rods, molding pellets and in resin form; tinted and colored (translucent to opaque); in a wide range of colors. Acrylics have high impact strength and are slow burning, can be worked easily; cut, drilled, heat-bent, cemented together, painted and polished by sanding. Acrylics are produced under various trademark names: Fiberglas (Rohm & Haas), Acrylite (American Cyanamide Co.), Lucite (E.I. du Pont de Nemours) and Perspex (Imperial Chemical Industries, Ltd.).

ADAPTATION Adjusting, amending or altering the scale or proportions of a design to suit another use or purpose. Making necessary changes to fit a design into a new location, within a new period or into a new material.

ADAPTER A connecting device that makes it possible to join two elements of different sizes or designs.

ADDITIVE See *admixture*.

ADJACENT STOCKROOM A term used in store planning for the space directly behind the selling area that holds the reserve stock, or the working stock. Also called the forward stockroom.

ADMIXTURE Any substance other than the aggregate, cement or water that is added to concrete or plaster, which affects the properties of the concrete or plaster. It might be an accelerator (to hasten hardening), a plasticizer (to increase workability or spreadability), a coloring agent, a water repellent, etc. Also called additive. See *aggregate*.

ADOBE The clay bricks, as well as sundried bricks, made and used in Mexico and the southwestern part of the United States for building or facing materials.

A-FRAME A term used in fixturing to describe the vertical sides of a rack or gondola resembling an inverted "V" with a horizontal crossbar. The raked angle at the bottom gives more rigid-

ity to the unit and the crossbar reinforces the legs. Similar to a sawhorse in appearance.

AGATE LINE A standard measurement in printing and advertising to describe the depth of columns in advertising and editorial space. Fourteen agate lines equal one inch of column depth.

AGGREGATE The material added to concrete, plaster, asphalt, etc., such as broken stones, sand, slag, gravel and marble chips. Also see *admixture.*

AGORA The Ancient Greek version of a shopping center, market-place, downtown shopping street or open air flea market where merchandising took place.

AIR BRICK A brick that is perforated with air holes which permit air to enter and circulate through a wall. Used in construction.

AIRBRUSH A small mechanical, pencil-like device with an adjustable nozzle that works like a gun to spray paint by means of compressed air. Used to obtain tone or graduated tone effects in artwork and on photographs.

AIR CONDITIONING The controlling or modifying of the air in a structure by making it warmer or cooler (the usual connotation), drier or more moist, mobile or static. In warm air heating, cold air is heated and circulated. Air conditioning may be the removal of moisture from the air.

AIR CURTAIN A term used in store architecture for the streams of high velocity, conditioned air which create a warm air barrier between the cold air outside and the warm air inside. Resists outside drafts and eliminates the need for a vestibule and the waste of valuable main floor selling space.

Requires open air grills overhead and directly below in the floor (a hazard for women's heels).

AIR DUCT A term used in store architecture for a passageway, pipe or enclosed channel made of metal, plastic, etc. Used for ventilating an area. Ducts are usually suspended from the ceiling and often require camouflage or cosmetic treatment. See *plenum.*

AIR RIGHTS The restrictions or zoning laws as set by a local government on the size, shape and height of a structure, and the amount of unused or unfilled space that must be left around that structure. May limit the signing above the building, as well as any extensions or superstructures that might be planned. See *building line.*

AISLE An open walking space between areas of merchandise or otherwise filled spaces in store layout and design. A passageway with entrances to the side areas. The minimum width of aisles in public buildings is usually determined by fire laws and building codes. Often signing and display platforms will face towards the aisle or walk-through space on a selling floor.

AISLE LINERS Light-looking, feature fixtures that are placed next to the traffic aisle on a selling floor. They carry a few garments and show merchandise "face-out" or front forward and often accessorized. A T-stand is a traditional aisle liner. A costumer or valet could be used as an aisle liner. New designs are appearing in the fixture market that show a choice selection and do not block the view or the entry into the area beyond the aisle. See *costumer, T-stand* and *valet.*

AISLE TABLE A promotional or feature table set in an aisle for impact selling. See *promotional table.*

ALABASTER A milky white, semitranslucent, marble-like material usually used for sculpture and ornamentation. It is rarely used an an external facing for a building, but is quite handsome on interior walls.

ALCOVE A recessed area of a room or a smaller room or enclosed area attached to a larger one that can only be entered by going through the main area. Originally, a bay or small space separated from the main room by a semi-partition, curtain, screen, etc.

ALDER (RED) A maple-like, American hardwood that can be stained to simulate mahogany or walnut. It is quite strong and often used for plywood cores.

ALENÇON LACE The "queen" of French handmade needlepoint lace that dates back to the 17th century in Alençon, France. Currently machine-made. The design, usually floral, is outlined in heavy thread on a fine net ground.

A-LINE SILHOUETTE A trapeze shape that flares out gently from the shoulderline to the hemline in an unbroken sweep. Introduced in 1955 by Christian Dior.

ALLEN WRENCH A six-sided metal rod (about ³⁄₁₆″ in diameter) with a right-angle bend at one end. This simple tool, about $3″ \times 3″$, is used to secure and tighten recessed head screws. Also called a hex wrench.

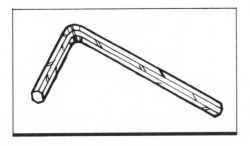

ALLOVER PAINTINGS Designs that are painted over a total surface without any groupings of colors or forms to create a special point of interest or central focal area. They are usually painted in a uniform manner and right up to the framing edge. This is typical of Jackson Pollock's work, and the later paintings of Monet.

ALLOY A metal produced by a mixture of two or more metals. See *pewter* and *bronze*. In the plastics industry, the blend of polymers or copolymers with other polymers or elastomers.

ALPACA A llama-like mountain animal of South America and the hard, shiny-surfaced fabric made from the wool of the Alpaca. The alpaca wool is sometimes mixed with silk, sheep wool or cotton.

ALTERNATING CURRENT See *AC*.

AMBIENCE The overall effect of the surroundings; the "look"; the atmosphere. The image created in a store, department, etc., by the combination of color, line, form, textures, lighting, decoratives, etc. See *amenities* and *image*.

AMENITIES The gracious parts of an architectural design. The parts that satisfy and gratify the aesthetics of the structure. The "image-makers" of the architecture: landscaping, plazas, walks, fountains, sculpture, benches, vistas and paintings. The environmental elements. See *arcade, arbor,* etc.

AMORTIZATION The process of paying off the cost of an item (building expense, special fixtures, mannequins, etc.) over a period of years, while enjoying the use of the item. Planning the use of an item with a proposed life of two, three, four, or more years, and deducting each year from the budget for the use of that item—until the item is completely paid for. A bookkeeping technique.

AMPERE The unit of measurement used to indicate the intensity of the flow of an electrical current through an electrical circuit. It is based on the flow resulting from one volt of pressure against one ohm of resistance.

AMPERSAND The symbol "&" for the word "and." A corruption of the term "and per se" (and by itself). Symbol is derived from the early scribes writing the Latin "et" for "and."

ANAGLYPH From the Greek word for "raised ornament." A design, ornament or decoration sculptured or embossed in low relief, such as a cameo. It is not as low as bas relief or as deep as high relief. Also called mezzo-rilievo.

ANAGLYPTA A raised ornament such as can be applied to walls and ceilings. In the past it was made of gesso and plaster compounds, but today it is produced of rag stock. The rag stock is liquefied, poured into forms and molded. The resulting raised decorations are similar to "composition ornament."

ANALOGOUS COLORS Colors that are next to each other, or neighboring, on the traditional color wheel: orange, red-orange, red, yellow, yellow-green, yellow. An example of an analogous color scheme would be red, red-violet, violet and violet blue.

ANCHOR-LOK SYSTEM Trademark for a modular system that uses round or square, ½-inch, #18 gauge steel tubing, connected by means of seven different Anchor-Lok fittings. These fittings are basically cubes with varying numbers of "fingers" or projections attached. The elbow has two pro-

jections at right angles to the cube, the tee has three projections, the cross has four projections, etc. The tube slides over these fingers, is then tapped, and is locked into place. The system is available in "triple plate chrome," satin bronze, and black. Assorted accessories for shelves, panels, leveling and coupling units are available. Produced by the Kason Fixture Ware Division, Binghamton, New York.

ANCHOR STORE The major retail store used to draw or attract consumers to a shopping center or mall. The retailer can be a tenant or the landowner or developer of the mall. Other stores will fill in around this feature attraction.

ANGEL'S HAIR Finely spun glass, often white, in long, lustrous, silky fibers that resemble floss, silk yarn, or "hair." Used for fantasy mannequin wigs, snow, clouds, or wherever a soft, puffy effect is desired. It can be an irritant and some people are allergic to the material.

ANGEL SLEEVE A long, loose sleeve flowing from the shoulder into a wide open end.

ANGLED FRONT A storefront that does not run parallel with the sidewalk, but angles in toward the entrance door or doors. The result is an oblique set of display windows.

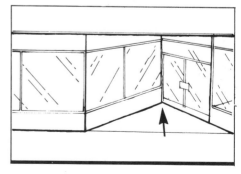

ANGLE IRON An L-shaped metal bar that forms a right angle. Used as a reinforcing agent in construction and fixturing.

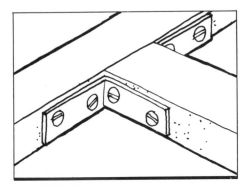

ANGORA The soft, fluffy yarn made from the fleece of the angora goat. Used to produce mohair.

ANILINE DYES Paints, inks, and dyes prepared from coal tar and mixed in an organic solvent such as alcohol, esters, ketones, and ethers. Usually brilliant, sharp, transparent dyes of high intensity and pureness of chroma.

ANIMAL GLUE The oldest type of glue made from the hides, hoofs, and bones of animals—often horses. Used on wood. It is strong, but has poor moisture resistance. It sets by drying and will become brittle as it ages and because of the thick glue line, it is best for loose-fitting joints.

ANIMATED DISPLAYS Mechanized displays. Wood, papier-mâché, or fiberglas forms or figures that are articulated, mechanized and wired to perform a desired movement or series of movements. The animation can be powered by electricity or self-contained batteries.

ANKLE ROD The short, upright bar that extends up from the floor base and inserts into the fitting above the mannequin's ankle. It is the usual way of keeping male mannequins upright, and is also desirable for female mannequins that "wear" pants. It is almost invisible and usually does not require the opening of any seams for the insertion of the supporting rod. Also see *base flange, butt rod* and *foot spike*.

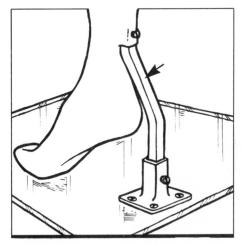

ANNEX An auxiliary structure created or designed to function as an addition to or in conjunction with an existing building or business. It does not have to be attached or even be adjacent to the main building, but there are decided advantages in the proximity between an annex and a main building.

ANODIZED A term used to designate a metal, usually aluminum or magnesium, which has been given a protective film or coating, often colored, by electrolytic means.

ANTIQUE FINISH An artificially created patina or aged effect on wood, metal, etc. It is often accomplished by applying a light coat of a darker shade of paint or stain over a lighter shade (or a lighter shade over a darker shade) and rubbing off the excess paint leaving a vary-tone finish which looks "old." Wood can also be "antiqued" by gouging, fly-specking, nicking or distressing.

APPAREL A broad term for clothing (suits, dresses, separates) and the appropriate accessories.

APPEAL The "attraction" or the "look" that will bring about a desired response or a sale. Usually a call to a specific taste level or to a particular type of customer.

APPLIQUÉ A design or motif that is cut out and sewed or pasted onto the surface of another material as a decorative trim. An applied decoration. A layered or superimposed ornament.

APRON *1. In store layout and design* The floor of the display window extending beyond the proscenium or valance frame of the window. The floor area between the actual glass line and the frame or border line. *2. In furniture construction (as illustrated)* The structural part of a table or chair directly beneath and at right angles to the table top or chair seat. In case furniture it is the perpendicular face beneath the lowest drawer. *3. In architecture* The protective covering, usually of lead or zinc, which covers the joint where the roof and the chimney meet.

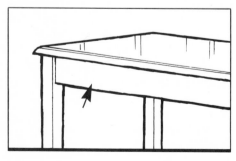

APTON SYSTEM One of the first square tube and joint systems used in store planning and fixturing. The Apton system uses square tubing of various lengths with "finger" projecting connectors of many configurations, which allow two to six tubes to connect at a single junction. Originally, it was available only in a baked black enamel finish, but it is now produced in other colors and in a chromeplated finish. The tubes vary from 1″ to 2″ in width and are available up to 8′ in length. Assorted accessory clips and devices are produced to enhance the use of this system. Also called dexion.

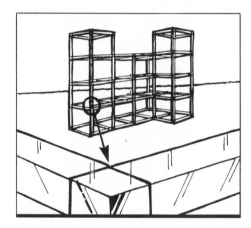

AQUARELLE A true watercolor painting produced by using transparent colors and water. The surface that is painted on is reflected through the applied paint and affects the tonal quality of the painting. It also refers to a printed picture which is colored with watercolors, by hand, but the paint is applied through stencils.

AQUATINT A form of intaglio etching that produces tones instead of lines. It produces an effect similar to a watercolor. In intaglio etching, the ink lies in the engraved furrows of the metal plate, rather than on the smooth surface.

ARABESQUE The complicated ornamental designs based on plant growth fancifully intertwined with lines and geometric patterns. A rhythmic, scroll-like pattern or design used by the Moors who were prohibited by their religion from representing animal forms.

ARBITRATION The presentation and eventual decision on matters in dispute between two or more parties. The problem in question is discussed and argued before an impersonal arbitrator (or arbitrators) who has been selected and agreed upon by all the parties concerned.

ARBOR, ARBOUR A bower, retreat or passageway usually formed by a lattice framework that supports climbing plants or vines.

ARCADE *1. In architecture* A series of arches and their supporting columns or piers that usually support a roof, wall or superstructure. A covered walk or passageway between two rows of arches, or between a row of arches and a wall or building. *2. In store planning* A walkway between shops or stores.

ARCADED FRONT A store front in which the display windows may be L- or Z-shaped, and the store entrance is set back from the street. This type of front allows the shopper to come in off the street and "window shop" in an enclosed and protected area. An island window may sometimes be included in this type of store front arrangement.

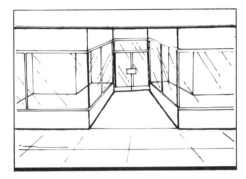

ARCH A self-supporting structure composed of bricks or stone blocks and capable of carrying a superimposed load over an opening. A semi-circular or arched structural element which spans an opening and can support a weight above that opening.

ARCH BRICKS The wedge-shaped bricks used in the construction of an arch. Also called a voussoir.

ARCHITECT The designer, detailer, specifier, and sometimes superviser and/or engineer in the erection of buildings and other structures, usually degreed and licensed. From the Greek word for "master builder."

ARCHITECTONIC A term that refers to the architectural qualities found in nonarchitectural designs such as a window display, a piece of sculpture, a painting or graphic design.

ARCHITECTURAL TERRA COTTA Hard-burned clay building blocks, which are usually larger than regular bricks. Available glazed or unglazed, plain or decorated.

ARCHITECTURE "The art which so disposes and adorns the edifices raised by man—that the sight of them contributes to his mental health, power and pleasure." John Ruskin.

ARCHITRAVE The lowest of the three main divisions of the Classic Entablature. It supports the frieze, and rests upon the columns. It is the equivalent of a lintel. See *lintel.*

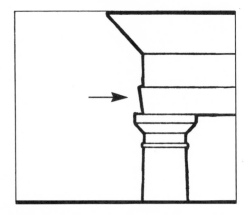

ARC LIGHT An electric light source. A voltaic arc between the ends of two carbon rods supplies the light. The term is often misapplied to any brilliant light.

AREA WALL A surrounding wall of brick, stone or concrete, or a retaining wall around below grade or basement windows.

ARENA The enclosed playing area or stage in the center of an amphitheater. The performing or showing area usually surrounded by seats—in a round or oval structure. From the Latin word for "sand." Originally applied to the sand-covered area where gladiator contests were held.

ARGON ARC WELDING See *welding.*

ARM A horizontal attachment or appendix on a vertical unit. A right-angled projection.

ARMATURE *1. In construction* The metal bars or rods or the internal skeleton or framework that supports or gives strength to a light or delicate structure such as a piece of sculpture or a paper construction. The bars may be made of other rigid materials. *2. In store display* The skeleton upon which the original clay sculpting of a mannequin or form is formed. The metal frame inside a molded form or the bendable and shapable skeleton in the "stuffed doll" type of mannequin.

ARMOIRE From the French word for a large, movable closet or wardrobe. Originally used to store armor. Today, it refers to any large cabinet with doors in which merchandise can be hung. It is not unusual for the cabinet to have a shelf or two to stack folded garments. In furniture, the armoire is comparable to the "chifferobe," which is a combination closet and drawer unit.

ARMORED CABLE See *BX cable.*

ARNEL A soft, drapable, crease-resistant fabric made from triacetate yarns and fibers. Trademark of Celanese Corporation of America.

ART DECO According to Bevis Hillier, "an assertively modern style, developing in the 1920s and reaching a high point in the 1930s; it drew inspiration from Art Nouveau, Cubism, the Russian Ballet, American Indian art and the Bauhaus. It ran to symmetry and the rectilinear." An applied art form rather than a fine art form, it found its greatest expression in decorating movie houses, ocean liners, skyscrapers, and hotel interiors of the 20s and 30s. Repetitive geometric lines and forms in bands and tiers.

ARTICULATED FORMS Forms similar to, or the life-sized variations of, the artist's wooden mannequins that can be repositioned into many different, life-like poses. Forms or mannequins with articulated or movable joints (elbows, wrists, knees, hips, tor-

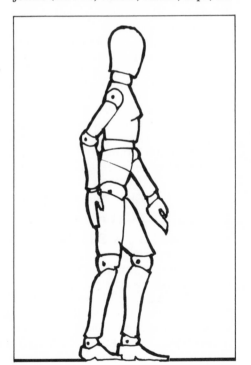

sos) that can be swivelled or turned into new positions.

ARTIFACTS Ancient materials or objects produced by man.

ARTIST'S PROOF The approved proof of an etching or engraving pulled when, in the artist's opinion, the plate is prepared and ready for the printing of the design. The criterion and standard for the projected printing.

ART NOUVEAU The "new art" of the 1890s in Europe and America strongly influenced by Gothic and Japanese art forms. A decorative art of flat patterns of twisting, whiplash, plant forms. Used in architecture, art and home furnishings. Some of the famous practitioners of Art Nouveau were: Aubrey Beardsley, William Morris, James Ensor, Horta, Van de Velde, Hector Guimard and Antonio Gaudi.

ARTYPE See *dry transfer*.

ASBESTALL Fire-resistant fabrics woven of asbestos and nylon yarns. Trademark of The U.S. Rubber Co.

ASBESTOS A noncombustible mineral fiber. It can be woven, with other fibers, into flameproof fabrics. It can also be pressed and shaped into rigid cemented sheets that can act as flame-retarding shields. Asbestos, though brittle, is noncorrosive and impervious to rain and rot. Currently falling into disfavor due to the respiratory diseases associated with prolonged exposure during the production of asbestos fibers.

ASCENDER The part of a lower case letter that extends above the body of the letter, such as the top part of the vertical stroke in "b," "h," or "t." See *descender*.

ASCOT A cravat or scarf, double knotted, with wide flat ends that are folded over and held in place with a stick or scarf pin. A wide kerchief or scarf, folded over and worn inside an open-collared shirt. Originally worn by 19th-century gentlemen with cutaway jackets.

ASH A blond or light-colored wood with an interesting grain that stains well. It is a very hard wood and not easy to work.

ASHLAR The pattern on masonry walls or facades of buildings created when squared stone blocks, usually with smooth faces, are laid in regular and even courses (rows) with clean, straight jointing.

"AS IS" A term used to describe irregular or damaged merchandise that is offered for sale at a greatly reduced price.

ASPEN A light-colored, soft, easy to work, American wood. It has a natural sheen and a silky texture, and the crotch cut is particularly decorative.

ASPHALT A black, tar-like material that can be melted and poured. Used in street and road paving as "asphalt concrete."

ASPHALT TILE A floor covering material, which is available in tile form in thicknesses ranging from $1/8$ to $3/8''$. It is fairly flame-resistant, fade-resistant, nonporous and easy to maintain though it can be ruined by grease and oil. Affected by extreme changes in temperature—becomes soft under great heat or very brittle with severe cold. The tiles can be laid on wood or concrete floors.

ASSEMBLAGE ART A broad term to cover all "composite art," three-dimensional collages, or collage sculptures which are created from pre-formed, natural, or manufactured nonart materials. Also called junk sculpture or combine painting.

ASSESSMENT The adjudged or appraised value of an item as set down by experts, assessors, usage or "supply and demand." Important in determining insurance rates and replacement values, e.g. a borrowed antique prop which is "misplaced" or broken.

ASSISTANT BUYER See *buyer*.

ASSOCIATED MERCHANDISING The coordination and presentation of "go together" merchandise in a particular shop without reference to which department buys which item. It could refer to showing shoes, bags, gloves, scarfs and hats in a special accessory shop, yet use the stock from the various departments that usually buy and sell those items. A selling technique used in boutiques and "shop-within-a-shop."

ASSORTMENT DISPLAY A display presentation that includes an example of every style or design carried in a particular store or department, such as the window displays in popular-priced shoe chains that are loaded with the hundreds of styles plus bags, hosiery, etc.

ASTRAKHAN A crinkly, curly fur of the karakul lambs from Astrakhan in Russia. Also designates a type of men's or women's hat made from broadcloth or karakul fur, or an imitation thereof.

ASTRAKHAN CLOTH A curly looped, heavy pile fabric that simulates Karakul fur. Used to trim coats and suits.

ASTYLAR A building facade that is without visible or exposed columns, pillars or masonry piers.

ASYMMETRICAL The opposite of symmetrical. Unequal. Not evenly balanced or proportioned. A favorite decorative line design during the 18th-century Rococo period.

ATELIER From the French word for a "workshop" or "studio." Usually associated with designers, artists or craftspeople.

ATMOSPHERE LIGHTING The use of light and shadow, and sometimes color filters, to create a specific mood or feeling in a display or in a selling area, restaurant, entrance, etc. See *back lighting* and *cove lighting.*

ATRIUM An open-air garden or court surrounded by rooms or selling areas. In some contemporary structures, a glass ceiling covers the atrium to offer protection from rain and snow and to control heat without detracting from the feeling of openness and light. In classical structures, the central room or the open courtyard of a home or public building partially or completely open to the sky.

ATTITUDE SHOP A fashion-wise, trendy or avant-garde shop or department which features the newest in "looks."

AUBERGINE A deep purple color. From the French word for "eggplant."

AUBUSSON A flat, uncut pile rug that is woven like a tapestry. The motifs are usually floral and scroll designs. This type of carpet is usually used to create an 18th-century French ambience especially when combined with Rococo or Neo-Classic French furniture. Named for the French tapestry works in the town of Aubusson, France, which date back to the 15th century.

AU COURANT The newest, trendiest, most current fashions and fashion accessories.

AUDIENCE The special customer or shopping group to whom the retailer is making his appeal. Also see *appeal.*

AUDITORIUM A large meeting place, hall or theater enclosure usually provided with seats (which may be movable or removable). Ideally designed for maximum visibility of the presentation area and with good acoustics.

AUGER BIT A spiraling or corkscrew-like boring bit available in a variety of diameters from $\frac{3}{16}''$ to $2''$. Used in conjunction with a brace to bore holes of a specific diameter. The diameter of the bit is the same as the desired hole and the spiral also serves to carry the shavings out of the hole as the boring tip descends. See *brace* and *bit.*

AUGER BIT

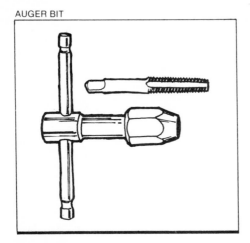

AVANT GARDE The most advanced, radical, up-to-date or extreme styles, art forms, or ideas at a particular time.

"AVERAGE GROSS SALE" The total dollars of all sales (the gross) divided by the number of sales needed to make up the gross figure.

AWL A pointed instrument. Used for punching small holes or marking surfaces.

AWNING A device used on exteriors to shield an open area or window surface from sun, rain and snow. Usually of canvas or any other dense fabric or vinyl material. Originally, a panel attached to the frame above the window and sloped down and out—away from the wall and window—to carry the rain and snow away from the building line. It may also be a sunshield or a decorative, temporary roof over a patio, arbor or entrance-door. Also used to add color and pattern to a facade, to cut down on window glare, or to camouflage a dull window construction.

AXMINSTER A tightly woven, cut-pile rug of unlimited colors, styles and patterns. Originally produced in Axminster, England, in the mid-18th century.

AXONOMETRIC A three-dimensional representation of a structure showing the plan and elevation, in a true and measurable scale, and how they appear and are joined together. It is not a perspective drawing which would show the relationship as seen by the human eye, but a working drawing for a designer or architect. Usually drawn at a 45° angle. See *isometric* and *oblique drawing.*

B

BABUSHKA From the Russian word for "grandmother." A peasant's brightly colored wool scarf tied under the chin and favored by the older country women. When a cotton or lightweight silk scarf is used and tied in back (at the nape of the neck) it is called a *"platok."*

BABY SPOTLIGHT A small, useful spotlight with a 4½" to 5" planoconvex lens for a 250 to 400 watt lamp. In many cases it has been replaced by the 6" Fresnel lens, 500 watt spotlight which is more efficient. See *Fresnel-type lens.*

BACK FIXTURE A fixture that displays merchandise and reserve stock and is located behind a counter serviced by a salesperson.

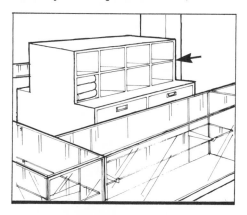

BACK LIGHTING The atmospheric lighting used behind the display or display area. See *atmosphere lighting* and *cove lighting.*

BACK PROJECTION See *projection.*

BACK SAW A short, fine-toothed saw reinforced along its back edge with an additional metal rib. It has a high tooth count (ten to twelve per inch) and is often used in conjunction with a miter box to produce clean, accurate angled cuts. See *miter box.*

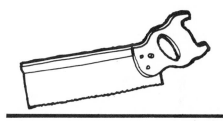

BAFFLE Louvers, grids, screens or any devices used to divert or direct the flow of air, light, attention or even human movement. A redirecting barrier.

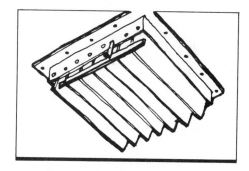

BAFFLE LIGHT See *cove lighting.*

BAGGED Merchandise that arrives at the store prepackaged and is presented on the selling floor "bagged," such as shirts, bras and hosiery. It may require merchandisers with special clips, hooks or clamps to accommodate the merchandise and the packaging. See *blister packaging*.

BAGHEERA A rough, crush-resistant, fine, uncut pile velvet.

BAKED ENAMEL A painted, varnished or lacquered surface which has been given a final drying in an oven or under great heat to insure a hard and lasting glossy finish. Any coating which resembles enamel and has been baked or heat-dried.

BAKELITE Trademark of Union Carbide Corporation for one of a group of thermo-setting plastics.

BAKER'S RACK A large, floor-standing, open shelf unit with ladderlike sides. Based on a design used by 19th century French bakers. Usually the baker's rack is made of wrought iron, painted black and trimmed with brass balls and finials as well as scrolls and swirls. The ladderlike sides made it possible to raise and lower the shelves

which are stretched between the uprights. More contemporary versions are made in chrome, brass, stainless steel, wicker and/or rattan.

BALACLAVA A heavy woolen helmet, usually knitted, that covers the entire head and leaves only the face exposed. Worn by soldiers in World Wars I and II, but named after Balaclava on the Crimean coast of Russia—the scene of the Charge of the Light Brigade in 1854.

BALCONY A platform, either cantilevered or supported, projecting out from a wall, from the facade of a building or over part of an auditorium.

BALLAST The electrical device that supplies the proper voltage and current to start and operate a discharge lamp (such as a fluorescent fixture). The most common is the electromagnetic type which is typically the "little black box" mounted inside the luminaire. Certain lamp types have "solid state" ballasts. See *luminaire*.

BALL BEARING A device designed to support and locate rotating shafts or parts, to transfer the load between rotating and stationary parts and to permit free rotation with a minimum of friction. The device is composed of

rolling elements (small round beads or balls of metal or plastic) interposed between an inner and outer ring. Sometimes separators or retainers are spaced between the rolling elements. The device is then sandwiched between the stationary member (usually the upright) and the part which will revolve (the flat or horizontal plane). For example, a "lazy susan."

BALLOON SKIRT A voluminous, full skirt which starts out cinched at the waist, flares at the hips and is narrow and banded at the hemline. Similar to the look of the "harem skirt" but without a center slit.

BALLOON SLEEVE See *melon sleeve.*

BALL PEEN HAMMER A metal-headed hammer with one end flattened into the traditional striking surface and the other end rounded into a ball-like protuberance.

BALMACAAN Originally a Scottish tweed or gabardine man's overcoat, loose and flaring, with raglan sleeves.

BALUSTER A turned spindle used as an upright support; may be part of a balustrade. Usually a wood turning.

BALUSTRADE A continuous railing or ornamental fence made up of a series of balusters.

BAMBIN, BAMBINO HAT A hat with a large, upturned brim that frames and surrounds the face in a halo-fashion. It was popular in the 1930s and named after the haloed Christ child plaques of Luca Della Robbia.

BAMBOO A woody, tall and thin tropical plant whose distinctive nodular stem is used for display settings and for furniture or ornaments. The look of the bamboo stalk is reproduced in metal and plastic. A very popular ma-

terial that suggests the Orient and the jungles.

BAMBOO TURNING Wood or metal rods that have been given the nodular or ringed look of bamboo stalks. A popular look in furniture and interior decoration.

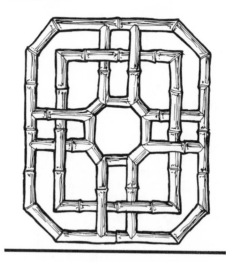

BAND *1. In architecture* A plain or molded flat strip or string course running horizontally across the face of a building or wall. *2. In furniture or interior decoration* A narrow strip of veneer or a painted line used as a border or edging trim on table tops, cabinet doors, etc.

BANDANA PRINT From the East Indian word for "tie-dye"—Bāndhnū. Large silk or cotton scarf designs with brilliant patterns or dots on darker backgrounds.

BAND COLLAR A small, soft, stand-up collar that is not notched or slit. Similar to the "mandarin collar" but it is not split and sits closer to the neck.

BANDEAU A headband, veil or hair tie.

BAND SAW A mechanical saw in which the cutting teeth are on a continuous metal band which runs over two wheels. Used for cutting curves, scrolls and irregular patterns. It is limited to outside cutting and will work on pieces only as large as its throat (the open space behind the exposed blade) will accept.

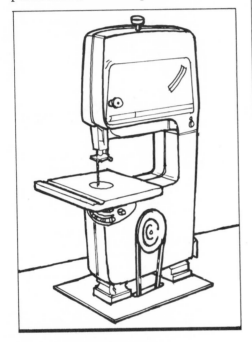

BANK (OF WINDOWS) A series of show or display windows, of merchandising tables or counters, or of other elements that are repeated in a group or continuous row.

BAR The horizontal cross stroke in upper case letters such as "H," "A," "E," and in lower case letters such as "t," "f."

BARGAIN SQUARE The arrangement of tables, fixtures or counters in a special area to encourage the sale of clearance or promotional merchandise. The area is usually attended by sales personnel. See *dump table* and *emphasis table.*

BARGEBOARD Originally the decorative woodwork that covered the joint between the roof and the gable end of a pitched roof. In the late 19th and early 20th century this board was scrolled and lacy-looking and full of jigsaw cutouts and highly ornate. Also called carpenter's Gothic and steamboat Gothic.

BARK IRON Iron rods that have been treated to have a rough texture similar to the bark of a tree. Most often used to make decorative displayers, étagères and towers.

BARN DOOR A lighting accessory used with spotlights to control the spread of the beam of light. Four adjustable flaps or doors (one on each side and one each on top and bottom) can be adjusted to control and direct the light and, also, to block off completely an area from the light. Usually attached to the front of the spotlight—in the color frame guide. Sheets of colors,

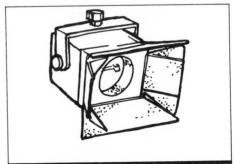

frosted gelatin or plastic, or spun-glass diffusers can be used with a barn door.

BARN SIDING The rough wood and/or shingles that simulate the aged and weathered wood on a barn. Used for display settings and wall surfaces.

BARONG TAGALOG The loose fitting men's shirt or blouse of the Philippine Islands worn instead of a dinner jacket. Sometimes made of banana fiber cloth and richly embroidered.

BARREL VAULT A semicylindrical roof constructed on the principles of the arch. A tunnel of brick, stone or concrete. Used in Roman and Romanesque architecture.

BASE *1. In architecture* The dado or lowest stage of paneling on a wall. *2. In fixturing (as illustrated)* The block or molding at the bottom of a piece of furniture. The lowest horizontal element of an upright unit. The base is weighted, constructed and proportionately sized to keep the unit erect and to prevent tipping, unexpected moving or sliding. If mobility is a desired feature, the base can be equipped with glides or casters.

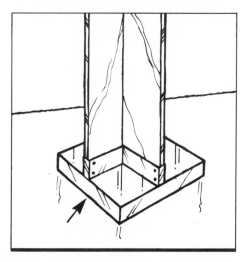

Since the base surface is larger than the vertical element, it is often more detailed and ornate and is available in many styles and finishes. See *counter units.*

BASEBOARD The horizontal board placed at the bottom of a wall, and resting directly on the floor. Usually a piece of molding, shaped and contoured to create a better flow from the vertical wall to the horizontal floor.

BASE COAT, BASE COLOR The first or background color upon which other colors may be applied.

BASE FLANGE A flat disc or plate with a perpendicular hollow tube extending up from the plate. The hollow tube will accept the mannequin's ankle or butt rod, and thus support the mannequin. The flat plate can be screwed or secured to the floor, a base or platform. See *ankle rod, butt rod* and *foot spike.*

BASEMENT The floor of a building partially or entirely below ground level.

BASEMENT STORE See *budget store.*

BASE PLATE See *base, glass base plate* and *plexiglass base plate.*

BASIC ITEM An item that a customer may call for during an entire season. The merchant should always have in stock to satisfy the demand.

BASKERVILLE TYPE The first transitional typeface of the 20th century. There is more differentiation between the thick and thin strokes, and the serifs on the lower case letters are much more horizontal than they were formerly. The italic letters differ greatly from the old-face italics. The slope is more regular and less angu-

ABCDEFGHIJKLMNOPQRSTUVWXYZ
abcdefghijklmnopqrstuvwxyz
$1234567890¢ ;;&?!()%° fifl

lar, and the letters K, N, T, and Y are swash letters. See *serif* and *swash letters.*

BASKET WEAVE An in-and-out weave of large, similar size weft and warp strands. Imitates the appearance of a woven, reed basket.

BAS RELIEF From the French word for "low relief." A form of sculpture in which the design is only slightly raised from the background. Also called basso relievo. Also see *anaglyph.*

BATEAU NECKLINE A straight neckline, on the back and front, that extends from shoulder to shoulder. A boat-shaped neckline.

BATIK A Javanese resist-dyeing technique that requires the artwork to be applied in wax which will resist the dye when the fabric is immersed or treated with the dyes. Only the background or unwaxed area will be stained. The process can be repeated many times so that multicolored patterns can be obtained. The streaked effect, associated with batik, is caused by some of the dye crawling under the wax. Batik can be imitated by machine printing.

BATISTE A fine, sheer cotton or cotton-blended fabric with vertical striations.

BATTEN *1.* A long piece of sawed wood used for flooring or wainscoting. A thin, narrow strip of wood used as uprights in lathing a wall. A strip of board that is used to fasten two other boards together by overlapping and being secured to them both. *2. (As illustrated)* An iron pipe used to support hanging drapes or panels in a display window or on a stage. The pipe may be hung off of a ceiling grid, and the panel or drape is lashed onto or threaded over the pipe. A similar bat-

ten will be used at the bottom hem or edge of the suspended unit to hold it taut. A curved pipe or batten is used when hanging a cyclorama or drape which will round out a corner of the enclosing area. See *cyclorama.*

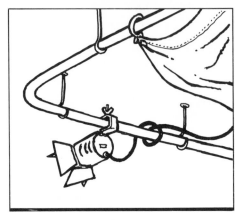

BATTLE JACKET A single-breasted jacket, semibloused and fitted at the waist. A World War II American soldier style. Also called Eisenhower jacket.

BATWING SLEEVE A funnel-shaped sleeve that fits into an armhole and extends from the shoulder down to the waist, and ends tight at the wrist. Almost a reverse of the angel sleeve.

BAY The spacing between columns on a grid pattern floor plan or layout. The greater the spacing between the col-

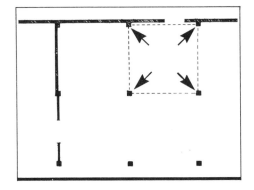

umns, (the larger the bays) the heavier the structural supports will be, and the more costly the construction. If columns are set 20' o.c. from each other, each bay will be 20' × 20'.

BAY WINDOW A window that projects out from the otherwise flat wall surface of a building.

BEAM A long, horizontal piece of timber or metal that rests on two or more supports and sustains a transverse load such as a ceiling or roof.

BEAMED CEILING A ceiling in which the exposed or encased beams are part of the decorative scheme of the area covered. The beamed effect can be "faked" with any of the many imitation or hollow beams available on the market.

BEAMSPREAD A lighting term that refers to the diameter of the circle of light created by a spotlight or floodlight. The farther the beamspread from the lamp, the less intense the area of light. "Narrow spots" are designed to throw narrow beams from medium to long range spotlighting, or provide high intensity spotlighting at close range. "Wide floods" are designed to spread a wide uniform beam over a larger area.

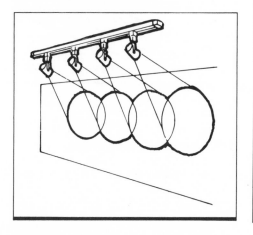

BEARING PARTITION, BEARING WALL An interior wall of one story or less in height which in addition to its own weight will assist in supporting a load from above (such as another story).

BEECH WOOD A strong, light-colored wood that resembles birch and maple. It is tough and straight grained. Often used for furniture frames and supports.

BEE LIGHTS Miniature screw-base type electric bulbs of very low wattage such as are used in strings of twenty or thirty for Christmas decorations. Tiny, tubular, globular or flame-shaped replaceable bulbs which operate on a transformer.

BEHIND-THE-SCENES The area behind the perimeter walls that separate the selling floor from the nonselling space. This area will contain service elevators, storage, employees' changing room, and toilets.

BELL BOTTOMS Trousers with full flaring bottoms, traditionally a part of a sailor's uniform. The wide bottoms made it possible for the sailor to climb, jump, and move about freely without feeling restrained.

BELLBOY'S CAP See *pillbox hat.*

BELL SKIRT A full, flaring skirt usually made up of gores (see *gored skirt*). Originally fashionable in the 1890s, and was reinforced and shaped with a haircloth stiffener or petticoat.

BELOW GRADE A finished level below the street or pavement outside. The amount of "below grade" can vary from a few inches or feet to a floor or more (for example basement levels).

BELVEDERE The uppermost story or level of a building with many openings (or windows) that allow a panoramic view of the area around and below. The story is covered with a roof. From the Italian word for "beautiful view."

BENDAY See *dry transfer*.

BENGALINE A heavy faille-type fabric with pronounced crosswise ribs. It may be woven of silk, wool, cotton, or manmade yarns and combinations of both.

BENTWOOD COSTUMER, BENT-WOOD HATRACK A reproduction or adaptation of a 19th-century design for an arrangement of coat hangers and hat hooks. The units were made of wood that had been softened by steaming and then molded into curved or scrolled forms. The traditional costumer is one of natural light-colored wood with four scrolled legs meeting approximately one foot off the ground, continuing up for about four or five feet and then curling off into an arrangement of coat hangers and hat hooks. Also available in assorted bright colors as well as chrome and brass metal variations. See *hall tree*.

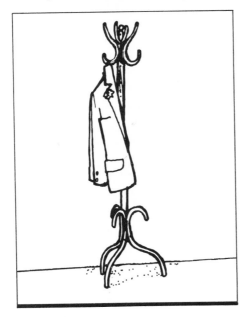

BERMUDA SHORTS Knee-length shorts.

BERTHA COLLAR A capelike collar, of varying length, that forms a cap over the sleeves, across the back and the front of a bodice. Popular at the end of the 1

BEVEL The angled or contoured profile of a flat surface such as a piece of wood and the inner surface of a frame.

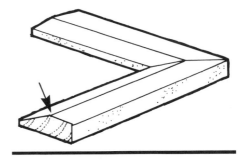

BIAS A line drawn or cut diagonally across a piece of fabric.

BIB The upper part of an apron or a jumper. A deep-fronted collar that extends down over the chest. An added front or chest piece. A small pad, tied around a child's neck to protect clothing.

BIG MEN SIZES Clothes sized for the stout man, usually weighing over 250 pounds. Sizes 48 to 54.

BIG TICKET ITEM A single, high-priced or expensive item such as furniture, major appliances, televisions, fur coats and jewelry.

BIKINI CUT A female mannequin with a removable leg; the break or cut line is close to the pubic area and thus will be hidden successfully by the bottom of a bikini-type swimsuit. A more natural look for displaying abbreviated swimwear and sportswear.

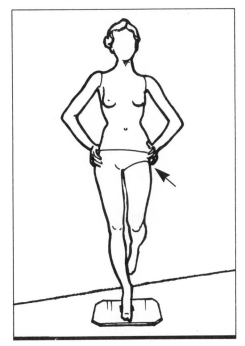

BILLBOARD A large framed area covered with panels of printed matter. Originally a form of outdoor advertising. Poster panels. Billboard posters are measured by "sheets" (a 6 sheet, a 12 sheet, etc.) and each sheet measures 28″ × 42″.

BILL OF LADING A signed, dated and stamped receipt issued by a common carrier (bus, train, plane) acknowledging the acceptance of merchandise (numbers of boxes, crates, etc.) and specifying the terms of the shipping contract.

BIN An enclosed receptacle or compartment. A container or box with five sides. Usually associated with cubbyholes or squared off divisions.

BINDER The substance or material in printing and graphics that affects the ability of an ink or paint to adhere onto the surface which is to be printed or colored.

BIRCH A strong, hard, light brown wood that can be stained to simulate many expensive woods. Used for doors, floors, interior trim and furniture.

BIRD'S EYE VIEW A perspective drawing or three-dimensional representation taken from a high horizon line or eye level. It is almost a floor plan or ground drawing with the vertical dimension actually rendered. A view from on top looking down into the area. An elevated viewing point. Also see *plan*.

BIRREN COLOR NOTATION SYS-TEM A color notation system used in graphics and printing devised by Faber Birren who believes in three basic forms of sensation—white, black and colors. His color theory is based on four "psychological primaries": red, yellow, green and blue. His system contains thirteen basic hues or colors and nine tonal steps from black to white.

BISHOP SLEEVE A long, full sleeve set into the armhole and shirred into a fitted band at the wrist. May be gently shirred into the armhole.

BIT The replaceable part of a carpentry tool that can be adapted to a variety of functions. The bit is the part of the tool that does the actual cutting, drilling, boring, etc., and will vary depending upon the specific diameter, depth, etc., required. See *auger bit* and *brace.*

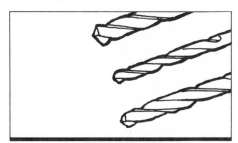

BLACK LETTER A bold-faced and angular style of lettering or type devised from 15th-century northern European manuscripts. Gothic Old English and the German Fractur typefaces are modern developments of this style.

ABCDEFGHIJKLMNOPQRSTUVWXYZ
abcdefghijklmnopqrstuvwxyz
$1234567890 :;&?!()* Esoeftz

BLACK LIGHT A special, ultraviolet, incandescent or fluorescent lightbulb that will cause surfaces treated with ultraviolet paint to glow in the darkness. The black light is directed onto the treated surfaces and the darker the area, the more intense and brilliant the treated objects or surfaces will appear.

BLACK LINE PAPER A chemically treated paper that will reproduce a drawing into black lines. Similar to blueprint paper.

BLAZER Originally, the bold-colored jacket worn by British college students for tennis or cricket and later adopted by Army and Navy officers as an informal country jacket. A lightweight jacket, trimmed with brass or emblematic buttons. An insignia or "patch" sometimes is applied over the breast pocket.

BLEACHING The removal of natural or artificial impurities, stains or colors from woods, fabrics, etc.; a lightening process. Bleaching, depending upon the material, can be accomplished by a chlorine process or exposure to light, air, etc.

BLEED *1. In paper* The printed matter that extends beyond the trim marks and, therefore will be cut off or will not show once the printed sheet is trimmed. A method of getting color out to the very edge or margin of the printed sheet or poster. Such bleeds usually extend out only ⅛" to ¼" beyond the trim mark. *2. In fabrics* when excess dyes run off during the washing of dyed fabrics, the fabric is said to bleed. See *creeping.*

BLIND A shade or screen or other masking device used to control light or air in an area. Window shades, Venetian blinds, shutters, louvers.

BLISTER PACKAGING A method of pre-packaging small merchandise on cards over which a plastic, see-through, bubble has been heat-sealed in place. The merchandise is visible and is protected in shipping and can be set out on the selling floor on the card.

BLOCK LETTER A sans serif typeface. A plain, unadorned letter with lines of uniform thickness. See *sans serif*.

BLOCK PLAN The primary allocation of space, location and areas, on a floor plan, based on the merchandising needs, traffic patterns, and anticipated sales. The required areas are blocked in roughly on the floor layout so that store management can get a visual picture as to how much space is needed, how much is left for growth, and what is left for "behind-the-scenes" activities, for the amenities and for dramatic or image-projecting effects.

BLOCK PLANE A small, hand carpentry tool designed to work across the grain and smooth out or shape the end section of a board. Sometimes 3″ long and very light; the most popular planes are 6″ to 7″ long. The blade is mounted at a lower level and is thus suitable for a thin shaving action.

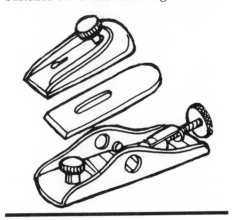

BLOCK PRINT Fabric or paper printed by hand by means of carved wood, metal or linoleum blocks or plates. The dye or paint is rolled over the raised surface of the block which is then pressed down onto the material to be printed. It usually requires a different plate or block for each different color.

BLOND WOODS Pale, beige-toned woods, or woods that have been bleached to a light color.

BLOUSE FORM An armless and headless bust form that ends just below the waistline. It may be equipped with an adjustable, up and down rod and a decorative base. Used to display ladies' blouses, sweaters and jackets.

BLOUSON A full shirt or dress top with a drawstring, elastic or belt at or below the waistline to create a billowing or poufy effect.

BLOWUP Photograph, illustration, etc. that has been enlarged, in some cases to "heroic proportions," from its original size. See *photo blow-up*.

BLUEPRINT 1. *In mechanical drawing* A positive print of white lines on blue paper (ferroprussiate), usually of floor plans, elevations, construction details, etc. The negative is a translucent drawing. *2. In offset lithography and photoengraving* A photoprint made from negatives or positives. Used as a proof. *3.* Commonly used to refer to the detailed and specific instructions for doing a task.

BOA A long, streaming (6′ to 8′ long) neckpiece made of feathers, tulle, fur, lace, etc., that wraps around a woman's neck and shoulders and flows down and out. See *stole.*

BOARDING The use of cardboard or other semirigid materials underneath a piece of merchandise, which is being pinned or shaped for display. For example a board underneath a shirt or blouse.

BOBBINET A semitransparent net available in widths up to 30 feet. Used in window displays. It is adaptable, drapable, and sheerer than shark's tooth scrim. A gauze curtain material used for theatrical effects that can be painted, appliquéd or cut-out.

BODICE The part of a woman's garment that extends up from the waist.

BODONI TYPE A style of Roman typeface, now called "Modern," designed by Giambattista Bodoni (1740–1813), an early designer of print and type. The descenders are elongated, the serifs are flat, and the main stress is vertical with the combination of full and thin hairlines.

ABCDEFGHIJKLMNOPQRSTUVWXYZ
abcdefghijklmnopqrstuvwxyz
$1234567890 :;&?!()%/—-‐'* fifl

BODY STOCKING, BODY SUIT A garment usually made of stretch knitted fabric that encases the legs, hips, waist and bust, and has narrow shoulder straps that extend up and over from a low-cut front to a very cut-out back. It eliminates the use of a bra or girdle in many cases. A one-piece body garment.

BODY TRUNK A male or female torso form that starts above the waistline and extends down to just below the knees to show shorts, underwear, swimwear, etc.

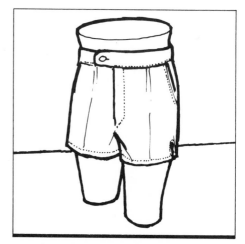

BOLD-FACE TYPE The heavier and darker typeface that is used for emphasis, and thus stands out from the text type with which it is used. See *full-face type.*

BOLERO A short, tailored jacket that ends at or above the waist, usually collarless and often sleeveless; often trimmed with braid or edging. Copied from a Spanish bullfighter's costume.

BOLTS Fasteners used in fixturing and carpentry. See *carriage bolt, machine bolt* and *stove bolt.*

BOISERIE The carved woodwork and paneling of 17th- and 18th-century French interiors. The woodwork was often picked out in gilt, and the interiors of the framed panels might be filled with raised designs, carved trophies, stretched fabrics, painted canvases, or mirrors. The frames, moldings and ornate wood trim of French period rooms.

BOND The method, arrangement and patterns that result when building units (brick, masonry, concrete, tiles, etc.) are cemented or put together to construct or surface a wall. Building units are usually organized in such a manner that the vertical joints are not directly over each other. Some

popular bonds are: common bond, checkerboard bond, Flemish bond and English bond.

BOOK OUT A term used to refer to the signing out of merchandise from stock or from a selling department to be used in a display away from the stocking area. The merchandise is signed out in a merchandise requisition book.

BOOM, BOOMERANG A vertical pipe used for mounting spotlights at the side or in front of a window display or stage.

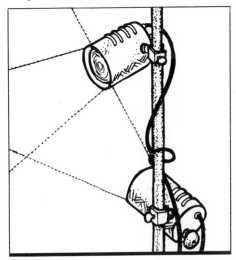

BOOTH A small, self-standing and self-contained service area within which a salesperson may stand or sit. A standing cubicle. Similar to a "kiosk."

BORAX A retailing slang expression used in the 1920s to refer to cheap, gaudy, obviously poorly made furniture. Originally applied to furniture one could get for premium coupons offered by the Borax Soap Company. In the 1940s–1950s it was used to describe imitation "streamlining"— overinflated and redundant curves and the repetitive bands used to decorate juke-boxes, etc. A cheap, obvious design or construction.

BORDER *1.* A partial, usually cutout, overhead valance used in a display window to mask the sides. A valance or semi-frame. *2.* An ornamental frame; a rule; a frame within a frame; a series of lines around a box of type or around an illustration. Used in printing or graphic design. Also spelled bordure.

BORDERLIGHT A striplight hanging from an overhead batten or pipe or ceiling grid to produce general overall lighting in a display window. See *striplights.*

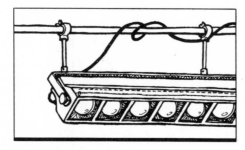

BORSALINO A fine Italian felt hat, usually made of natural fur that has been aged for three years, and the felted body is aged for still another year. Hand-crafted and detailed.

BOSQUET A small clump or grouping of trees or tall plants in landscaping.

BOSTON BLINDS See *vertical blinds.*

BOTTEGA The studio or workshop or place of "business" of an artist or craftsman. From the Italian word for "shop."

BOUCLÉ A fabric with small, regularly spaced loops and flat twists that are woven into the texture of the twill weave fabric. The fabric can be made from most fibers and the "rough" effect accounts for the name. From

the French word for "buckled or crinkled."

BOUFFANT From the French word for "puffed or poufy." Full skirted dress shape.

BOURGES ARTIST'S SHADING SHEETS See *dry transfer.*

BOUTIQUE A shop or shop-within-a-shop that sells a particular or specialized type of merchandise such as an individual designer's collection. A special appeal or ambience directed at a definite target market.

BOW COMPASS A drafting instrument used for drawing small accurately scaled circles. The radius of the circle is determined and the compass is adjusted to the desired radius by a setscrew which works against a spring.

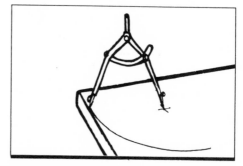

BOWLER A hard, dome-shaped hat designed in the mid-19th century by the Englishman, William Bowler. Similar to the American derby. See *derby.*

BOX COAT A straight, loose-fitting coat popular in the 1930s and 1940s, originally worn by coachmen in the early 19th century. The coachman drove from the "box" of the coach, and thus the name.

BOXER SHORTS Shorts with a stitched down elasticized waistband that gives a fullness to the shorts around the hips and backside. A fashion take-off on the prizefighters' costume. Also worn as men's underclothing, women's and children's playclothes.

BOX NAIL A thin nail used for rough woodworking.

BOX PLEAT Folds in fabric or in another material that are arranged in pairs—one overlap is to the right and the companion fold is to the left. When the resulting fold or inset is hidden between the two folds, it is called an inverted pleat—a reverse of the box pleat.

BOYS' SIZES A retailing term referring to sizes for pre-school, nursery and kindergarten age boys, sizes 4, 5,6,7. At this age, there is usually no defined waistline.

BRACE *1. In fixturing or construction* A stretcher, cross-piece or angled element used to reinforce and strengthen a construction. *2. In carpentry* The instrument that holds or turns the bit. Usually equipped with a crank or handle for turning. See *auger bit* and *bit.*

BRACES The British term for "suspenders."

BRACKET A horizontal projection that is hooked, attached, or bolted to a vertical surface. This projection or shelf support makes possible a horizontal, weight-bearing surface such as a shelf or hangrail. See *standard.*

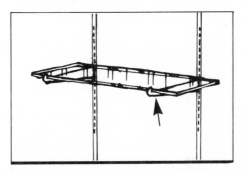

BRAD An almost headless carpentry nail that is used mostly for finishing work where the heads are usually countersunk below the surface of the material.

BRA FORM A headless and armless female bust form that ends just below the bustline. The forms are scaled to wear the size 34B. Junior bra forms

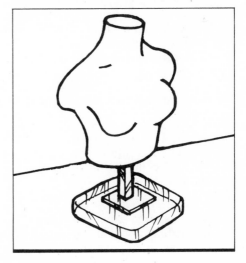

are proportioned to a 32A bust. Also see *braselette form.*

BRANCH STORE A subsidiary store, sometimes in the suburbs or in outlying areas, operated by the parent or flagship store. It will carry most of the same merchandise at the same price and will be involved in similar sales promotions. Media advertising will often include the branch store. See *flagship store.*

BRAND NAME The specific, recognizable and/or trademarked name of the manufacturer affixed to merchandise. The name that makes quick customer identification possible due to advertising and media exposure. Sometimes the designer's name. See *store's own brand.*

BRASELETTE FORM A headless and armless female bust form that ends at the hips. A longer version of the bra form that can also be used to display lingerie and slips. Proportioned for a 34B bust size. Also see *bra form.*

BRASS A bright, gold-toned metal alloy (one part zinc to three to seven parts copper) that has a tendency to oxidize and thus discolor. It requires a coating of clear lacquer to act as a sealant to prevent discoloring or tarnishing. A harder, more chip-resistant coating is achieved by oven-baked drying of the lacquer finish. Brass is softer than steel and more workable, and can be chrome-plated for a silvery finish.

BRAZING The act of joining two surfaces of similar or dissimilar metals with a layer of soldering alloy applied under very high temperatures. See *welding.*

BREEZE BRICKS Standard-sized bricks prepared from coke breeze concrete instead of the usual baked clay.

It is possible to nail or screw into breeze bricks.

BREEZEWAY A covered or roofed-over connecting unit between two structures. Usually a light and airy arcade, arbor or trellis device that allows air to circulate, provides a free view of the surroundings, and offers protection from sun, rain and snow. It can also refer to a long, canopied passageway.

BRETELLES The French term for "suspenders."

BRETON HAT A turned up, medium-sized brimmed hat made of straw or felt. Originally worn by the peasants of Brittany, France.

BRIDAL REGISTRY A service desk or area for brides-to-be that keeps a file on the bride's preferences in silver, china, linens, etc. Gifts can be purchased in these classifications by checking the registry and making selections within the confines of the bride's stated preferences, and against what has already been purchased. The registry is usually located near the bridal salon or in the china and glass departments.

BRIGHTNESS A term used in store lighting for the strong, bright part of a ceiling or wall light fixture that is most obvious from the floor. The blinding glare that can be reduced by use of a color lens, a filter or a baffle around the lamp. See *barn doors.*

BRISE SOLEIL An architectural device, either fixed or movable, that acts as a screen or shield to block the unwanted sunrays. A canopy, awning or overhang designed as "part" of the building and not just an "add-on."

BRISTOL BOARD A pasted board made of a rag content paper used in drawing or signing. Mill Bristol, with a textured or smooth finish, is usually manufactured in a 22½″ × 28½″ size. Originally, a kind of cardboard produced in Bristol, England.

BRITE CHROME See *polished chrome.*

BROADCLOTH A tightly woven, plain cotton fabric, with a lustrous finish and crosswise rib.

BROADLOOM Seamless carpets, woven in a myriad selection of natural and man-made fibers, in widths ranging from 6′ to 9′, 12′, 15′, and wider on special order. The carpets are available in endless patterns, colors, textures and weaves.

BROADSIDE A term used in advertising and signage for a large printed sheet of paper, usually intended as a mailer, that can be folded into a more convenient size for mailing. Originally, a 16th- and 17th-century popular ballad, often based on news or political items, that was printed on a single sheet of paper, ornamented with a woodcut and sold on the streets.

BROCADE A raised or enriched fabric with fanciful patterns of flowers, scrolls and arabesques, and produced in multicolors on a jacquard loom. From the low Latin for "to embroider" or "to stitch."

BROCATELLE A heavy damask-like fabric with a slightly raised or embossed pattern. An imitation of Italian tooled leather.

BRONZE A brownish-gold colored metal alloy (mainly composed of copper and tin); not very bright or shiny. As bronze ages and reacts with chemicals in the air, it takes on a greenish tint and matte surface called a "patina." In fixturing, the "bronze" finish is often a matte, rubbed-down

metallic ocher finish. See *statuary bronze.*

BRONZING Printing or decorating with ink or paint to which a sizing or glue has been added. While the paint is still tacky, a bronze powder is added. It adheres to the painted or inked surface and imparts a metallic glint.

BROWN PRINT PAPER Similar to blueprint paper but the white lines are developed onto a brown background. Also see *black line paper.*

"BROWNS" A class or general name given to brownish wrapping papers of all kinds that are usually derived from a raw stock or hemp rope waste. Examples are: bag brown, brown print, corrugated brown, kraft brown and tarred brown.

BROWNSTONES Originally the architectural term used to describe the three-, four-, and five-storied townhouses built in connecting rows during the 19th and 20th centuries and faced with a soft, red sandstone.

BRUSHED FINISH *1.* A sueded finish on fabrics. *2.* See *satin finish.*

BRUSSELS CARPET An uncut loop pile wool carpet that has unusually fine wearing abilities. Also called a round wire carpet.

B.T.U. (BRITISH THERMAL UNIT) The amount of heat required to raise one pound of water one degree Fahrenheit.

BUCKRAM A heavily sized, stiff, semirigid plain weave fabric. Used to stiffen or shape other, softer materials.

BUDGET A plan, based on an intelligent estimate of future expenses balanced against expected revenue or income, which will be in effect for a specified period of time.

BUDGET STORE Usually a part or division of a department store that sells lower-priced lines than are found in the rest of the store. Previously referred to as *basement store*.

BUILD UP A term applied to the grouping of geometric shapes and forms to create multi-levels for the display of small associated merchandise such as cosmetics, toiletries, small leather goods and shoes. It is a method of highlighting and giving special attention to several items by presenting each on its own mini-platform, yet keeping the assorted but related merchandise together as an integrated group. See *risers*.

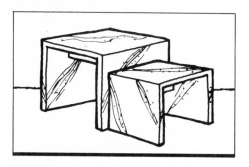

BUILDING LINE The line of the outside face of a building, and the line on a given plot beyond which the law or building codes forbids a building to be erected. The codes allows for a certain amount of the plot of ground to be set aside for parking, sidewalks, plantings, park space, etc.

BUILT-IN SALE A traditional, once-a-year or twice-a-year major sale for a particular group of merchandise such as a furniture clearance sale or a white sale.

BULLET CATCH A retractable nipple attached to an upright hollow tube. When this tube is placed within another hollow tube, designed with pre-drilled holes along its length, the retractable nipple will extend and catch through one of the aforementioned holes. This stop action will hold the inner unit at a certain height in relation to the outer unit. To raise or lower the inner unit, the nipple is pushed in passed the hole and the inner unit is then raised or lowered as desired. The nipple is allowed to extend and line up with the desired hole at the desired height. Used to raise and lower the height of a fixture or displayer. Also see *push-button catch*.

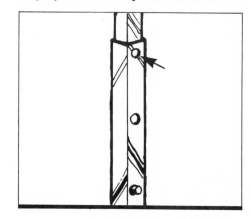

BUNDLE See *roll (of wallpaper)*.

BURIN A cutting tool used in etching or engraving. A metal needle, sharpened to a square or diamond shape, and contained in a wooden handle.

BURL A wartlike growth on a tree or the root of a tree which, when sliced for veneering, produces knotted, swirled or pitted decorative markings instead of the usual graining.

BURLAP A coarse, loosely woven, plain weave fabric made of jute, hemp or cotton. Usually beige-brown in color and associated with bags and sacks for foodstuffs (potatoes, coffee, tea, spices) or protective wrappings on import crates or packages. Available in a wide range of colors and widths and premounted onto paper backings. Used for decorative displays and wall surfaces.

BURNISH A method of polishing or brightening or smoothing an object or surface by applying friction, or rubbing.

BURNOOSE, BURNOUS A full, long circular cape with a hood and neck opening. Originally worn by Moors and Arabs in northern Africa.

BURNT SIENNA A permanent, fine, red-brown color which is quite brilliant and rich. A warm, deep, earth color.

BUSH JACKET The traditional safari or "great white hunter" jacket usually made of wind and waterproof materials. Cuffed sleeves and belted in the middle, with an assortment of breast and hip pockets (bellows) for carrying shells, other hunting paraphernalia and for generally keeping ones hands warm.

BUSTER BROWN COLLAR A starched, medium-sized collar, usu-ally worn with a soft bow tie or scarf, which was popularized by the costume worn by the early 20th-century cartoon character with the Dutch hairdo.

BUSTIER A strapless top or the top of a dress that is held in place by a clinging knit fabric or by elasticized threads woven through or stitched into the fabric.

BUSTLE An extended pouf or exaggerated flare or drape below, behind and beyond a woman's waistline. A fashion conceit of the 1870s–1880s and into the 1890s with the emphasis on the rear end.

BUTCHER BLOCK Originally the massive solid block of wood used as a cutting and chopping block in butcher shops. Currently, the term refers to wooden shelves, planks, cubes or surfaces made up to resemble a mosaic of vertical strips of wood unified into a dense, solid block. The strips are glued together and bonded under pressure. The surface is decorative as well as functional since by alternating grains, lengths, widths and types of wood, myriad patterns and color variations can be achieved. Usually made of hard rock maple. Butcher Block has been simulated in laminates.

BUTTERFLY NUT A threaded securing fixturing and carpentry device such as can be used at the end of a bolt or threaded rod. The two "wings" or extended ears make it possible to grip, turn and thus secure the nut. Also called a winged nut.

BUTTERFLY ROOF The opposite of a gabled roof. In this case, the sloping surfaces are higher at the outer edges of the building and slope down and meet, in a valley, at the center of the building—like a butterfly ready for flight with the wings angled up and out from the body. A look that suggests movement, flight, the out-of-doors. See *gabled roof.*

BUTT FITTING The square metal receptacle equipped with a setscrew which is set into the mannequin's butt or upper thigh, and receives the butt rod which angles up from the metal, glass, or plastic mannequin base plate. See *butt rod.*

BUTT HINGE A simple hinge composed of two leaves, which are secured to two butting members such as on the edge of a door and a side of a door frame. When the hinge is attached to a movable member such as a door and to a stationary frame, it is possible to swing the movable member back and forth while it is secured to the frame. The pin joint, between the two leaves, is visible.

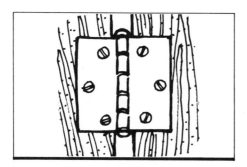

BUTT JOINT A simple and not very strong construction method of joining two members. One piece is set at right angles to the other piece and then the two members are glued, screwed or nailed together. The pieces butt up against each other.

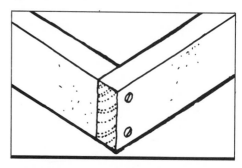

BUTTRESS A wall or abutment that is visible on the outside of a structure and is used to help support and reinforce an external wall which is very tall or which is carrying a heavy load from a superstructure.

BUTT ROD The square metal rod on a mannequin that extends up, at an angle, from the metal, plastic or glass mannequin base plate. The upper and free end of the rod fits into a square opening on the mannequin's butt or upper thigh. See *butt fitting.* The butt rod, when secured in place, keeps the mannequin erect and in the pose it was meant to hold. Also see *ankle rod, base flange* and *foot spike.*

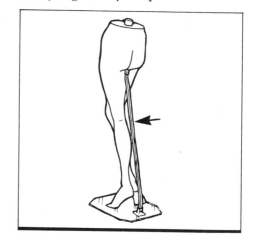

BUTYRATE See *cellulose acetate butyrate.*

BUYER The individual who is responsible for selecting, purchasing, and controlling the "in and out" of the stock of a specific department or area. It is the buyer who knows what merchandise is expected and when, in what colors and sizes, and the depth of inventory that will be maintained. It is usually the buyer who must decide when the merchandise will be "cleared" (clearance sales). The success and health of a department depends upon how well the buyer balances all of his/her duties. The buyer may be assisted by one or two assistant buyers who may be delegated some authority.

BUYING GROUP, BUYING OFFICE An office or organization of noncompeting stores, located in a resource city and set up to service and benefit the store members. The major function of the buying office is to supply a buying service for their members. Also called resident buying office.

BUY-OUT *1.* A retailing term used to describe the materials or fixtures purchased from a supplier who is not the manufacturer of the item. The supplier (or jobber) will purchase said items from the original manufacturer at a discounted price and add on to it for his expenses, handling, administrative costs, sales commissions, profit, etc. *2.* The term refers to those fixtures or merchandisers that are not part of the architect's or outside store planner's package of required fixtures. The fixtures the store can and does buy on its own without the architect's involvement.

BX CABLE An electrical term for insulating wire which is helical (spiral) bound of interlocking, flexible steel strips and inside a cable. The cable is fairly rigid so it can be manipulated up and through openings and will bend and arc as needed. BX cable is usually required in public buildings to carry electrical wires to and through the walls of the building. Also called *armored cable.*

C

CABINET Case furniture constructed of metal, wood or man-made wood sheets with shelves or drawers. Used to house, store or contain goods. From the French word for "receptacle" or "closet."

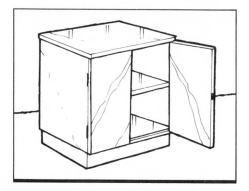

CABINET DISPLAYER See *armoire*.

CABINET PERSPECTIVE See *oblique drawing*.

CABINETRY, CABINET WORK Fine, elegant carpentry work which is usually reserved for interior fixtures and built-ins; cabinets, bookcases and shelving units, tables, displayers, etc.

CABINET VITRINE See *vitrine*.

CABLE *1.* A twisted, rope-like, decorative molding. *2.* A heavy, wire rope of many strands, sometimes twisted, or a group of vertical wires used as a single member in creating tension. *3.* A waterproof and insulating electrical conductor. See *BX cable*.

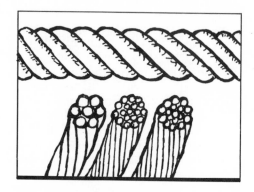

CABLE WIRE See *BX cable*.

CADMIUMS Yellow and red pigments derived from cadmium sulphide or a blending of cadmium sulphide with cadmium selenide. They are brilliant in hue, opaque, and permanent. Cadmium red can be substituted for vermillion.

CAFTAN A long, Oriental, coatlike garment with long, full sleeves that often cover the hands of the wearer.

CALCIMINE A cold water mixture of glue and whiting that may contain a coloring agent. Used as a whitewashing solution for walls, ceilings, etc. Not too permanent or durable a finish.

CALENDAR YEAR The standard year in retailing measured from January 1 through December 31. See *fiscal year*.

CALENDERED PAPERS/FABRICS Papers, boards or fabrics with extra smooth, glazed finishes which are produced when the material is passed between hollow, heated cylinders or sets or stacks of horizontal cast-iron rolls at the end of the finishing machine.

CALICO A cotton fabric with a plain weave that is usually printed with a small allover pattern, similar to percale.

CALIPER *1.* A measuring instrument used in mechanical drawings and carpentry consisting of two arms joined at a pivot or screw top which can be adjusted to determine distances, diameters or thicknesses by measuring the space between the arms. *2.* A standard of measurement for the thickness of paper, usually stated in thousandths of an inch.

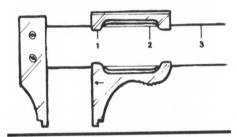

CALLIGRAPHIC TYPE Typefaces based on script or freely drawn letters. Loose, nonmechanical styles of typeface.

CALLIGRAPHY The art of writing beautifully. The brush strokes used by the Chinese to produce their written characters. In painting the term refers to free and loose brushwork.

CALPAC See *cossack cap.*

CAMAÏEU The French word for "monochromatic."

CAMEL'S HAIR The wool-like underhair obtained from a camel. The color will vary from an ochre-tan to a deep brown, but the color "camel" is usually associated with the golden-beige color. The wool is soft and lustrous and is often blended with sheep wool.

CAMEO PAPER A smooth, dull-finished paper used in printing and advertising when soft effects are desired.

CAMISOLE Originally a corset cover or underbodice. Currently, a top with a neckline that is cut straight across and over the bosom and held up with wide or narrow shoulder straps. Also a ruffled and lace trimmed top of a fitted slip.

CAMP According to Susan Sontag, it is a form of "dandyism" in an age of mass culture. "It is so bad—it is good." The emphasis is on theatricality, exaggeration, and extravagance. It is elegance, texture and style rather than function or content. There is often something "cliquish" about camp, a sort of private joke to be enjoyed by those "in the know." The digging up and rejuvenation of old or passe fads. Possibly from the French, "se camper"—to posture boldly.

CANDELABRA-BASE BULB A bulb with a screw base that is approximately ½" in diameter. A candle or cone-shaped lampbulb that is available in up to 60 watts. See *flame bulb* and *flicker bulb.*

CANDLEWICK FABRIC An unbleached or colored muslin used as a base for fuzzy tufts arranged in stripes or patterns. A pseudo-chenille fabric.

CANE The stems of palms, grasses, or plants similar to rattan or bamboo which can be woven or plaited into meshlike materials. Used for decorative inserts in case goods, screens, chair seats and/or backs.

CANOPY *1. In lighting (as illustrated)* An enclosure or cap placed between the stem of the fixture and the outlet box in the ceiling. It makes it possible to conceal wire connections in the area between the outlet and the fixture. *2. In interior design* A covering or drapery placed over a piece of furniture or on poles or rods.

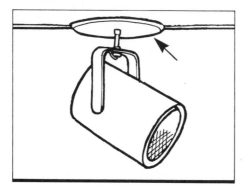

CANOTIER A straw hat or boating hat such as was popular at the turn of the 19th century.

CANTILEVER A beam, balcony, shelf, or other container that projects out from a flat surface and is not supported or reinforced by any structural members at the far end, i.e., an overhanging cornice or an unsupported mezzanine over a selling floor or auditorium. Marquees over store fronts are usually cantilevered.

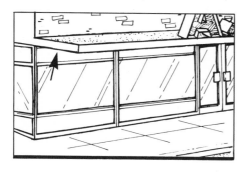

CANVAS 1. A heavy bleached or unbleached cotton or linen fabric with a light, even weave. 2. A firm, closely woven fabric used as a paint surface for oil painting. 3. A stiff openweave material used for needlework.

CAP See *wig foundation.*

CAPE A sleeveless outer garment to be worn by either sex. It may be full and flaring and circular in pattern, or seamed to fall fairly straight from the shoulders. Length may extend to the hip or to the floor.

CAPELET A short cape, usually ending above the waist.

CAPE SLEEVE Loose, flaring sleeve hanging freely from the shoulder at front and back. Similar to a cape. Often extends into the shoulder in a raglan effect.

CAPITAL *1. In architecture and design* The head or top of a column, pillar, anta or pier usually decorated with carvings and moldings. See *Composite order, Corinthian order, Doric order, Ionic order,* and *Tuscan order* for descriptions of the classic capitals of the Greek and Roman periods. *2. In business* The money, property of other assets of an individual or company used or being used to produce more wealth. The assets that remain after the liabilities are deducted.

CAPITAL EXPENDITURE Materials, machines or property that are purchased by an individual or company and that can be added to the value of fixed assets of that organization such as fixtures, mannequins and sign printing machines. The cost can be amortized over a long period of time.

CAPITAL LETTERS The upper case letters as opposed to the lower case letters used in headings and captions.

The first letter of the first word in a sentence.

CAPRI PANTS Women's tight-fitting pants with very narrow, tapered legs. Often with slits at hem to aid in getting them over feet.

CAPROLAN A nylon fiber with a high abrasion resistance. Used to produce upholstery fabric and also to manufacture carpets. Trademark of Allied Chemical Corp.

CAP UNIT See *end unit*.

CAR CARDS Printed advertisements that appear in the overhead panels of buses and trains. They are usually 11" tall and can measure 21" (for a single slot), 42" (for a double slot). There are also odd sizes like 11" × 14" and 11" × 28". The end panels in these public vehicles usually accommodate posters 22" × 21", 27" × 21" and 44" × 16".

CARCASE, CARCASS *1. In fixturing and furniture* The basic framework of a wooden piece of furniture without veneer, applied panels or moldings, carving, glazing, etc. The raw, constructed skeleton. *2. In architecture* The load bearing part of a structure or building without doors, windows, plaster, finishing surfaces, etc.

CARDBOARD A generic term for stiff, rigid papers which are 0.006 of an inch, or more, in thickness.

CARDED Merchandise that is delivered to the store attached to display cards (or blister-packed) such as earrings, buttons, some lipstick and eye makeup, and small toys. The merchandise is put out onto the selling floor in its carded form and may require selling fixtures equipped with special hooks, clips, clamps, or holders. See *blister packaging*.

CARD (OR SIGN) HOLDER A frame or container used to display a message or price-bearing card. Usually designed with a device to make it self-standing, or to attach it to racks, stands, shelves, uprights, etc.

CARDIGAN A straight, collarless, hip-length sweater or jacket—with or without buttons—for men and women. Originally a short military jacket in a knit-worsted fabric designed and worn by the Earl of Cardigan during the Crimean War.

CARD TOPPER A card, usually 3½" × 11" or 3½" × 7", used to announce seasonal or promotional information, that is inserted on top of a fixture which contains the special merchandise. These are not price cards, but are usually used in and on fixtures throughout the store to give impetus to a special event, holiday or featured item. For example reminders for Mother's Day, Valentine's Day, "Shop Early," Lay-a-Way, etc.

CARPENTER'S GOTHIC See *bargeboard*.

CARRIAGE The framing timber that is the direct support for the steps in stairway construction.

CARRIAGE BOLT A connecting piece of hardware that consists of a

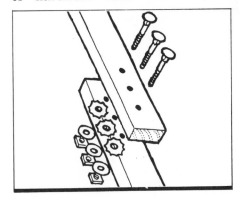

threaded shaft which graduates into angular shoulders below the rounded head. The angled shoulders prevent the bolt from turning once it has been driven into the wood.

CARRIAGE TRADE A term used to describe customers who expect better merchandise and individual attention. Originally the term referred to the wealthy patrons who arrived at a store by carriage and expected, and were given, very special treatment.

CARRIER A horizontal supporting or weight-bearing device into which other elements can be attached, hung or hooked.

CARTOON From the Italian word, "cartone" for a large sheet of paper. *1. In interior design* A full-size drawing for a painting, worked out in detail, and ready to be transferred onto a wall, canvas or panel. One of the steps in the preparation for a fresco or wall mural. *2. In graphic arts* A caricature or humorous drawing.

CARTOON-STYLE LETTERING A spontaneous, freehand lettering, usually *italic,* which suggests excitement, action and is attention getting. It is calligraphic in character, soft rather than hard, crisp and sharp, and very informal.

CARTOUCHE An ornament in the form of a scroll unfurled; a field or panel or inscription, a conventionalized shield or oval. An ornate frame surrounded with rococo swirls and/or arabesques. It may also refer to a sculptured ornament upon which an inscription is carved.

CARTWHEEL HAT A woman's hat, usually made of woven straw with a low, flat crown and a very wide, straight, stiff brim. A fashionable

and romantic hat since the 18th century.

CARVED RUG A rug with assorted levels of pile—depending upon how they were cut. The varying heights of pile create shadows and patterns in what might be an otherwise one color design.

CASE A cabinet or storage unit that contains merchandise within its constructed sides or on top of the unit. It can be a shelf unit with a table or counter top, or a drawer unit with a dump table top, etc. See *museum case, security case,* and *showcase.*

CASE GOODS Fixturing or furnishing units designed to contain, hold, store, or display items such as chests, cabinets, bookcases, étagères, vitrines and drawer units, etc.

CASEIN GLUE A high strength and moisture-resistant glue made from milk-protein powder mixed with water. It is especially good for poor-fitting joints and for use on oily woods.

CASEIN PAINT An interior paint that uses a casein solution instead of the usual drying oil. It is mixed and thinned with water. The hiding or covering property of the paint is lime, powdered chalk and kaolin. Available in a wide range of colors including deep and brilliant hues.

CASEMENT CLOTH A sheer, lightweight fabric used for curtains in display settings and in home furnishings. Provides a maximum of light with some privacy.

CASEMENT WINDOW Side-hinged window which swings, door-like, in and out, rather than up and down as other framed windows do.

CASH BEFORE DELIVERY See *C.B.D.*

CASH DISCOUNT A percentage reduction on the cost of an item for prepayment or immediate payment of a bill. The terms and percentages are usually indicated on the bill of sale.

CASH IN ADVANCE See *C.B.D.*

CASHMERE A soft and luxurious fabric produced from the hair of goats.

CASH ON DELIVERY See *C.O.D.*

CASH WRAP A specially designed counter, fixture or table that will house or hold a cash register (or cash drawer), materials for wrapping, boxing and/or packing, as well as the surface necessary for the wrapping operation. Usually located in the forward sales area.

CASLON TYPE A style of old typeface named after the 18th-century designer, William Caslon. The "C" has two full serifs, the "M" is wide and square, and the "S" is a light letter. Most of the *italic* capitals appear to be irregular in their leaning angles. There are many variations of Caslon Type: Caslon Old Face Heavy, Old Face Open, Old Face Open Heavy, etc.

ABCDEFGHIJKLMNOPQRSTUVWXYZ
abcdefghijklmnopqrstuvwxyz
$1234567890   :;&?!()

CAST A plaster of Paris reproduction of a statue, decorative capital, piece of molding or dimensional detail. Used in fixturing.

CASTER A swiveling wheel or ball-like roller attached to the undersurface of a unit to make it mobile.

CAST-IN-PLACE Concrete work poured and cast into forms on the exact location where the resultant structure will stand rather than precast or prefabricated in a plant or factory and then brought to the site. In England, it is referred to as "in situ."

CAST IRON Iron with a high carbon content. Usually hard, brittle and nonmalleable (incapable of being bent or shaped under heat or pressure).

CAST STONE An imitation stone often made from concrete, poured into a mold and sometimes prelayered with crushed stone, gravel or other natural materials. Used to face buildings. Also called reconstructed or patent stone.

CATALOG STORE A retailing term to describe a combination "store-warehouse" where the merchandise that is available may be seen on display and in catalogs. Customers make their selection from one of the above and then will either pick up the packaged merchandise at a cash desk, or at the rear of the warehouse upon presentation of a paid receipt. Customers may have the merchandise sent to them if the store is "non-stocking," or return, upon notice, to pick up the merchandise when it arrives at the catalog store from its supplier.

CATHEDRAL CEILING A high pitched ceiling which may be enhanced with windows (like a clerestory) to permit extra light into the area. Sometimes a low wall with a windowed roof which pitches back to meet the higher wall of a building.

CATHEDRAL GLASS A textured, rolled translucent glass. The uneven surface, which can be tinted, tends to partially obscure the view.

CAULKING The process of filling in the cracks, crevices and slots after a piece or structure has been assembled. It is also the repair work done with plaster, cements, putty, etc., around moldings, door and window frames, between bricks and stones, and other exterior surface openings.

CAVITY WALL A "hollow wall." A wall created by two masonry walls spaced approximately 3 inches apart, but joined together with metal ties or bonding bricks. It is like two separate vertical partitions, separated yet tied together. The approximately 3-inch air space between the walls permits the moisture that penetrates through the outer wall to drain off into this space.

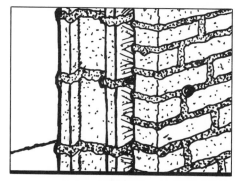

C.B.D. (CASH BEFORE DELIVERY) The terms for a sale where the product will be delivered only after the final payment or the complete garment has been received. Also called cash in advance (C.I.A.).

C-CLAMP A general, all-purpose, holding device, shaped like a "C" with an adjustable screw which opens or closes the open arc of the "C." By tightening the screw, the clamp is secured and holds whatever member or members have been set into that opening.

CEDAR A fine-grained, colorful wood with a particular fragrance associated with chests and closet linings.

CEILING WASHER A lamp fixture that directs the light up towards the ceiling—like an electrified wall urn.

CELADON A light, grayish sea-green color. The word is also used to describe pottery or Chinese porcelain of this pastel color.

CELLULAR BOARD Board that is corrugated or lined on one or both sides. Used in decorative displays and signing.

CELLULOSE ACETATE A generic term for a tough, flame-retardent and transparent film that can be bent, cut, formed or cemented. Manufactured under trademarks by Celanese Products, Inc., Eastman Chemical Products, Inc., etc. It is often used in display as a vacuum formable material or as a protective laminate. It absorbs moisture and is not recommended for long-term outdoor use. Also called acetate.

CELLULOSE ACETATE BUTYRATE (CAB) One of the strongest of the cellulosic plastics that has good transparency and colorability. It is recommended for outdoor use, signing and decoratives. It is generally supplied in pellet form and can be processed. Molded or thermoformed parts of CAB are recommended where hard wear is expected and longevity is desired. Also called butyrate.

CEMENT BLOCK, CEMENT BRICK A building unit which is precast in cement and is usually 8″ × 8″ × 16″. It is often bonded with cement mortar (a mixture of cement, sand and water). A fireproof building material. See *cinder block.*

CENTER PUNCH A hand punch consisting of a short metal bar with a hardened conical point at one end.

CENTRALIZED BUYING A retailing term given to the selection and purchase of merchanse for an entire chain or group by a specialist or head buyer. The display director may purchase props, mannequins, etc., for all the display departments in the various suburban stores under their control and get special rates, discounts, preferred handling, or special changes or variations because of the combined volume and buying power which is centralized in one person.

CENTRAL WRAP A major "cashwrap" desk, centrally or prominently located on a selling floor which will handle self-selection sales from several selling areas or departments. See *cash wrap.*

CENTURY TYPE A modern typeface designed before the 20th century for *Century* Magazine. The hairlines were made thicker and the serifs were shortened from the type previously used by the magazine, resulting in a blacker and more readable type.

ABCDEFGHIJKLMNOPQRSTUVWXYZ
abcdefghijklmnopqrstuvwxyz
$1234567890¢ :;&?!()˙

CERAMALUK 4 A new, high-pressure sodium lamp produced by Westinghouse. Yellower than the incandescent lamp, but is much improved to render colors acceptably at the warm end of the color scale. See *high-pressure sodium lamp.*

CERAMIC TILE Baked glazed tiles of assorted shapes and sizes. Available in a wide range of colors. Used to cover walls, floors, counters, etc.

CERAMIC VENEER Large, architectural terra-cotta tiles in thicknesses varying from 1⅛″ to 2½″ applied as a facing material over brick, concrete, wood lath, etc. Used on exterior and interior surfaces.

CERTIFICATE OF OCCUPANCY (C.O.) A license, supplied by the city government, which must be obtained when an existing building or construction, not previously used as a retail operation, is converted to that use. It involves the approval of zoning laws, health laws, fire standards, etc.

CERULEAN BLUE A bright, clear, greenish-blue or turquoise blue made from cobalt and tin oxides. It is a permanent color in either oil- or water-based paints.

CERUTTI The French term for *planter's hat.* See *Panama hat.*

CHAIN STORES A group of stores, usually selling the same or similar merchandise under the same name, that are centrally owned, controlled and managed. A chain may consist of a "flagship store" in an inner city location plus a group of suburban stores, or a group of stores of almost equal size and stature in a variety of locations.

CHAIR RAIL A molding strip usually set horizontally along a wall, about 30″ up from the ground. Originally, it protected the wall surface from being scraped or scarred by chair backs rubbing against the wall. See *dado.*

CHALLIS A soft fabric, made of wool, cotton or silk, with an overall pattern of small, multicolored elements.

CHAMFER An angled or beveled edge on a corner.

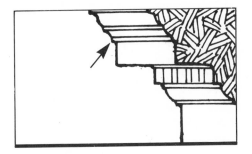

CHANG-FU The traditional and basic long, informal Chinese robe with the standing collar.

CHANG-SHAN The simple, long gown worn by Chinese men for formal wear. It is sometimes topped with a black jacket.

CHANNEL A three-sided strip of metal, wood or plastic similar to a "U" with right angles. This device can serve as a restricting path, a glide, or a cap to cover wiring, pipes, etc. See *standards.*

CHANNELS *1. (As illustrated)* The long, shallow, concave grooves that run vertically on the shaft of a column, and are separated from one another by a narrow edge or ridge called a "fillet." *2.* Structural steel shapes.

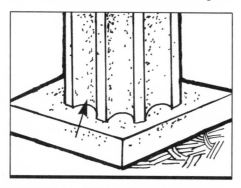

CHARCOAL DRAWING A loose, free-hand drawing made on special paper by means of a charcoal stick or pencil. A quick, free sketch.

CHASE LIGHTS A series of lamps that flash on and off in a set pattern, reminiscent of the lights that seem to "run" around theater marquees. The set of lights usually comes with its own timing device that sets and controls the flashing pattern. Also called running lights.

CHASE STRIP LIGHTING See *chase lights.*

CHAUSETTES The French term for anklets or socks.

CHECKERBOARD BOND See *bond.*

CHECK OUT A cash-wrap fixture located at an end of a selling floor through which customers must pass to get out of that selling area. Usually, the funnel end of a controlled customer traffic pattern.

CHEMISE Originally, the long body garment worn by Medieval men and women, called a "chainse." By the 13th century, it became "sherte" or "chemise." An undergarment made of a fine, soft material. In the 19th century, the garment became a knee-length unit and was worn under the corset. It was the forerunner of the embroidered, ribboned and laced lingerie. A one-piece silhouette, straight from shoulder to hem, which may be lightly sashed or belted. A shift or sheath.

CHENILLE A fabric with a high pile and a plushy surface. From the French word for "caterpillar." Chenille fabrics can be made to create a velvet or cut-velvet effect if woven on a jacquard loom.

CHENILLE CARPET A thick, soft pile, plushy carpet which can be woven in assorted designs, many colors and patterns.

CHEONGSAM, CHEONG SUM The traditional Chinese, Korean, or Hong Kong sheath; slitted on one side to 4 or 5 inches above the knee, straight-lined and topped with a high-standing collar and front closing slanted to the side with frogs or buttons.

CHERRYWOOD A reddish-brown wood which darkens with age and bears a resemblance to mahogany. Mainly used for small woodwork, inlays and decorative elements.

CHESTERFIELD COAT A single- or double-breasted, fly-fronted coat with a black velvet collar. Named after the 4th Earl of Chesterfield, Philip Dormer Stanhope, and originally a knee-length coat in the 1840s.

CHESTNUT A coarse-grained, soft wood, similar in appearance to oak. Used in woodworking.

CHEVIOT A rough napped, loosely woven wool fabric. Originally woven from the wool of the cheviot sheep of the Cheviot Hills in Scotland.

CHIAROSCURO A piece of artwork rendered in black and white with strong contrasts produced by the use of light and shade. From the Italian word for "light-dark."

CHIFFON A soft, lightweight, sheer fabric.

CHIFFOROBE A piece of furniture that is a combination of a many drawer unit (chiffoniere) and a movable closet (wardrobe). Thus—a chifforobe. See *armoire.*

CHILDREN'S SIZES A retailing term referring to sizes for girls and boys of nursery school, kindergarten age, sizes 3, 4, 5 and 6X (a tall size 6). A child that is taller and thinner than the toddler.

CHINA SILK A lightweight, plain weave silk fabric. Semitransparent.

CHINESE PAPER See *rice paper.*

CHINO A strong, sturdy, medium-weight twilled cotton fabric used for summer military uniforms and work clothes. Originally called "khaki"—the Hindu word for "dust colored—when the 19th-century British soldiers in India dyed their white uniforms with coffee and curry powder. Americans in the Philippines did the same with their uniforms and called the tan-beige fabric "chino."

CHINTZ A fine cotton fabric with a printed design which is often highly glazed and calendered. Rather stiff but when unglazed and "limp" it is called "cretonne."

CHIPBOARD *1.* A single-ply board, made of coarse stock, which is neither rigid or dense in construction. Usually prepared up to a maximum thickness of 72 points (0.072 of an inch). Used in signing and decorative display. *2.* See *particle board.*

CHISEL A metal bar tool, often with a wooden hand grip, which ends in a sharp wedge-shaped cutting edge. Used as a clean-up tool by gouging or clearing out excess wood from rabbitted, mortised, or routed surfaces.

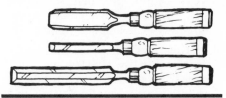

CHOKER COLLAR A very high collar which is boned at the sides and back to stand up almost to the chin. A fashion conceit of the 1890s and early 1900s. Revived in the mid 1960s.

CHROMA, CHROME The strength, intensity and purity of any given color or hue. Yellow is in the center of the spectrum and is the most brilliant, but of the palest chroma because it has the least saturation. Blue is the darkest and has the greatest saturation. Red has a medium chroma.

CHROME PLATING The process of electrode depositing of chromium onto another metal, usually steel, to create a corrosion-resistant finish with a bright, silvery shine. It is actually a nickel-chromeplating with 99% of the deposited thickness being nickel. The chrome acts as a sealant to prevent the nickel from oxidizing and discoloring. The mirror-like finish depends mostly on how well the metal, which is to be plated, was prepared before the nickel and chrome was added. See *spit out*.

CHROMO A color print.

"CHUBBIES" A retailing term for sizes 7½ to 16½. The same age and height as Girls' sizes 7 to 16, but for the fuller or heavier figure.

CHUCK An attachment used to hold a piece of work, or a tool in a machine. Similar to a vise.

C.I.A. (CASH IN ADVANCE) See *C.B.D.*

CINCH A tight, wide belt, sash or "girdle" used to create a smaller waist or emphasize the smaller middle.

CINDER BLOCK Portland cement combined with cinders, varying in color from white to gray to tan, made up into blocks usually 8″ × 8″ × 18″. A building block both economical and texturally interesting.

CIRCLE *1. Diameter*—a line drawn through the center of a circle connecting the opposite sides of a circle. To determine the lengths of a diameter of a circle: (A) If the radius is known, diameter = twice the radius. (B) If the circumference is known, diameter = circumference divided by Π (3.14). *2. Radius*—one half the diameter or a line drawn from the center of a circle to any point along the outer edge of the circle. To determine the length of the radius of a circle: (A) Radius = diameter divided by 2. (B) Radius = circumference divided by 6.28 *3. Circumference*—the distance around the

outside of a circle. To determine the circumference of a circle: (A) Circumference = Π (3.14) × diameter. (B) Circumference = 2 × Π (3.14) × radius *4. Area*—the quantitative measure of a flat surface or plane. The space inside a circle. To determine the area of a circle: Area = Π (3.14) × radius × radius or Π × r^2.

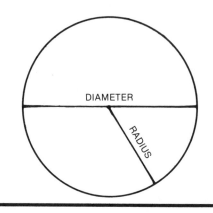

CIRCUIT A closed loop of wire or any other conducting material through which an electric current flows. It is usually the path of a good conductor which leads from the source of electrical energy to a device such as a lamp or heating unit, and then back to the source.

CIRCUIT BREAKER An automatic switch that opens and breaks the flow of electric current through an overloaded circuit. A safety device which replaces the fuse.

CIRCULAR SAW An electric-powered table saw sometimes with a tilting arbor. The table surface remains level to work on, but the blade tilts for angular ripping or cross-cutting. It is possible to make rabbet and mortise cuts as well as cut rough lumber down to size. The blades are replaceable and by changing the blade and the setting of the position of the blade, it is possible to perform many different operations.

CIRCULAR SKIRT A skirt which, when laid flat, is a complete circle with a smaller circle cut in the center for the waistband. The full flaring bias-cut skirt revived with Dior's "New Look" in the late 1940s and popular throughout the 1950s.

CIRCULATION The movement or flow of traffic, pedestrians, shoppers, etc., in a store. The ability to get around easily or to move in an orderly or prescribed manner. See *traffic*.

CIRCUMSCRIBE To draw an outline about an object. To restrict or set within limits or boundaries.

CLADDING The non-load-bearing interior or exterior surfacing material used to cover the framework and/or roof of a structure. It may be decorative as well as functional and can serve as a weatherproofing agent. Siding material.

CLAPBOARD WALL An exterior wall surfacing consisting of horizontal wood boards or planks overlapping the planks underneath.

CLARE OBSCURE The 18th-century anglicized form of the French "clairobscur," a method of painting in lights and shades. See *chiaroscuro*.

CLASSIC *1.* The architecture, arts, sculpture and literary accomplishments of the ancient Greeks and Romans. *2.* Anything of quality and excellence (of good taste) which survives in the world of fashion change and is accepted as a standard or criteria.

CLAW HAMMER The standard hammer with the metal head on a shaped wooden handle. One end of the head is flattened out into a striking surface, and the other end resembles two, slightly separated, bent fingers used to grasp and pull out nails, etc.

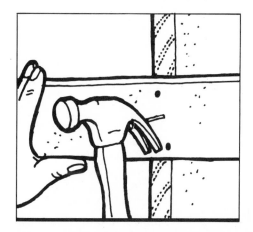

CLAY COATED, CLAY FINISH A paper or board with a high degree of smoothness which has been obtained by filling the surface pores with fine clay. A paper or board coated with fine China clay, which has been mixed with a thin, glue-like liquid. An enamelled paper.

CLEARANCE *1.* The space between two enclosing horizontal surfaces. The space between the threshhold and the underside of the door lintel, between the tread of a step on a stairway and the closed ceiling above it, between the top of a built-in fixture and the ceiling above it. See *headroom*. *2.* The act of getting rid of something; clothes that were not salable, a style that never took off, a color that lacked appeal, a size with no back-up stock or a stock of only one size, merchandise that is "worn," "as-is," faded or damaged. It can be the dregs of the season that has passed or merchandise that would not pay to keep till the next season or year. A "Clearance Sale" is often a means of recouping some part of the original cost of the merchandise and reducing the loss by "dumping" it.

CLEARANCE CENTERS See *outlet store.*

CLEAT A method of reinforcing the joint of two adjacent surfaces. A strip of wood secured over two other pieces of lumber, which have been butted or glued together.

CLERESTORY (CLEARSTORY) A window placed near the top of a wall, but above the level of an adjacent roof. An example would be the windows in the nave wall of a church, above the roof of the side aisles. This window permits extra light to flow in.

CLINCH PLATE A metal plate set between a work table and a piece of wood being worked on so that when a metal fastener such as a nail, tack or brad goes through the piece of wood, the end of the metal fastener will go back on itself or "clinch" or angle back into the wood rather than fasten itself to the work table.

CLIP STAND A counter unit or fixture provided with clips for displaying carded or bagged merchandise or any merchandise which is best shown and stocked by being clipped.

CLOCHE A deep, close-fitting woman's hat with a very narrow or without a brim that completely encases the head from low down on the forehead (or eyebrows) to the nape of the neck. Popular during the 1920s and 1930s, especially with the short, bobbed hair styles of that period.

CLOGS Wood-soled shoes made with leather or fabric straps, laces or toe pockets. They were originally raised up on metal rings or platforms, and effective for walking on cobbled streets. Today the wooden platforms are the soles of these outer shoes. Also called pattens.

CLOSED BACK WINDOW A fully enclosed display window with a back wall, floor and ceiling. There will often be a door or sliding panel in the back wall to permit movement, in and out of the window with mannequins, merchandise, props and for personnel. A stage. Also called a self-contained window.

CLOSED CIRCUIT TELEVISION (CCTV) In-store television used as part of the store's security system or for special in-store presentations or events.

CLOSED DISPLAY Merchandise displayed under glass—in a case, in a counter, in a shadow box. The opposite of an open-to-touch-and-take display.

CLOSE OUT The final sale to clear out a specific group or type of merchandise which will no longer be ordered or stocked by the store or manufactured by the manufacturer. The "close-out" is usually drastically reduced in price, "no return" policy, and the merchandise may be available only in broken sizes or colors (not all sizes and not all colors).

CLUSTER LIGHT FIXTURE Several light fixtures arranged on a single upright, column or pole used for exterior illumination of stores, in malls, on walkways, in parking lots, etc. Since the cluster of lights uses a single pole, it requires only one electric feeder line and the light can be focused in various directions.

CLUSTER LIGHT FIXTURE

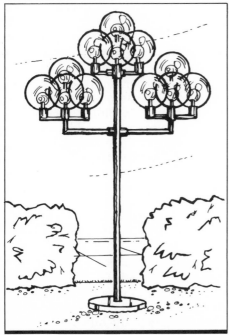

C.O. See *Certificate of Occupancy.*

C.O.D. (CASH ON DELIVERY) The terms for a sale which require the final payment or the balance of payment due to be rendered upon receipt of the merchandise.

COACHMAN COAT A late 18th- and early 19th-century coat worn by both men and women. A long cloth coat with buttons down the front, and layered with three or four capelets over the shoulders and down to the mid-back or waist. A semi-fitted coat with a short overcape. See *box coat.*

COAT DRESS A simple, tailored dress with a front button closing similar to a coat or wrap.

COAT FORM A headless and usually armless male form that ends above the hips and can be raised or lowered on an adjustable rod. The form is used to show coats, jackets or sweaters. Most are flat-fronted, with little chest muscle development, and the "arms," when available, are either bendable rods or sleeve pads.

COBBLES, COBBLESTONES Originally rounded fieldstones of about 6 to 8 inches, used in paving public thoroughfares. Today, the paving blocks that are cut from hard stones, rounded and smoothed and then used for streets and roads. Houses have also been faced with cobbles.

COCKTAIL DRESS A semiformal dress for late afternoon or evening "dress-up." Decorative and/or elegant —festive but not formal.

COGGING A form of joinery in which pieces are joined at right angles to each other. The underside of the upper member is grooved out to receive and hold the lower unit snugly.

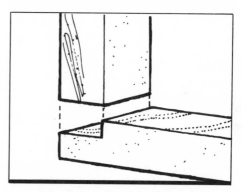

COLD CATHODE LIGHTING An instant starting type of fluorescent lamp which uses cylindrically formed electrodes. Like neon tubing, cold cathode lighting can be bent to conform with architectural details and thus can be used for lighting coves, handrails, ceilings, arches and fins. It has a useful life of up to 25,000 hours which approaches "permanent lighting," and no wiring troughs or ballasts are needed for installation.

COLLAGE From the French word for "glue" or the process of glueing together. A picture, design or ornament built up with pieces of paper, cloth, wood and/or other materials which are glued or stuck onto a canvas or other surface. See *montage.*

COLLAR BEAM A horizontal wood unit used to tie two opposite rafters together at a center point on the rafters. It usually takes place above the wall plate level in a collar roof.

COLLECTION A group or line of designs created by a designer or couturier for a specific season, a special store or for a particular manufacturer who will produce them. The collection could be a complete line of dresses, suits, separates and perhaps accessories created by a designer and introduced to the press and the major retail buyers at a fashion showing. Orders are then taken and stock is produced accordingly.

COLONNADE A row of columns or uprights that support a single entablature or lintel. See *breezeway.*

COLORFAST The ability of a fabric to resist a color change or fading when subjected to a normal exposure of sunlight, heat, gas and laundering.

COLOR MODIFICATION The change of color that takes place when a painted or dyed surface is subjected to colored light. The modification of the painted color is the same as though pigment, (the color of the light) were added to the painted or dyed surface.

Thus, a red light on a yellow surface will produce an orange effect.

COLOR RENDITION See *C.R.*

COLOR SEPARATION In preparing artwork for reproduction, it is the separation of colors into individual negatives by means of color filters. The filter screens out all other colors but the yellows, reds, or blues that are contained in the multicolored design. The yellow negative will pick up the yellows present in the greens and oranges and flesh tones in the design. The blue selects all the blues in the violets, greens, magentas, etc. A fourth negative contains the blacks in the design.

COLORWAYS The various color schemes in interior design or home furnishings in which a pattern or design is produced. The number of colorways refers to the number of color arrangements printed or screened on a paper, fabric, etc., of a particular design.

COMBINATION SAW A saw blade that can be used for rip sawing or cross cutting. It can cut with or across the grain of the lumber.

COMBINATION SQUARE A marking or measuring tool with an adjustable sliding bar. The tool is calibrated so that one can measure. Also has a marking guide for 45 and 90 degree angles.

COMBINE PAINTING See *assemblage art.*

COMMISSION *1.* The order or contract for the creation or design of a building, piece of sculpture, artwork, mural, special fixture or displayer. *2.* The money paid to the salesperson involved as the "go-between" or "arranger" between the contractor and the contractee.

COMMON BOND See *bond.*

COMMON LUMBER A grade of softwood. It is not as good as the "select lumber," as it contains more blemishes and defects. Common lumber is suitable for general construction or utility work since it does not finish particularly well. The grades of common lumber, in descending order, are: Construction Grade (#1 Common), Standard Grade (#2 Common), Utility Grade (#3 Common), Economy Grade (#4 Common). Also see *select lumber.*

COMMON NAILS The usual and familiar flat-headed carpentry nails that are thicker than box nails, which are also flat headed. Casing and finishing nails are almost headless.

COMMUNITY CENTER/ROOM An area in a store set aside for public or group use. It might be used for social gatherings involving the community, meetings, a lecture area, a gallery, a special events section. One of the "amenities" of store planning.

COMPASS A drafting instrument for drawing circles of assorted sizes consisting of a needle point and a lead or inking arm. The radius of the circle would be determined by the distance between the needle point and the lead or inking arm. Also see *bow compass.*

COMPLEMENTARY COLORS The complement of a color is the color directly opposite it on a color wheel. Each primary color (red, yellow, blue) has its complement which is produced by mixing the other two primaries. Red is the complement of green which is produced by mixing yellow and blue. Blue is the complement of orange. Violet is the complement of yellow.

COMPLEXION BULBS A 10-watt frosted lightbulb, approximately 1½" in diameter. It emits a soft light and is often used around makeup mirrors or as part of a chase striplight arrangement. Also called cosmetic bulb.

COMPONENTS All the parts of pieces of essential elements of a unit or design.

COMPOSITE *1.* A halftone photograph made up of several different pictures or parts of pictures. *2.* A montage. *3.* A pictorial composition made up of bits and pieces from various sources.

COMPOSITE ORDER A variation of the Corinthian architectural order. It combines the volutes of the Ionic order superimposed over tiers of acanthus leaves. See *Corinthian order.*

COMPOSITION The arrangement of various and often assorted elements, lines, forms, colors, etc. into a pleasing and organized whole. See *collage* and *montage.*

COMPREHENSIVE See *working drawing.*

CONCEALED WALL SYSTEM A slotted upright or standard flushed or slightly recessed into the wall or into a vertical surface. A cleaner, less obvious use of standards since the vertical hardware is less obvious.

CONDENSED TYPE A narrow, slender and elongated typeface. Usually, the condensed version of any style of lettering will appear more elegant and refined than the standard typeface.

ABCDEFGHIJKLMNOPQRSTUVWXYZ& . , : ; ! ?
abcdefghijklmnopqrstuvwxyz 1234567890$

CONDENSER A device for storing or intensifying an electric charge or for compressing air.

CONDUCTION The passage of heat, light, sound, etc. through a material. See *conductor.*

CONDUCTOR A material through which heat, light, sound, etc. will flow freely with little or almost no resistance. Some materials are better conductors than others for specific purposes, e.g. copper is a good conductor of heat and electricity and therefore most often used for electrical wiring.

CONDUIT A pipe or enclosed channel for transporting water, electric current, etc.

CONE-SHAPED LAMP A small light-bulb, similar to a candle flame, sharply pointed at the top usually with a small candelabra screw-type base. Used for Christmas tree and outdoor decorations.

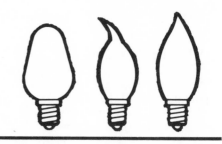

CONNECTING BAR See *cross bar.*

CONSERVATORY A greenhouse, usually glassed-in, filled with plants and trees. A retreat or "jardin d'hiver."

CONSUMER The purchaser, the customer, and/or the end user of a store's merchandise.

CONTACT CEMENT Strong, water-resistant and instant-setting glue with a neoprine base. It is especially useful on veneers, laminates and leather. It is quick setting and the parts that are to be joined cannot be repositioned once the glue has set.

CONTEMPORARY The current, present day, "as-of-this-moment" trend, style, form of decoration or ornament.

CONTINUOUS HINGE An elongated version of the butt hinge. Usually attached along the entire length of the swinging member and on the frame which will sustain it. The standard length of a continuous hinge is 6 feet. It is also available as a "take-apart" or

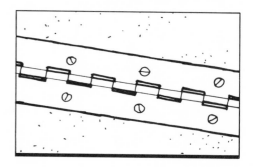

"lift off" continuous hinge which makes it possible to change or alternate the swinging member while the frame remains fully attached to the hinge.

CONTINUOUS TONES A photographic image which has not been treated with a film screen of cross-ruled lines or vignetted dots, but does contain varying tones from black to white.

CONTRACT A signed and legally binding agreement between two or more parties in which one party agrees to supply a service or product, and the other party agrees to the payment for that service or product in money, other goods or services. *In retailing* Usually a commission is accompanied with a contract listing all that is expected and how the renumeration will be effected.

CONVERTIBILITY A term used for fixturing that can be altered or converted from one use to another without great effort or cost; from hanging to shelving, from single to double hang, etc.

COOL COLORS The colors that appear cool and psychologically affect the viewer as cool. These colors tend to recede in a room or in a color scheme. Green-yellows, greens, blue-greens, blues, blue-violets and violets.

COOL WHITE The bluish color emitted by a particular fluorescent tube. "Cool" as compared to the pinkish "warm" cast of an incandescent lamp.

COOPERATIVE DISPLAY, COOPERATIVE ADVERTISING A term used in retailing to describe a joint effort by a national manufacturer (or supplier) and a local store to promote a particular product by sharing in the costs of promotion, advertising, displays, etc. The money that is contributed is referred to a "vendor money."

COORDINATES A term used in retailing and fashion to describe the various parts of an outfit or a design concept. It may refer to the tops, sweaters and/or jackets that are designed to combine with specific skirts, slacks or shorts for a total effect. Usually, coordinates are displayed together, or very near each other in a department.

COPING SAW A saw consisting of a spring steel blade held taut across the open side of a U-shaped frame and a wooden handle at one end. Similar to a scroll saw. The saw is designed to be used at an angle and to turn in all directions. Especially useful in cutting curves, complex profiles and "fancy-work." See *scroll saw.*

COPPER A reddish-orange metal which is an excellent conductor of heat and electricity. It is often combined with other metals to form alloys such as bronze. It discolors easily and must be treated with a clear plastic coating to prevent oxidation. It is often used as a complement to natural woods.

COPPER PLATE GOTHIC A sans serif typeface.

CORDALON See *wigs.*

CORDUROY A cotton or man-made fiber fabric in which the lengthwise ridges or cords are cut to produce a velvet-like pile. From the French "Corde du Roi."

CORINTHIAN ORDER The most elaborate and ornamented of the original classic Roman architectural orders. Slender and graceful, the capital is enriched with tiers of carved acanthus leaves and four volutes.

CORK TILES Squares of cork which has been pressed and baked into a solid homogeneous block and then sliced and cut. A resilient material used for floor, wall and ceiling surfacing. Cork that has not been combined with resins and surface-treated may stain, discolor or crumble.

CORLON Sheet vinyl flooring with a hydrocord back, usually produced in a variety of widths. It can be used over suspended, on grade, and below grade subfloors. Trademark of Armstrong Corp.

CORNER BLOCK A reinforcing brace in carpentry. A block used to form a junction between two pieces of wood joined at right angles, such as the point where a chair leg meets the seat rails.

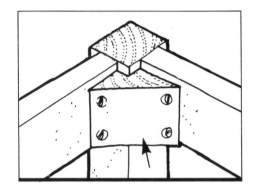

CORNER WINDOW A display window with glass openings facing out on two perpendicular streets. It faces two traffic patterns and is usually given a major display treatment. The corner window is often triangular in plan.

CORNICE *1. In architecture* The projecting upper portion of a classic entablature. *2. In interior decoration* A decorative cap or band over a curtain or drapery arrangement. A valance, lambrequin or pelmet.

COROMANDEL SCREEN A Chinese lacquered screen often decorated with an allover design, in low relief, or a fanciful landscape picked out in gilt. Introduced into Europe by the East India Company in the mid-17th century. Used in decorative displays and furnishings.

CORRIDOR A tubular passageway or connector between various elements, areas or rooms in a structure. Usually enclosed by parallel walls and a ceiling, and broken with doors, arches or openings leading to various areas.

CORRUGATED FASTENERS A rippled piece of metal with one edge sharpened—approximately 1″ wide and anywhere from ¼″ to 1″ deep. The sharpened edge is struck into two pieces of wood and holds the two flat surfaces together at the same level. Often used on mitered joints. Sometimes called "wiggle nails."

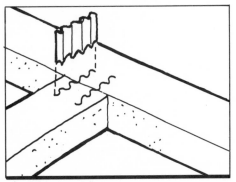

CORRUGATED PAPER A rippled or grooved paper or board, often light brown in color, which may be lined on one or both sides. A wrapping paper which is cellular in construction and can be fairly rigid.

CORSAGE *1.* An 18th- and 19th-century term for a low-cut bodice. See *décolletage. 2.* A small floral arrangement fastened to the bodice, shoulder or waist of a costume.

COSMETIC BULB See *complexion bulb.*

COSSACK CAP The tall, soft, crushable and jaunty hat worn by the Cossack officers. Usually made of astrakhan.

COSTUMER A free-standing fixturing unit, used on a floor, ledge or counter depending on size, upon which the assorted components of an outfit can be shown. It may be possible to show a coordinated jacket, skirt, blouse, bag and shoes on a single upright element fitted with adjustable arms, clips, hangers and carriers. The attachments can be raised or lowered and oriented in different directions. See *draper* and *valet.*

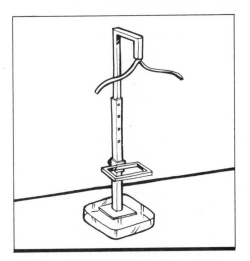

COTTON ROPING Lengths of twisted cotton fibers that resemble nautical roping but are softer, more pliable and more decorative than the sisal or hemp roping. Available in assorted diameters, and in white, but can be ordered or dyed in colors to match. Used in decorative displays.

COUNTER FIXTURES, COUNTER UNITS Any one of many specialized merchandisers or displayers which is set on a counter or table and used to display and/or hold small merchandise such as scarfs, ties, jewelry, cosmetics, slippers and hosiery. By the nature of its location and use, it is usually small (under 3½'), narrow (about 20"), and portable. Ideally, it should not obstruct the salesperson's view of the customer, or visa-versa. Counter units should facilitate the handling and sampling of the merchandise and, if possible, prevent pilfering. They may be constructed of metal, wood, plastic, etc., or combinations of any of the above, and wherever possible adjustability is desirable. Counter units are considered part of the store's decor as well as part of its fixturing and therefore much emphasis is given to the selection of bases, finishes and decorative details.

COUNTERFLOOR The sub-flooring beneath a main floor consisting of battens laid over floor joists. See *sleepers*.

COUNTERSUNK A term used in fixturing and cabinetry to describe a screw or fastener which when tightened and fully in place does not extend above the surface plane of the unit. A concave depression surrounds the screw or bolt hole. It prevents snags and tears in merchandise and on the customers.

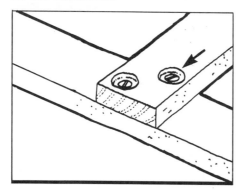

COURSE A horizontal row of bricks, stones, masonry blocks, etc.

COURT An open, unroofed area which is surrounded partly or entirely by a building. See *atrium*.

COUTURE From the French word for "sewing." The term describes custom-made clothes. Haute couture refers to high fashion designs.

COUTURIER French term for male designer or proprietor of a couture house. Couturiere (female).

COVE A quarter-round concave molding which covers the angle between ceiling and wall or floor and wall. A cornice attached to the ceiling.

COVE LIGHTING A form of indirect lighting. The light source is concealed from below by means of a cornice, cove, valance or partially dropped ceiling, and the light is directed up to a reflecting surface. A soft subdued way of lighting an area or wall. Also called atmosphere lighting, back lighting and baffle light.

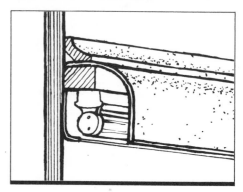

COVER PAPER Many and various types of paper or board used on the outside of booklets, magazines, brochures, etc.

COVERT CLOTH A twill-woven, sturdy woolen, worsted or man-made fiber fabric with a hard or soft finish. Coating or suiting fabric.

COWL NECKLINE A soft, draped neckline similar to that created by having a hood hanging down the back. Loose, unstitched folds that cover part of the shoulders and may hang low over the bosom.

CR (COLOR RENDITION) The ability of a lamp or light source (incandescent, fluorescent, H.I.D.) to show color effectively, i.e., the ability of a fluorescent lamp to present a red garment as a warm red and not greyed down or neutralized.

C-RACK A fixturing unit which in plan view is a one-half round or 180 degree arc. In actual floor use it is a semicircular rack. Also called half-circle rack. A pair of C-racks can be combined to make a two-part round rack, or joined end to opposing end to form an "S" rack. By combining C-racks, which can be made adjustable, into a continuous serpentine pattern, it is possible to make a vari-leveled department or area divider. A variation of the "C" rack is the "U" rack in which the ends are extended beyond the arc.

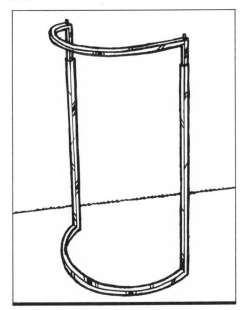

CRAFT UNION A labor union that restricts its membership to professional or skilled craftsmen in the same field, i.e., scenic artists, cabinetmakers, costumers, etc.

CRASH Coarse, uneven, rough fabrics made of cotton, jute, linen or mixtures. Similar to burlap.

CRAVAT A neck scarf or tie.

CRAWL SPACE Any area, usually unfinished and not a full story high, used for access to pipes and ducts. A person can get in and out, but not necessarily while walking erect. Often the underfloor space where the evacuation has not been carried down a full story. See *plenum*.

CRAYON DRAWING A loose, not very detailed kind of drawing produced by a soft black or colored wax crayon on a pebbly or rough surface. These soft crayon drawings can be reproduced as line etchings while hard crayon drawings on smooth board can be reproduced by halftone processes.

CRAZE The erratic, finely cracked surface pattern on glazed pottery or tile which is also used as a decorative pattern on plastic laminates. Crazing may also occur on treated wood veneers possibly from shrinkage and the effects on paint or varnished finishes.

CREDIT RATING The estimate of the ability of an individual or of a business to repay loans based on previous experiences. It is also an indication of the financial stability of a manufacturer and his ability to produce an order without defaulting or going into bankruptcy.

CREEPING The flow or spread of ink or paint beyond the limits of the set pattern or design. See *bleed #2*.

CREPE A fabric with a crinkled surface which can be obtained by hard twisting the yarns, embossing, chemical treatment, etc.

CREPE PAPER Paper which has been tightly crinkled or minutely shirred or corrugated so that the paper has a certain degree of elasticity or stretch. A decorative paper, available in a multitude of colors, used for window display backgrounds or making artificial flowers and party decorations.

CRESCENT WRENCH A small, hand-held vise with a pair of jaw-like clamps, set at an angle to the holding handle. Similar in appearance to a lobster's claws. A ratchet device in the head controls the opening and closing of the jaws.

CRETONNE A cotton unglazed chintz, usually printed with a large, allover pattern.

CREWEL A type of embroidery worked with wool yarn on natural unbleached linen or cotton. The designs are usually large, winding and vinelike with oversized, stylized flowers, birds, etc.

CREW NECKLINE A high, flat round neckline which sits against the throat. A sweater neckline originally sported by boating crews.

CRINOLINE A stiff petticoat, the horsehair or braid used for stiffening petticoats, or the "cage" that serves to fill out the skirt from underneath. A stiff or starched slip used to fill out and flare out a skirt. It made its reappearance in 1947 with Dior's "New Look." See *circular skirt.*

CROCKING The tendency of excess dye to rub off a dyed or printed fabric.

CROP MARKS The marks used to indicate where a piece of artwork or copy is to be trimmed, cut or cropped for it to fit into a specified space.

CROQUIS A preliminary sketch or rough draft.

CROSSBAR A rod or horizontal unit between two vertical supports or brackets. It may also function as a reinforcing or bracing element in a unit as well as a hang rod.

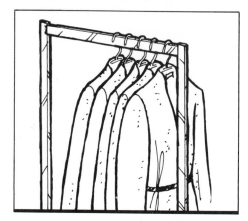

CROSSCUT SAW A sawing carpentry blade designed chiefly to cut across the grain of the wood. The cutting teeth are sharp and straight like a band of "V's." There are usually eight, ten or twelve teeth to the inch.

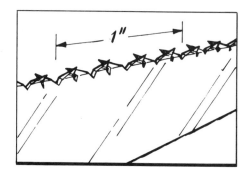

CROSS SECTION *1.* A profile view through an object showing the inner construction and details, etc. *2. (As illustrated on following page)* A sectional drawing.

CROSS SECTION

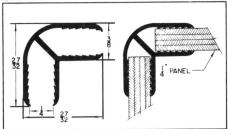

CUBAGE A term used in store planning and layout for the width and depth of an area multiplied by the height. The utilization of the air space, above the floor level, for additional and maximum merchandise and display use.

CUBICON SYSTEM A modular system based on heavy duty fiberboard rectangles with rounded corners. Each face or side has four slots and the units can be hooked into one another (through the slots), stacked upon each other, or set next to each other. There is a variety of rectangular sizes available and all sorts of "Mondrian-type" wall arrangements can be created. Free-standing units are also possible. Various channels, connector bolts and wall mounting angles are available. Produced by Cubicon Corp., St. Louis, Missouri.

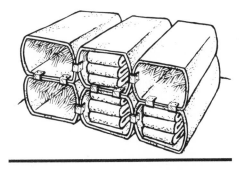

CUBISM One of the major forerunners of abstract art. It is the analysis of forms and their relationship to each other and to space in general. It sometimes expresses the idea of an object rather than a particular view of it. Picasso and Braque were the main exponents of this art form.

CUL-DE-SAC A term used in store layout and planning for a "dead-end." An area or room with only one way in and does not lead to another merchandising area.

CULOTTES Pants that are wide and full enough to look like a skirt. A stitched down or divided skirt. In floor-length designs, with flared or belled trouser legs, the culottes are called "pajamas" or "palazzo pants."

CUMMERBUND A wide, soft sash worn around the waist as a finish to the top of a skirt or trousers. It replaced the vest or waistcoat for men's summer formal wear and is now worn year-round. From the Persian word "kamarband" and originally a carry-all.

CUNEIFORM WRITING Wedge-shaped characters used by the Assyrians and Babylonians as a form of writing. The characters were pressed into damp clay tablets.

CURRENT The rate of and the direction of the flow of electricity. Usually expressed in "amperes."

CURSIVE TYPE Typefaces which simulate hand writing. Script type.

ABCDEabcdefghijklmnopqrstuw

CURTAIN WALL *1. In exterior construction* A thin, nonbearing wall supported independently of the wall below. A large-surfaced facade of glass and metal such as is found in the early works of Mies Van de Rohe, Gropius, Behrens and Dudok. These sweeping clean walls were made possible by advances in the metal and plastics industries in overcoming problems of waterproofing, insulating, expansion and contraction. *2. In interior construction* A valance suspended from the ceiling structure, usually in front of a wall fixture or merchandising wall, to create a recessed or built-in look. It often camouflages a lighting system. Similar to a cornice or valance.

CUSTOM MANNEQUIN A mannequin especially sculpted and made to order for a particular customer or may be based on an actual person. It may be a special head which can be used on an existing "line" body, or it may be an all new form with the "store's" own particular image or "look." It can also refer to a different finish, glaze, or makeup.

CUSTOM MANUFACTURING The production of merchandise to the specific orders and/or requirements of a given customer. A manufacturer may also produce a "line" or merchandise which he can "customize" for a customer.

CUT An engraving of any kind. A design or illustration which has been engraved or etched into a plate and is available for reproduction. Originally it referred to as a woodcut.

CUT AWL A lightweight, hand-manipulated power tool designed for intricate profiles and scrolls on lightweight materials such as cardboards,

composition boards and thin plywoods. It works best on a padded bench or table so that the cutting blade, which will extend below the flat surface of the saw, can bite into something soft and disposable. The machine has two guiding knobs set on either side of the cutting blade. The cutting is controlled by means of pushing forward or backward on the knobs and thus guiding the blade.

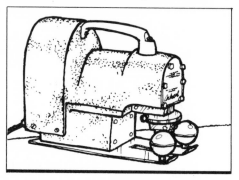

CUT PILE Fabrics such as plush and velvet where an extra set of warp or filling yarns are woven into the fabric and the thread loops are cut into a plushy pile.

CYANOTYPE A blueprint; a blue photographic print on specially sensitized paper. See *blueprint*.

CY-BELLE See *wigs*.

CYCLORAMA (CYC) A large curved or arced background or drop which semi-envelops an area and gives the impression of endless space or sky. There should be no sharp angles or straight lines to detract from that flow of space.

D

DACRON A strong, resilient polyester fiber. Combines well with cotton, wool and other man-made fibers. Trademark of E. I. du Pont de Nemours.

DADA An anti-art, anti-logic, anti-order, pre-surrealistic art that developed from 1915 to 1922. Marcel Duchamp was one of the leading exponents of this "avante garde" art form. From the French word for "hobbyhorse."

DADO The area below the chair rail molding. The lower section of a wall, sometimes given a different surface treatment, separated from the area above by a molding strip.

DADO JOINT A joining technique that serves to reinforce the vertical member of the joint. The horizontal member is prepared with a groove or rabbet into which the vertical member fits snugly. Also called a rabbet joint. See *notched joint.*

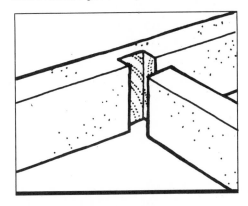

DAGUERREOTYPE The first practical photographic process invented by Louis Daguerre (1781–1851). A faint image was produced and had to be viewed from an angle for true clarity.

DAMASK A floral or geometric pattern fabric, made of almost any natural and man-made fibers or blends. Patterns are lustrous on a dull ground. Reversible fabric.

DART A tuck in the fabric to achieve a better fit in the garment, usually at the bustline, waistline or over the hips.

DAYLIGHT A term used in store lighting to describe the color of light emitted from certain fluorescent tubes to approximate the color of daylight—out of doors. A cool-yellowish color.

DC (DIRECT CURRENT) An electric current that flows in one direction only. See *AC.*

DEAL Southern yellow pine wood that is usually used for the carcase or base of furniture which is to be veneered. A soft wood. Also refers to planks of pine wood and to objects constructed of that material.

DEALER DISPLAYS Point-of-purchase displays that are supplied by the manufacturer or dealer to promote the sale of their merchandise. Displays are usually self-contained and will sometimes be designed to carry a certain amount of stock along with the name and promotional information. See *point-of-purchase displays* and *point-of-sales.*

DECALCOMANIA A decal or transfer piece of decoration. The artwork or message is printed on special, thin paper—in reverse—and when the paper is moistened the design "transfers" to the new surface. The now blank thin sheet of paper is discarded.

DECKLE EDGE A rippled, irregular edge with a "torn" appearance made by machine or by hand. Usually associated with the finish of handmade paper or parchment.

DECK PANTS Leisure pants that end slightly below the knee and, as the name suggests, are ideal for boating. Similar to the 18th- and 19th-century sailor's pants, which were considerably shorter than they are today.

DÉCOLLETAGE A low-cut front and/ or back neckline. See *corsage*.

DÉCOUPAGE A graphic or decorative display art form similar to collage or montage. The application of bits and pieces of assorted materials, textures, etc., to create new and pleasing designs.

DEEP OFFSET HINGE A device that makes it possible for a door or panel to be set back or recessed, yet swing open —clear of the corner posts. One end of the hinge has a right-angled setback to accommodate for the jog in the unit. Used in cabinetry and fixturing. See *jog, offset,* and *setback*.

DEMOGRAPHICS The study of population statistics based on sex, income levels, educational background, shopping habits, religion, politics, etc.

DENIER The size or number of filaments or fibers in a yarn or thread. The higher the denier—the coarser or heavier the yarn.

DENIM A firm, heavy twill weave, cotton or blended fabric. Term derived from serge de Nîmes, a fabric made in the French city of Nîmes. The filler

yarns are usually white and thus account for the whitish cast of the finished fabric.

DENSITY The proportion of fixturing or merchandisers to the total area of the selling space in store planning and layout.

DENTELLE The French word for "lace."

DEPARTMENT A subdivision in store selling that handles a special type of merchandise and has its own buyers and administrators.

DEPARTMENT STORES Large retail operations that sell a wide variety of merchandise from soft goods to hard goods—from fashion garments and accessories to furniture, garden hoses, house paints, nuts and bolts.

DEPRECIATION *1. In business* The loss of use, value, effectiveness or stylishness of an item over a specified period of time. Assets such as fixtures, merchandisers and mannequins are expected to function over many years, but they depreciate in value or resalability over the anticipated life span. *2. In accounting* The "wear and tear" of capital improvements.

DERBY HAT See *bowler*.

DERNIER CRI A French expression for "the very latest."

DESCENDER The downward strokes of certain letters that continue down below the body of the letter. The tails of letters such as the lower case "y," "p," "q," "g," and "j." See *ascender*.

DEVELOPMENT A group of buildings, structures or businesses with a common purpose and, hopefully, profit. An area planned and laid out to accommodate a group of stores, or homes, with parking spaces, plant-ings, roadways, community areas and other amenities.

DEXION SYSTEM See *Apton System.*

DIAGONAL BRACE An angled strip of wood to strengthen and hold square a frame or framed panel.

DIAMETER See *circle.*

DICKEY A detachable insert that simu-lates a shirt front—with or without a tie. A bib, either of fabric or plastic, that may be substituted for a shirt on a suit or coat form.

DIE CAST A process by which molten metal or plastic material is shaped and formed in a mold under heat and/or pressure. In die casting it is possible to reproduce a given design with great precision and accuracy so that it fits, assembly is feasible, and the die cast part can be replaced by another from the same mold without any adjustments.

DIE CUTTING The use of a cutting tool under pressure through several layers of paper or board to yield a cutout with a specific contour and/or interior cuts or scores.

DIFFUSE EDGE The soft edge or outer perimeter of a beam of light which is not sharp or clearly defined. A hazy-edged spot.

DIFFUSER A shield or mask that soft-ens the beam of light from the lamp source. A textured glass or plastic, an eggcrate or filter to cut down on the sharpness or harshness or direct glare of a light. Also see *diffusing glass.*

DIFFUSING GLASS Glass that has been textured by means of rolling to cut down the transparency of the glass and also to soften the light as it comes through the allover patterned surface.

DIMMER A mechanism for changing the intensity of light in a given area by means of cutting down on the amount of electric current that is al-lowed to pass through the electric wires to the lamps. The "resistance dimmer" is the only one that will work on direct current (DC), while "autotransformer," "electronic react-ence," "electronic and magnetic amplifier" dimmers will work on alternating current (AC).

DINNER JACKET First appeared in England in 1880 as a "dress sack coat." It was a dress coat, without tails, used for dinner and dances "at home"—small parties rather than formal balls. In the U.S., it was called the "Tuxedo" after the elegant and affluent village of Tuxedo Park, New York, where it was first popularized.

DIRECT LIGHTING A lighting plan in which the electric fixtures and lamps are clearly visible and not "hidden" or camouflaged. Lighting fixtures that are seen, such as fluorescent ceiling fixtures, chandeliers and droplights.

DIRECT MAIL An advertising device that makes use of mailing lists (such as the store's list of charge customers) to focus on the most likely customers for a particular product or promotion.

DIRECTORY A signing device to supply location information within a store or department. It may be wall mounted or free standing.

DIRNDL SKIRT A full skirt gathered at the waist. Based on a Tyrolean design, it is often peasant-like and executed in bright colors and provincial patterned fabrics.

DISCOUNT STORE A retail operation selling merchandise at "cut-rate." The merchandise is discounted from the suggested retail prices set by manufacturers, or the standard markup of other retailers.

DISPLAYER A fixturing unit that shows a garment, or piece of merchandise, or a group of coordinated or related pieces. It may, but does not necessarily have to, hold stock or an assortment of the merchandise, but it

should show the featured piece to its best advantage. A displayer is a highlighter for visual impact. See *Teestand.*

DISPLAY STORE A store that contains only a sampling of the merchandise available by mail order or phone from the main store, which has a complete stock.

DISPLAY TYPE Type that is larger than 14 point or the usual body type of the message. Usually used for captions and headlines.

DISTRESSED An "aging" process in wood finishing such as scarring, shading, drilling minute "worm" holes and spattering or "flyspecking." An antiquing effect which suggests "wear and tear."

DIVIDER 1. (*As illustrated*) A store layout unit designed to separate two areas, or to create two areas out of one space by dividing it physically and visually. A screen, merchandising unit, cabinet, decorative platform with panel or piece of furniture, which is finished, decorated on both sides and semi-opaque. Often the dividers are temporary so that the floor space can be altered or redesigned to

suit new spatial requirements. *2.* A window device, such as a screen, panel or curtain, that separates a run-on window into parts, the back of an open-back window from the interior of the store, or a display area from a selling space. *3.* A drawing instrument for measuring, marking and transferring measurements or dimensions. Two arms ending in points and joined at a pivotal or set-screw head. A caliper.

DJELLABA A full-length cloak with full sleeves and hood open at the neck and worn by men or women. A Moroccan hooded cloak.

DOCUMENTARIES Wallpaper and fabric designs that are based on or taken from authentic period designs.

DOG COLLAR A tight-fitted necklace, several strands high and held together with vertical bars. Similar to a dog's collar. It was fashionable in the 19th century and worn with high, shirtwaist collars or with décolletage necklines. A choker.

DOLLAR SALES PER SQUARE FOOT The net sales of a department store, specialty store or an individual department divided by the square-foot area of the store or department. The higher the dollars in relation to the square footage, the better it is for the store or department.

DOLLY A low platform or pallet, mounted on wheels. Used for moving heavy or awkward objects.

DOLMAN, DOLAMA A full-length, flowing open robe with long, full, slitted sleeves that is worn as an outer garment, often over a caftan or sheath. It is Oriental-Turkish in origin and has been adapted over the centuries. Today, it is popular as an evening wrap, executed in velvet, brocade or fine wool.

DOLMAN SLEEVE A sleeve cut all-in-one with shoulder. Sometimes similar to batwing sleeve.

DOME SKIRT A skirt that has been stiffened or reinforced to stand out at the hips and then fall straight down to the hemline. Popular in the late 1940s and into the '50s.

DOMESTICS The "bed and bath" grouping of merchandise: sheets, pillowcases, quilts, comforters, blankets, towels, shower curtains, etc. The merchandise that stars in "White Sales."

DOMINO PAPER An early wallpaper decorated with small, allover designs —often square or diamond shaped. It also refers to the marbleized papers printed from blocks, and colored by hand. Originally produced in Italy in the late 16th and early 17th centuries.

DORIC ORDER The oldest and simplest of the classic architectural orders. A simple, flattened bowl-like capital sits atop the fluted shaft.

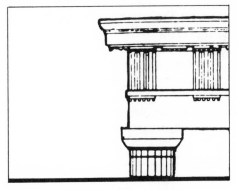

DORMER, DORMER WINDOW A window or enclosed structure that projects up from the sloping surface of an angled roof.

DOUBLE DECK STOCK The use of a mezzanine in the storage area for greater cubic space. A secondary storage or stocking area built *over* the floor-based stock shelves or bins.

DOUBLE GLAZING A window covered with two sheets of glass with a minute, rarefied air space between the two sheets to serve as an insulant against the passage of heat—in or out.

DOUBLE-HEADED/DUPLEX NAIL A nail with two heads spaced one above the other. The top head remains exposed and uninvolved with the materials to be joined. When the joint has to be disassembled, it is simpler for the clutches of the claw hammer to grasp the top head and pull the entire nail out. It is especially useful in temporary constructions such as displays and stage settings.

DOUGLAS FIR A relatively inexpensive wood with a curly grain used for making plywood and laminated sheets. It resembles white pine and stains well.

DOUPIONI, DUPPION, DUPPIONE Irregular slub silk yarns used in weaving shantung and pongee.

DOVETAIL CUTTING SAW A small hand saw, of the back saw type, especially suited to the angled cuts involved in making a dovetail joint.

DOVETAIL JOINT A secure, interlocking-type of joint in which wedge-shaped projections on one piece of lumber interlock with wedge-shaped

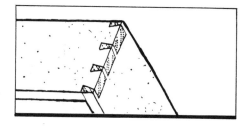

grooves on another piece of lumber. Often found in the front and side joints of drawers.

DOWEL A round rod of wood, metal or plastic.

DOWEL STAND A central vertical rod attached to a base with various sized rods projecting through the longer vertical rod to display necklaces, chains, ties, towels, cups, etc.

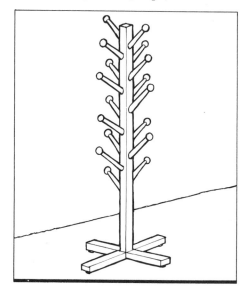

DOWNLIGHT A lighting fixture with a reflecting surface, shade or shield that directs the beam or spread of light down towards the floor area—rather than up to the ceiling.

DOWNSLANT See *waterfall*.

DOWNSTAGE The area closest to the glass in a display window. The part of the stage closest to the audience.

DRAFT A line drawing, often geometrically or mechanically projected, of a proposed structure or design. A preliminary sketch or drawing.

DRAPER A gooseneck stand or counter costumer used to show assorted components of an outfit (jacket, skirt, pants, sweater, tie, etc.). A hanger on a vertical rod with accessory attachments.

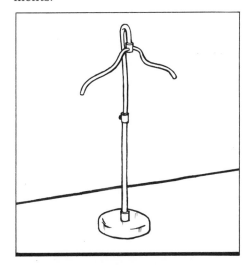

DRAW CURTAIN A fabric drapery or panel suspended from sliding or rolling carriers which are set into a track mounted overhead. The curtain is opened by means of drawing the panels to one side or the other.

DRAWING The art of representing images, shapes, patterns or three-dimensional elements on a two-dimensional surface. It may be executed in one of many media: watercolors, oils, charcoal, pastel, pencil, etc. Usually a freehand rendition as opposed to a mechanical drawing.

DRAWING BOARD *1*. A bristol board or similar heavy board, which is made of low-grade inner sheets lined or covered on both sides with sheets of good, coated paper. *2*. The surface or table upon which an artist works—usually adjustable.

DRESS FORM A headless, armless and legless form extending from the neck down to below the hips. It is usually made of papier-mâché and covered in linen, jersey or velvet. There is usually a fitting on the bottom of the form to receive a rod which may be attached to a base, a fixture, a platform, etc. The form averages between 36″ to 38″ in height, depending upon the neck extension.

DRESSING ROOM See *fitting room.*

DRESSMAKER FORM A standardized duplication of the human torso, canvas-covered and cotton-padded, set on a wire basketlike structure supported on an ornate cast iron or brass base, with or without casters. Used by designers, tailors, seamstresses, etc., to fit, pin and drape designs or patterns. Available in a variety of dress sizes and also customized for specific bust, waist, and hip measurements. Also called model form.

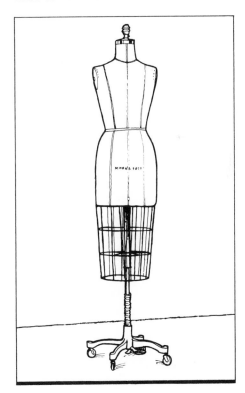

DRIERS Additives used to speed up the drying time of paints and printing inks.

DRILL *1.* A tough, durable, heavy twill cotton or man-made fiber fabric similar to denim. *2.* See *hand drill* and *power hand drill.*

DRILL PRESS An upright power tool used to drill holes. It usually consists of a base, mounted on the floor or onto a bench, a vertical column (shorter for bench mounting), the drill table and the mechanism which includes the spindle, speed reducer and motor.

DROP A decorative pendant such as a vertical foliage spray that hangs down against a column or wall or a cascading end of a pull-back curtain. Also a panel of fabric (net, muslin, burlap, etc.) attached to the top and bottom of a wood strip (batten) or pipe and suspended from overhead as a divider, a decorative background, or a setting. A "cutout drop" will have certain areas of the panel cut out and the openings are often reinforced with a piece of gauze or net.

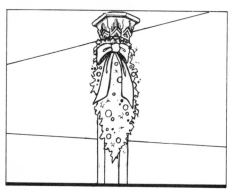

DROP CLOTH A tarpaulin. A large protective cloth used to cover mannequins, fixtures, furniture, etc., and keep them clean when they are not in use or protect them while work is going on around them.

DROPLIGHT A light fixture which hangs down from the ceiling on a flexible cord or a cord entwined around a chain.

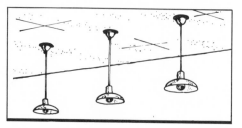

DRY BRUSH TECHNIQUE A technique used in graphics with a brush that is slightly inked or barely dipped in paint and stroked across the design or piece of artwork for tonal effects.

DRY CEILING SURFACES Ceilings finished with assorted sheets or panels rather than with plaster which is a wet application. Typical dry ceiling surfaces are sheetrock, metal sheets, acoustical tiles, cork, wood or carpeting. Selection of material will vary with use, decorative quality desired, price, building or fire codes, etc.

DRY GOODS A term used to describe textiles, piece goods, yard goods, notions and trimmings as well as women's and men's accessories and furnishings made of textiles.

DRY TRANSFER A vinyl, self-adhering sign system in which letters are transferred from the plastic sheet onto a surface. Hundreds of typefaces are available from 6 pt. to 288 pt., in black and white as well as in some colors. Characters are printed on a plastic film base, which is coated with an adhesive on the back. When pressure is applied by rubbing the printed character with a wedge-shaped tool onto a surface placed under the plastic sheet, the character is transferred onto the surface. The dry transfer process also applies to ornamental bands, numbers, tone and shading patterns such as dots, lines, checks, weaves, etc. Vinyl sheets are sold under such trademarks as Artype, benday, Bourges Artist's Shading Sheets, Prestype and Letrasign.

DRYWALL Veneering a partition with precast sheets of paper-covered plaster (plasterboards) make a wall "dry" as opposed to covering a partition with plaster, spread in place which makes a wall "wet." See *gypsum board* and *plasterboard*.

DUCK A tightly woven cotton or man-made fiber fabric, usually with a plain, flat weave, Similar to canvas.

DUMMY *1.* Slang for a mannequin, but most commonly used to describe the dressmaker or model form. *2.* A term used in graphics to describe a rough layout done in scale and in proportion to the finished artwork and/or copy. It shows the general plan and style that is contemplated. A mock-up.

DUMP BIN A "point-of-purchase" container, box or enclosure into which

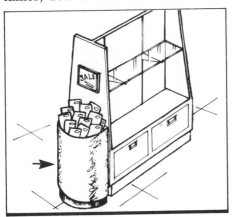

small merchandise (usually sale priced) is loosely tossed. A point-of-sale cardboard box with signing for display and stacking of featured merchandise.

DUMP TABLE A table on the selling floor, usually with a rim or rail, into which sale or specially featured merchandise is "tossed." Often associated with discount merchandise and a "helter-skelter" or "mish-mash" look. See *bargain square* and *emphasis table*.

DUPLEX PAPERS Papers finished with different colors and/or textures on each side. This type of paper is prepared by pasting two dissimilar papers together. Used in printing.

DWARF WALL A wall or partition that does not reach the ceiling.

DYNEL A modacrylic fiber. Used for upholstery and drapery fabrics as well as for carpeting. It has resiliency and strength and is resistant to chemicals. Trademark of Union Carbide Corporation.

E

EASEL *1.* An adjustable folding frame or tripod used in fixturing to hold a surface perpendicular to the ground. *2.* A sign holder. *3.* A die cut and scored cardboard flap which is attached to the back of a board to keep the board vertical and erect. Used for announcements. *4.* An adjustable frame to hold a canvas during the execution of a painting.

EASEMENT The facilitating of access to roads, utilities and passage over or right-of-way across another's land by means of negotiated terms. Permission to step on, park on, or erect on somebody else's property.

EBONY A hard, dense, dark brown-black wood with a fine grain.

ECLECTIC, ECLECTICISM The collection and mixture of assorted art forms, motifs, and concepts from various periods and styles. A melange of periods, styles, fashions, and fads. The adapting and using of assorted past styles in a contemporary manner. The Victorian 19th century was considered an era of "eclecticism." Older patterns and styles were borrowed and adapted to the new mechanized processes of the times.

EDISON BASE BULB See *medium screw base.*

E.D.P. See *electronic data processing.*

E.D. & P.A. Exhibit Designers and Producers Association.

EGGCRATE A baffle for diffusing light from ceiling-hung fluorescent fixtures. A rectangular attachment, which is divided into many smaller rectangles, and resembles the folded cardboard fillers used to separate eggs in the old cardboard cartons.

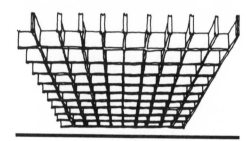

EGG HEAD An oval, abstract head without features or anatomical details. It may be used as a head for millinery or as an abstract head for mannequin or form. Available in a variety of non-skin tones and in metallics. Sometimes available with "faces" painted on head.

EGGSHELL FINISH A pebbly finish on paper or board resembling the textured surface on an eggshell. A matte, stippled effect. The finish is not aligned with the grain of the paper.

EGYPTIAN TYPE A display type also known as "antique." It is distinguished by thick, slab serifs and heavy main strokes, with little or no variation in thickness. First appearance approximately in 1815.

EISENHOWER JACKET See *battle jacket.*

ELECTRIC ARC See *welding.*

ELECTROBRITE Trademark for a zinc finish on metal, which resembles chrome in color and sheen.

ELECTRONIC DATA PROCESSING (E.D.P.) The collecting and communicating of assorted data, statistics, prices, accounts, etc., by means of a computer and special computer systems. See *Fortran.*

ELEVATED WINDOWS Display windows raised from 12 inches to 2 feet above the sidewalk level.

ELEVATION An architectural drawing of a flat, two-dimensional view of a room or building or object, usually to scale, to show relative size of architectural and decorative details. Heights and widths can be shown in an elevation. For the depth, one must refer to a plan view of the same object.

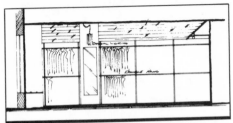

ELEVATOR WINDOWS Display windows with floor levels which may be raised or lowered to create special vi-

sual effects, or to make possible the dressing of the window at basement level. The completed window is then raised up to the desired height in relation to the viewer on the street level.

ELLIPTICAL SPOTLIGHTS A term for the elliptical reflector in a spotlight that throws a stronger beam of light from a greater distance than the traditional reflector spotlight. By use of framing shutters, the elliptical spotlight becomes a projector-type instrument. When a light source must be placed a great distance from the subject or area to be lit, the elliptical spotlight works better than the standard spotlight.

ELM A tough, strong wood that is light brown, tinged with red, and has darker brown ring marks. It stains well and the strong figure marking shows well with polishing.

ELMER'S GLUE See *polyvinyl white resins.*

ELURA See *wigs.*

EM A printing unit of measurement which represents the square of any type size: an 8 point em is 8 points wide by 8 points high, 72 points = 1 inch.

EMBLEMATIC ART The use of simple, recognizable emblems or symbols as a basis for creating a flat image on a flat surface. The use of stripes, targets, chevrons, flags, letters, numbers, maps, etc., provides the subject matter. The art is in the colors, harmony and scale used to interpret these simple forms. Frank Stella, Jasper Johns, Robert Indiana and Kenneth Noland are leading exponents of this art form. See *supergraphics.*

EMBOSSING The process by which a design or motif is raised up from the surface of the paper or board, by means of pressure applied to a die from underneath. An embossed or relief impression can also be obtained in certain printing processes where the lines of the design, etched into the die, appear in relief on the printed surface.

EMBROIDERY A raised pattern or design on fabric produced by means of stitching thread or yarn through the fabric, usually in special stitches.

EMPHASIS TABLE A table on a selling floor with an arrangement or display of featured merchandise. Often used in shoe, giftware, home furnishings departments or where the featured merchandise does not hang—as on a costumer or T-Stand. See *bargain square* and *dump table*.

EMPIRE STYLE French fashions worn under the reign of Napoleon I, 1804–1815. Women wore low-cut square-necklined dresses belted or banded directly under the bosom creating the illusion of a high waistline. Worn with Spencer jackets.

EMULSION A vehicle or medium in painting consisting of water and oil. It cannot be mixed unless combined with an emulsifier such as albumen, casein, egg or wax. Used in printing and graphics.

ENAMEL *1.* A high shine coated paper or board. *2.* A colored glaze used to decorate metals or ceramics. After firing, the paint becomes hard and permanent. *3.* A high luster paint finish.

ENCLOSED MALL A shopping center contained beneath a single roof and sharing the common amenities of plants, fountains, sculptures, seating, and "outdoor" restaurants. The en-

closing or containing ceiling may be primarily glass and serve as a pseudo-atrium. See *atrium*.

ENCLOSED PLAN The sales floor is divided into separate, and sometimes enclosed, shops or departments with individual ambiences and special treatments, colored walls, flooring, lighting, etc. There is limited flexibility for changes and remodeling, and usually requires more sales help, better security, etc.

ENCLOSED WINDOW A boxed-in window consisting of three full walls, the display window glass and a lighting system. Usually equipped with a door or sliding partition for entering and exiting.

ENCLOSING WALL An exterior, non-bearing wall connected to columns, piers or the floors.

END OF AISLE See *aisle liner* and *end unit*.

END UNIT An additional table or extension surface at the end of a stocking fixture—similar to a dump table or bin at the end of a gondola. Usually used in well-trafficked areas to pre-

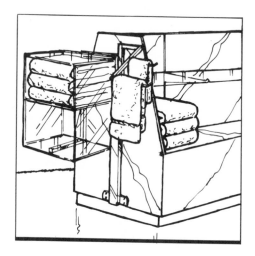

sent additional merchandise. Also known as cap unit.

END USE An object or piece of merchandise displayed in the manner it is intended to be used. For example a suit complete with blouse, scarf, shoes, bag and gloves or a chair in a vignette setting with the proper drapery fabric, carpet or rug, table, lamp and other accessories.

ENGAGED COLUMN A circular column shaft partially embedded into a wall or surface and thus only part of the roundness is visible.

ENGLISH BOND See *bond*.

ENGRAVING A general term that covers a multitude of techniques for reproducing prints or line artwork. The usual technique is to cut the design into a hard material such as steel, copper or wood. The design may be incised (cut below the plate surface) or raised up (the surface around the line is cut away). Then the design is inked and impressions are made by pressing a paper (or other printing surface) against the inked surface. Some engraving techniques are: woodcut, line engravings, drypoint, etchings, linocuts, aquatints, mezzotints, and intaglio engraving.

ENTRESOL A half story or mezzanine. See *mezzanine*.

ENVIRONMENT All the elements involved in store planning to make up the total surrounding. In a selling area it includes: the floors and the flooring, the walls (textures, colors and appliqués), the ceiling and the lighting, the fixtures, decorations, arrangement of merchandise, and the open spaces, the aisles, the seating, the gracious touches such as plants, sculpture and display areas.

ENVIRONMENTAL DESIGN The arts and sciences involved in creating a "man-made environment," be it a home, a school or a department store. It is the involvement and integration of architecture, interior design, landscaping, lighting, acoustics, flow, engineering, etc., to create a pleasing, satisfying whole.

ENVIRONMENTAL SELLING A merchandise presentation showing an assortment of items in a setting similar to how and where the customer might use them. As an example: a bedroom vignette with sheets, pillowcases, quilts and comforters, and maybe even terry robe, towels, slippers, soap, etc. See *vignette*.

E.O.M. End of Month.

EPOXY An extremely strong adhesive or sealant, which is available in kit form. It is also available as a liquid resin which must be catalyzed to become effective as a coating or cement. Epoxy is also used in molding, casting, laminating and as a means of encapsulating other materials. The epoxy resins are thermosetting and are widely used in the reinforced plastics field since they have good adhesion to glass fibers.

EPOXY RESIN GLUE Originally developed for joining non-porous materials. Does not shrink much upon curing and will combine with glass, plastic or other woods. It is very strong and comes in two-part formulation, which must be mixed before using. The mixture, under normal circumstances, is workable for about two hours and securely sets in about eighteen hours. The setting can be accelerated by the application of moderate heat (from a lamp).

ERTÉ A famous French artist-designer who began in Paris with Paul Poiret (c. 1910). Noted for the costume designs and sketches he created during the 1920s and 1930s.

ESCUTCHEON A decorative shield or plate used in heraldry and hardware.

ESPADRILLES Casual shoes with braided cord or rope soles with canvas or other fabric uppers. Originally worn by the Italians and the French of the Midi (the south).

ESPALIÉR A wooden lattice upon which trees and shrubs are tied back and "trained" to grow in decorative patterns. The decoratively branched trees are referred to as "espaliér."

ESPLANADE A grand concourse or a flat landscaped area with walkways, drives and plantings—usually with a view.

ESTIMATE An intelligent evaluation based on experience, available data (even if incomplete), and expert opinions. A predetermination of costs before actual construction begins. Budgets are usually based on estimated expenses.

ÉTAGÈRE A French term for a displayer shelf unit, a "what-not" or curio cabinet without doors. An open, multi-shelf, displayer-fixture.

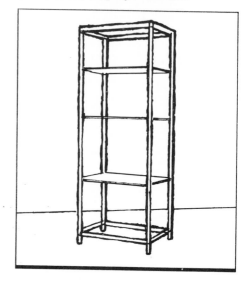

ETCHING The printed reproduction produced from an etched plate. A form of engraving. The design is either scratched (drypoint) or chemically etched through the protective covering on the surface of the copper or zinc plate to form an intaglio pattern of lines and dots below that surface. The finished plate is then heavily coated with ink which is, in turn, rubbed off leaving the ink only in the ruts and ridges below the surface of the plate. The prints are pulled on a press where great pressure is exerted to force the ink up from the etched furrows onto the paper.

ETHNIC MANNEQUIN A black, oriental or racial-type mannequin with a particular skin tone, or face or body physiognomy.

ETON JACKET A straight-cut jacket, from waist-length to top of hip-length, with wide notched lapels and an open front. Originally worn by the students at Eton College in England.

ETRUSCAN ORDER The "Tuscan" order. The Roman version of the simple Doric order.

EUROLYN See *wigs*.

EXCHANGE DESK The counter or enclosure, usually removed from the selling floor, where customers may bring back merchandise to be exchanged, credited to their account or returned for cash or "store money." The exchange desk is often hooked into a computer set-up to credit accounts and record transactions, as well as set up to contain case register or cash drawer. Since cash may be involved, the exchange desk is located in a high security area.

EXPANDED TYPE A wide, spread out typeface which is broader and more extended than would be usual for that particular type. See *condensed type*.

EXPANSION BIT A carpentry bit with a cutting blade that can be adjusted to various sizes or diameters.

EXTENDERS Inorganic printing and graphics compounds, which are usu-

ally fairly clear and colorless, that are mixed with pigments to increase the flow and covering ability of the pigments.

EXTRUDED A continuous shaped piece of metal or plastics formed by being forced through a die or mold under great pressure. For example: hollow tubes, channels, angles and decorative moldings.

EYEBALL LIGHTS Spherical, ball-shaped housings for spotlights and floodlights. Also called globe lights.

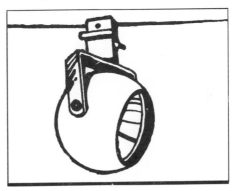

EYEBALL SECURITY A theft-control system or part of an overall security system which relies upon the direct observation by guards and/or store personnel for the protection of the merchandise. The "watchful worker" may or may not be in a uniform.

EYE BOLT A long metal screw with a ring at one end (the eye) and a nut or wing-nut at the other. It is possible to attach to the exposed ring or "eye" after the bolt has been secured into a bearing surface.

EYE LEVEL The horizon line to which, in a perspective drawing, all receding parallel lines converge—to meet at the vanishing points (which are located at eye level). The horizontal extension of a viewer's line of sight—about 5 feet off the ground for a stand- ing viewer. Displays set over 5 feet off the ground are often above the viewer's or "shopper's" eye level. Also see *horizon/horizon line, perspective,* and *vanishing point.* (See illustation under *perspective.*)

F

FACADE The principal front or face of a building, structure, architectural piece of furniture, decorative object, etc. The main, exposed frontal view which often is especially faced, veneered, ornamented or signed. See *facings*.

FACE The printing surface of a piece of type. The part of the die or type that will reproduce when inked and impressed on paper.

FACE BRICKS Bricks that are especially selected for their color, texture and finish to be used in exposed areas such as on the facades of buildings and fireplaces.

FACE OUT Merchandise that has been hung with a full frontal showing and towards the approaching shopper rather than displayed in a shoulder and sleeve presentation associated with round racks and closets. The face-out, front-on, forward presentation provides a better view of more of the garment and the styling. The first face-out garment on a rack or waterfall is often completely trimmed and/or accessorized. See *shoulder out* and *waterfall*.

FACINGS Finished or better quality surfacing materials used to cover the front facade or face of a structure that has been constructed of inferior or non-decorative materials such as a marble veneer over a poured concrete wall. See *facade*.

FAD A novelty and often a passing fancy. A trendy costume or gimmick that can be "dated" and "passe" by the next season—the papagallo (parrot) screaming all over T-shirts, sweaters, pins, etc. Sometimes a fad can be universally accepted and become a style such as Western-styled boots in New York City.

FAIENCE French for "pottery." Terracotta. A glazed tile used for facing walls or floors.

FAILLE A crisp ribbed fabric with the corded effect produced by heavier filler yarns.

FANLIGHT A window, usually decorative, set above a door or entranceway. A fanlike arrangement is still very popular.

FASCIA, FACIA 1. *(As illustrated)* The horizontal panel finishing the top of a wall hanging or shelving unit. 2. The band between built-in cabinets and the ceiling. 3. One of the three bands that make up the architrave, which is

the lowest part of the entablature. *4.* A flat band or vertical face in the architrave, but may also be the top or protruding or projecting edge of a building.

FASHION "What merchandising is all about." The new trends and looks created by designers, made by manufacturers, presented by the media and display people, and then, hopefully, sold by merchandisers and retailers. Whims, fads and novelties that can become styles or classics if and when they are accepted by the buying public. The answer to the ever present question—"What's new?"

FASHION COORDINATOR The individual or department responsible for analyzing the fashion trends, and then supervising the selection, coordination, accessorizing, and displaying of the correct merchandise in the various related departments. The title may also refer to the person in the visual merchandising department who is responsible for coordinating and accessorizing merchandise which is to be displayed.

FASHION CYCLE A term used to describe the arrival, the peak and the decline of a popular fashion trend.

FAT-FACE TYPE See *full-face type.*

FAVRILE Late 19th-century iridescent glass produced by Louis Tiffany. Often decorated in the Art Nouveau style.

FEATURED ITEM The merchandise that is getting special attention, that is being promoted and starred in a display.

FEATURE FIXTURE See *aisle liner* and *T-stand.*

FEATURE TABLE See *aisle table* and *promotional table.*

FEDORA A man's soft felt hat with a snapbrim and a center crease across the crown. Named after the heroine of a Parisian drama of 1883.

FELT A nonwoven fabric made by matting and interlocking fibers or yarns under heat and pressure. A fabric *without* weave, pattern or grain.

FENESTRATION The window and door arrangement of a building, and the relationship of openings to the balance of a facade.

FERRULE *1. (As illustrated)* A metal cup of lipped dish used as a protective end cap for a wooden leg, and as a reinforcing agent. *2.* A metal band on a paintbrush that holds the bristles onto the wooden stem.

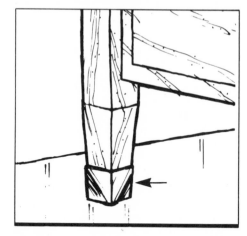

FESTOON A curved or inverted arc created by a piece of fabric or a chain or ribbon hanging limply between two points—one usually higher than the other. A garland, drop or swag.

FEZ A truncated cone-shaped brimless hat made of felt and usually ornamented with a long pendant tassel from the center of the crown. Originated in the city of Fez in French Morocco, and was originally a dull crimson color. Part of the Turkish official dress in the early 19th century.

FIBERBOARD A pulped wood panel, usually 4′ × 8′, without grain and formed by compression under great pressure. There are many trademark names for this type of product: Masonite, Beaverboard, Homosote, etc. It may be used as an underlayer for flooring or roofing materials as well as for partitions, ceilings and the carcases of inexpensive furniture. See *pegboard.*

FIBERGLAS, FIBERGLASS Fine filaments of glass fiber and for the cloth woven from these fibers. Strong, soft, pliable fibers which are resistant to heat, soil and chemicals. Fiberglass, in wool-like pads and covered with paper, is an excellent insulating material and when saturated with polyester plastic it can be molded into chair seats, planters, containers and other decorative units. Trademark of Owens-Corning Fiberglas Corp. Glass fibers are also manufactured by Pittsburgh Plate Glass Company (PPG) and Johns-Manville Corp.

FIBER RUG A rug woven of kraft or sisal fibers and usually reversible. A hard, flat surface.

FIELDSTONE Usually rough, rounded and irregular-shaped stones picked up in fields through which glaciers, at one time, passed. When joined into walls, or used as a facing for a structure, it presents a haphazard, jigsaw effect with the mortar adding decorative outlines around each stone. A casual irregular effect especially when compared to an ashlar facade. See *ashlar.*

FILAGREE, FILIGREE Ornate and fanciful, intertwisted metal wirework. Open, lacy grillwork.

FILAMENT TUBE The enclosure or envelop for the filament and halogen gas in tungsten halogen lamps. Usually made of quartz. See *tungsten halogen lamp.*

FILLERS The pastes or liquid substances used to fill the pores of coarse-grained woods before the final finish, or to fill cuts, gouges or other imperfections in the wood. Fillers will give the wood a smooth, flat surface, but may cause a somewhat poorer adhesion on the finish. The paste fillers are recommended for open-grained woods and are often available in colors. Paste fillers can be thinned with turpentine or naptha until they are the proper consistency for brushing. The liquid filler is generally a cheap varnish to which silex has been added and is best suited for close-grained hardwoods.

FILM STENCIL The gelatin-covered film used in preparing screens for silk screen reproductions.

FINGER JOINT A movable and interlocking cabinetry joint used between a fixed and a movable member.

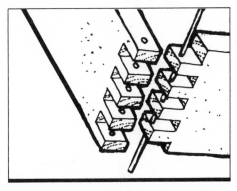

FINIAL A decorative turning, knob or caplike ornate element placed at the end of a pole, rod, pipe, or upright bar.

FINISH *1.* The surface texture or pattern of an object or material such as smooth, rough, shiny, eggshell, bumpy and striated. The feel or hand of a fabric. *2.* The treatment of fabric or paper such as napping, embossing, glazing, waterproofing and crinkling.

FINISHING NAIL See *flathead nail.*

FIREPROOF A material that prevents combustion and resists heat for a long and continuous period of time. Material will neither burst into and support a flame nor weaken internally and collapse from the exposure to heat. Reinforced concrete is a fireproof material in that the concrete protects and insulates the internal steel structure which could collapse from too long an exposure to heat.

FIRE RETARDANT See *flame retardant.* The latter term is preferred.

FIRE-RETARDANT WIRED GLASS Chromium-dipped wire embedded in a sheet of glass. In the rolling process the glass can have a variety of patterns or textures.

FIRESTOP A plug to fill the narrow open space in a hollow wall and prevent the spread of a fire. The plug may be only 1″ thick but up to 10′ wide.

FIRE WALL A wall constructed of fire-retarding materials and designed to hinder the spread of fire.

FISCAL YEAR A retailing term used to describe a business year of twelve consecutive months that may begin at any time and run through a complete operating and financial cycle. A fiscal year could begin on February 1 and end on January 31 of the next year, or run from June 1 to May 31.

FISHING LINE A fine, but strong, nylon cord such as is used on fishing poles. It is almost invisible but tough and used to hang, drape, tie-back and shape merchandise and props. A "must" in the display person's tool box and essential in "flying" merchandise. See *flying.*

FITTING ROOM A room where a customer will change or try on merchandise to make a selection. Type, size, lighting and furnishings will vary with the type and image of store.

FIXATIVE A thin varnish sprayed over pencil, chalk or pastel drawings to protect or "fix" them from rubbing or smearing. Available in spray cans. A fine spray of shellac dissolved in methylated spirits.

FIXTURES The furnishings of a retail operation: cases, counters, cabinets, closets, etc. They may be built-in, screwed on, nailed down, bolted through, as permanent elements in store planning and design or may be movable and "rearrangeable." The counter display units, T-stands, round racks, etc., stand free around the store. See *freestanding fixture.*

FIXTURE LAYOUT A plan that shows the perimeter walls, partitions, aisles, counters, selling fixtures and behind-the-scenes services. It is used to locate and apportion fixture stands, platforms, display areas, etc.

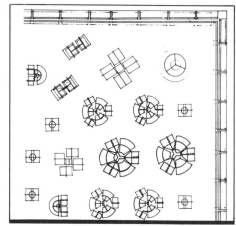

FLAGSHIP STORE The downtown or main store in a chain operation. It could be the "mother" store to the branches—or the special image or "presentation" store.

FLAGSTONE Flooring or pavement material. Large flat plates of stone which are cut into regular tiles or left as irregular shapes. Slate is often used for flagstone floors.

FLAKEBOARD See *particle board.*

FLAME BULB A lamp bulb with a conical glass casing, which is twisted and swirled at its end to resemble a candleflame. See *candelabra base bulb* and *flicker bulb.*

FLAME RETARDANT Chemical used to impart flame resistance to a material, but does not make it fireproof. The retardant may slow down the burning process.

FLANGE *1. (As illustrated)* A projecting collar, lip or rim which aids in the attaching or reinforcing of a unit. A flat dish with an attached cup, usually threaded, into which a member is screwed or bolted. It serves as a base or floor plate. *2.* Additional fabric taken up at the shoulder and armhole intersection in the form of a pleat.

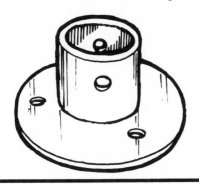

FLARED SKIRT A skirt wider and fuller at the hemline than at the hipline.

FLASHER A device that screws into the lightbulb socket before the lamp is inserted and causes the lightbulb to flash on and off by interfering with the flow of current. Sometimes a set of miniature lightbulbs comes with a flasher bulb, which breaks the current and causes the lights to flash on and off.

FLASHING *1.* Sheet metalwork, usually made of lead or zinc, placed over windows, doors, dormers, gable walls, around chimneys, etc., to prevent leakage. It covers and protects the joints between the roof finish and the aforementioned surfaces. *2.* An inexpensive makeshift plating, which imparts a chromelike finish of no lasting significance. *3.* A sheeting of metal to cover and seal exposed angles and joints.

FLAT A framed panel used in window display and theater set design, which may be painted on, printed on or onto which artwork can be applied. The basic unit in stage set design.

FLAT-BED CYLINDER PRESS A type of printing press in which the printing form with the type rests on a plane surface and is passed alternately under the inking rollers and a rotating cylinder, which presses the paper against the moving type.

FLATHEAD NAIL The common nail for rough woodwork. Large flatheads are best for soft materials since the nailhead can work its way down below the exposed surface of the material. The finishing nail has a small head and is extremely versatile. Also called finishing nail.

FLATTING AGENT A substance added to paints, varnishes and dyes to reduce the gloss on the finished surface. Used in printing and graphics.

FLAX A fiber from the flax plant used in the production of linen.

FLEMISH BOND See *bond*.

FLEX ARM Flexible metal wire extensions from the "arm sockets" of coat or suit forms, which can be bent and reshaped into various natural arm positions. The "arms" are similar to a BX cable or a gooseneck. With flex arms it is possible to break the rigid "dummy" look of a coat or suit form and give the garment a natural look. See *BX cable* and *gooseneck*.

FLEX-ARM DISPLAYER A counter or ledge fixturing unit, similar to a costumer, except that the hanger or shoulder element, on top, continues down, into flexible cable "arms." It is like a "stick figure" in that it is possible to place a dress, jacket, blouse or sweater on the displayer and bend the "arms" into animated positions. The flex-arm displayer is also available for wall or column attachment. Also see *gooseneck*.

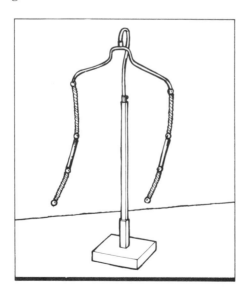

FLEXIBILITY Quality or design in fixturing that allows for change, movement and adaptability to new uses, sizes, locations, etc., such as raising and lowering hang rods or adding new arms and/or attachments.

FLEXIBLE CURVE A drafting tool. A flexible strip of material (usually pliable metal and hard rubber or plastic) which can be bent into assorted arcs and curves that can be traced or scribed onto another material. It is different from a French Curve. (in which all the curves are prescribed) in that with a flexible curve the designer can create his own curves or arcs.

FLEX MIRROR Small pieces of mirror cut into squares, diamonds, rectangles, etc.) that are glued onto a pliable, fabric backing. It is thus possible to wrap "mirror" around curves and angles.

FLEXWOOD See *weldwood flexwood*.

FLICKER BULB A candle-shaped bulb that flickers and spurts and simulates mechanically a candle flame. See *candelabra-base bulb* and *flame bulb*.

FLINT PAPER A shiny, highly polished and coated paper, which is prepared by rubbing flint stones across the paper. Similar to an enamel finish. See *glazed paper*.

FLITCH *1. In construction* A metal plate used as a splint or reinforcing agent on a wooden beam which is not strong enough to support its load. *2. In woodworking* Any part of a log which is sliced into veneer sheets.

FLITTER Tiny bits of finely chopped brass and tin (gold and silver) which sparkle and glitter. The minute sparklers can be glued onto paper, fabric, etc., and used in decoratives.

FLOATING FURNITURE Modern fixturing, cabinets, shelving, drawer units, etc., hung or suspended from the walls. The case pieces do not have legs and are usually bracketed off stiles or upright wall standards, which are bolted into the wall or partition.

FLOCKING A type of printing process in which finely powdered fibers are sprayed or dusted onto an adhesive-sized material. Flocking can be done in an overall or decorative pattern or design. Powder adheres to only that part of the surface that has been sized. Used on wallpaper and fabric.

FLOODLIGHT An incandescent lamp or bulb that throws a broad beam or wash of light over a wide area. Most theatrical floodlights work on the ellipsodal reflector principle (see *elliptical spotlights*), but with a matte finish that distributes the light smoothly and without a sharp edge. Floodlights are available in a variety of wattages —from 75 watts and up.

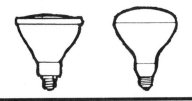

FLOOR PLAN See *bird's eye view* and *plan*.

FLOOR PLUG An electrical outlet set flush into the floor, rather than into a wall, into which extension circuits can be attached.

FLOOR UNITS Freestanding, self-supporting fixturing racks, stands, merchandisers and displayers on the selling floor as distinguished from those designed for use on counters, ledges or windows.

FLORAL CLAY A putty-like material used for creating floral arrangements, but will hold light objects on shelves or in place.

FLORIST TAPE A crepe paper-like binding tape that is used for holding flowers together in a corsage or arrangement. It has a self-sticking quality in addition to its stretchability.

FLUORESCENT LIGHTING A lighting system based on a glass tube which is coated on its inner surface with a substance that glows when a gas-conducted current is induced in the presence of mercury. Fluorescent lamps require much less power or wattage to operate and are more economical. Though, usually, less attractive and not as easy to direct as a source of light, the economy factor makes it the most popular lighting material in the commercial field.

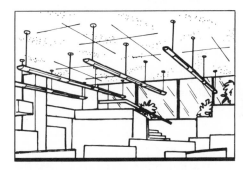

FLUSH The absence of an indent. An evenly drawn design ending in a straight margin. A body of copy which is perfectly aligned at the left margin and/or the right margin. Even with or even to another edge.

FLUTED Parallel vertical grooves running the length of an upright shaft such as a fluted column.

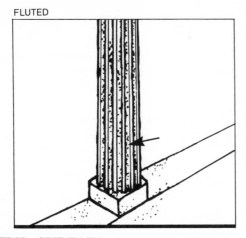

FLUTED

FLY CURTAIN A curtain that is opened or closed by being raised or lowered by means of a rope-line rigging or a counterweight system. Used in window display and theatre set design.

FLYER An advertisement prepared in the form of a handbill for giveaway distribution.

FLYING A form of merchandise presentation that does not use mannequins or forms, but depends upon the pinning, wiring and poufing of the merchandise to create a seemingly animated and floating display. A European technique, economical and effective, that requires time and talent to be done well. With the use of fishing line, piano wire, pins and tissue paper, the merchandise can take on the contours of form and body in an abstract and decorative manner.

FOAM CORE A laminated sandwich of a styrofoam center between two sheets of heavyweight paper usually produced in $4' \times 8'$ sheets. A lightweight, rigid material that can be cut or scored and treated decoratively with paints, silk screened or textured or specially coated sheets of paper or vinyl. Used in displays.

FOAM RUBBER A rubber material made from the sap of the rubber tree (latex) which is whipped with air to make a light, porous and resilient material. Used for stuffing mattresses, pillows, upholstery fillings and padding. The firmness of the foam rubber depends upon the air content.

F.O.B. (FREE ON BOARD) Pricing on an item that includes the delivery and loading of that item onto a specified carrier (train, bus, truck, plane, etc.). The customer assumes all costs and responsibilities for the item from the point of transit.

F.O.B. DESTINATION, FREIGHT COLLECT The buyer pays and is responsible for the freight charges, but the seller owns the goods in transit and will make any claims necessary for damage or merchandise missing in transit.

F.O.B. DESTINATION, FREIGHT COLLECT & ALLOWED The buyer pays the freight but then charges it back to the seller by deducting that amount from the invoice. The seller also owns the goods in transit and will be the one to file any necessary claims.

F.O.B. DESTINATION, FREIGHT PREPAID Freight and filing claims are the seller's responsibility and cost. The seller also owns the merchandise in transit.

F.O.B. ORIGIN, FREIGHT COLLECT See *F.O.B.* In this instance, the buyer pays for the freight charges, owns the merchandise while it is in transit and must file any claims for any mishaps or losses that may occur from the time the merchandise is placed on the carrier—to its arrival at the buyers place of business.

F.O.B. ORIGIN, FREIGHT PREPAID The seller pays and bears the cost of all freight from his plant to the customer's door.

F.O.B., FREIGHT PREPAID & CHARGED BACK The seller pays the freight costs and then bills the buyer for those charges. The buyer owns the merchandise in transit and is responsible for filing claims.

FOIL Shiny metallic papers and boards. A very fine sheet of a metallic substance that has been hammered and rolled to its present thinness.

FOLDING SCREEN HINGE A double-acting hinge which makes it possible to fold two joined panels in either direction. Panels can make a forward facing "V" or a reverse of the "V."

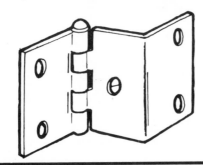

FONT A complete assortment of one size of a particular style of type, which includes all the large and small caps, lower case letters, numerals and punctuation marks. These are all contained in a "font case."

FOOT BRACKET A "sandal strap-like" contraption which is attached to a flange or base and will accept and hold a leg form or pantyhose form in an upright position. It is usually made of a clear plastic material.

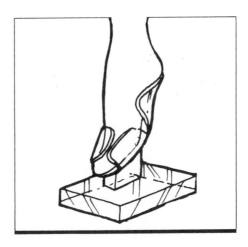

FOOTCANDLE A unit of illumination based on one square foot of surface upon which one lumen of light is uniformly distributed.

FOOTPIECE See *toe cap.*

FOOT SPIKE A short square metal rod used to support and hold a mannequin upright. It extends up from the metal, glass or plastic mannequin base and is inserted into the matching hollow fitting with a set screw, which is embedded in the mannequin's leg midway between the heel and the calf. See *ankle rod, base flange* and *butt rod.*

FORECAST A preview or prediction on the trends, styles, colors, and fabrics that will be important in *fashion* in the coming selling season. Some retailers will base their stock purchases for the new season on "fashion forecasts" as they appear in trade publications—*Women's Wear Daily* and in national magazines—*Vogue* and *Harper's Bazaar* or in mailings from buying offices or fashion coordinators, many months in advance of the actual season.

FORE PLANE A long, hand plane used for leveling or smoothing out long planks or large wood surfaces. It is usually about 18″ long and the cutting blade, which is adjustable, protrudes from the bottom surface of the plane.

FORM A three-dimensional representation of a part of the human anatomy such as the torso, the bust, the area from shoulder to waist or from hips to ankle. See *blouse form, bra form, coat form, model form* and *torso form.*

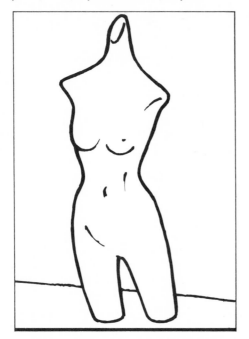

FORMAL Regular, symmetrical and traditional in effect. A carefully balanced arrangement.

FORMICA See *melamine formaldehydes.*

FORTRAN A symbolic computer language disigned and used to simplify the programming of scientific or mathematical programs.

FORTREL Trademark for a polyester fiber which is wrinkle-resistant, quick drying, wash and dry. Manufactured

and sold in the U.S. by Fiber Industries Inc., jointly owned by Imperial Chemical Industries Ltd. and Celanese Corp.

FORWARD STOCK ROOM See *adjacent stock room.*

FOUNDATION *1. In construction* The basic layer or construction between the ground below and the structure above. It is engineered to accommodate the supporting capabilities of the ground topography below and the structural requirements that will be needed above. *2. In fashion* A boned, fitted and constructed undergarment that is a combination corset and brassiere. Introduced in the late 1920s.

FOUNDATION WALL The part of a load bearing wall below the level of the adjacent grade—or the first floor beams or joists.

FOUR-WAY RACK See *quad rack.*

FOYER The intermediary space between the entrance and the working, selling or living space beyond. A passageway that leads from the entrance to individual, closed off or marked off areas.

FRAME *1. In graphics and decoration* The surrounding case or structure for the protection and enhancement of drawings, paintings, mirrors, etc. It can be made of carved wood, trimmed with moldings or embellished with gesso composition. A containing structure. *2. In cabinetry* The skeleton or basic construction of a wood unit. See *carcase.*

FRANCHISE An agreement or arrangement between an individual or a retail operation and a manufacturer or corporation to market the corporation's (or manufacturer's) product in a specific, and often exclusive, area. It may include the use of the franchiser's (the corporation's or manufacturer's) name, and the benefits that can be had from group advertising and/or promotions. Operation that may be individually owned.

FREE FLOW STORE LAYOUT An asymmetrical, loosely rather than rigidly organized floor plan which leads the shopper easily through turns, bends, in and around departments, island displays, etc. A flexible, movable and rearrangeable floor plan.

FREE FORM An irregular, flowing abstract shape. Amoebic. An asymmetrical, non-confined form or design which is created by freehand drawing rather than with a compass or curve, e.g. a design concept popularized by Hans Arp and Jean Miro, and used in the applied arts. Kidney, boomerang and egg shapes for furniture, fabrics, and jewelry.

FREESTANDING FIXTURE An individual unit, unsupported and not necessarily related to any other unit in the immediate vicinity of the selling floor. It functions on its own, though in some cases, it may be designed to combine with other, similar units to make a larger entity. It usually does not require any special attachment to floors, walls or ceiling. (See illustration under *merchandiser.*)

FREESTANDING STORE A store or retail operation that is not part of a shopping complex or mall, but one that stands and exists on its own—unattached. There can be other freestanding stores in close proximity.

FRENCH CURVE A drafting tool or template consisting of many arcs and curves. The designer or draftsman can reproduce the desired arc or curve by following the edge of the template at the desired arc or curve.

FRESCO A wall painting or mural technique in which a watercolor medium, such as tempera, is applied to a freshly, and still wet and absorbing, plastered surface. The color dries lighter and becomes integrated into the plastered surface. From the Italian word "fresh."

FRESNEL-TYPE LENS A piece of heat-resistant cast glass with one plane face and one consisting of concentric portions of lenses of different diameters and approximately the same focal length. It is thus possible to create a thin lens of short focal length, which is impossible in the usual plano-convex lens. It is placed in front of the light source or lamp and used to direct or redirect the light rays. It is a very efficient way of spreading the beams of light. Century and Kliegel both manufacture a complete line of Fresnel-type spotlights as do other stage lighting manufacturers. See *baby spotlight.*

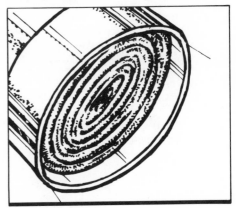

FRIEZÉ, FRISÉ *1.* Carpeting made in a tight, hard twist of heavy, wool yarns. *2.* A pile fabric with uncut loops. A curly, loopy textured fabric.

FRINGE An ornamental edging used to band or finish garments, hems, draperies, shawls, etc. A continuous band or ribbon with hanging, twisted threads, loops, and/or tassels. The fringe may be cut, looped or tied into tassels.

FRINGE BENEFITS Compensations above and beyond the stipulated salary such as health and/or life insurance, bonuses, discounts on purchases, pensions, supplementary unemployment benefits and free meals.

FROG Ornamental fastening of heavy cord twisted into loops, which serve as a buttonhole.

FRONT OUT See *face out.*

FRONT PROJECTION See *projection.*

FRUITWOOD The woods from fruit-bearing trees such as cherry, pear or apple. Particularly popular in "provincial" furniture and settings.

FULL-FACE TYPE A wide, heavy and broad typeface which results in a bold, black letter. The capitals usually occupy the whole depth of the type body. Also called fat-face type. See *bold-face type.*

FULL FIGURE MANNEQUIN A larger sized mannequin for the fuller, plumper figure. It will usually wear a size 14½ and, depending upon the pose or head position, stand about 5'9". The bust, hips and waist measurements are proportioned to suit the large, half-size garment.

FULL SERVICE DEPARTMENT STORE A department store that carries fashion merchandise and accessories (the soft goods), as well as home furnishings and other hard goods. See *hard goods.*

FURRING The application of thin strips of wood, laths or battens to coat or clad a wall, usually at 16-inch intervals. Used to smooth irregularities in the surface and/or to create space for air to circulate before the application of a final veneer or finished wall-facing material.

FUSE A replaceable link in the electrical current system which contains a low melting point metal. In case of an overload of current, the metal in the fuse melts and breaks the flow of current. A safety device which may also serve to release a fire door, sprinkler valves, etc. The melted fuse can be replaced and the current will then flow again.

FUSTIAN A suede- or velvet-like, heavy cotton fabric.

G

GABARDINE From the Spanish for "protection against the elements." A durable fabric with diagonal ridges.

GALLERY A wide corridor. A large, wide, high-ceilinged room or passageway. An open, walk area around the top of a building. The upper balcony of an auditorium. A decorative fencing or railing around the upper edge of furniture or trays.

GALLEY A shallow tray used to hold type that has been set in the composing stick or on the typesetting machine. The galley measures 2 inches long and from 4 to 7 inches wide with a thin brass bottom and three perpendicular sides that are approximately 1 ½-inch high.

GALVANIZED A zinc coating on iron used as a protection against rust. A dull, gray finish.

GAMBREL ROOF A gable-type roof with a double slope on each side. The lower slope is steeper than the upper one. A Mansard roof starts as a hipped roof and then is also double sloped.

GARAMOND TYPE A Roman typeface originally designed by Claude Garamond in the 16th century to replace the Gothic style then in use.

GARCY The manufacturer of slotted upright standards of various widths and thicknesses, types and sizes, spacing of slots, as well as hundreds of accessory units to enhance the usefulness of these standards such as brackets, rails, clips, and end caps. The name "Garcy" is often used to identify the standards themselves—"Garcy Strips." See *standards*.

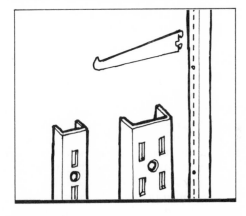

GARLAND A wreath or rope of foliage, flowers, fruit, etc., usually with ribbon ties at the ends. Used as swags, drapes or circlets.

GAUCHO PANTS Bell-bottomed or flared pants that end at midcalf and are reminiscent of the pants worn by South American cowboys.

GAUGE A standard measurement, dimension or quality. The gauge of a piece of metal, the thickness or density of a wall. A means or standard for comparing, judging or estimating.

GAUZE Sheer, semi-transparent fabric made of cotton, silk or man-made fibers and available in a variety of weights. The fabric is usually available in widths ranging from 3' to 6' (nylon net) but is also made in wider widths for use in theater design. See *bobbinet* and *shark's tooth scrim.*

GAZEBO "Merchandising in the round." A merchandised and stocked structure, which is often a high point or a focal point in a department or on the selling floor. The structure may be round, hexagonal or octagonal and is provided with several openings so that the customer can shop from inside or outside of the structure. It is similar to the summer house or garden house of the 19th century which was often made of latticework and was lacy and light-looking. The gazebo can be used as a boutique, a "shop-within-a-shop" or as a "highlighter."

G.C. (GENERAL CONTRACTOR) The individual or company that, under contract, assumes the responsibility for all the construction work in store planning including electrical work, decorating and fixturing, or only those stipulated responsibilities of the construction work.

GENERAL ILLUMINATION The overall lighting used to create a shadowless interior. Lighting that blankets an area with an even level of light.

GENERATOR A machine that converts mechanical energy into electrical energy.

GESSO A plaster-like composition which can be molded to create a sculptured or bas relief finish. It also refers to a dense, brilliant white ground which is very absorbent such as gypsum or chalk.

GIBSON GIRL The "Shirtwaist Girl" of the early 20th century made famous by the American artist Charles Dana Gibson. Her traditional outfit consisted of a "habit-back" skirt, a simple, starched white shirtwaist with "leg o'mutton" sleeves, an ascot at the neck, and a straw sailor hat atop her piled-up pompadour.

GIFT ITEMS A broad classification for home accessories that overlap into china, glass, and silverware. Small decorative items used to enhance the home: bon bon dishes, decanters, serving trays, crystal figures, ceramic figurines, vases, urns, bibelots, and collectables. Gift items are used for gifting on holidays, weddings, anniversaries, housewarmings, etc.

GILET A type of vest or sleeveless blouse or bodice worn under a jacket. A bib or dickey that fills in the neckline of a dress or blouse.

GIMP, GUIMPE A woven binding material or edging used to finish hemlines, cuffs, collars, also upholstery seams and drapery trim.

GINGHAM A yarn-dyed, light- to-medium-weight cotton fabric woven in a check or stripe pattern.

GIRDER A heavy beam used over wide spans to support smaller beams or concentrated weights.

GIRDLE FORM See *panty form.*

GIRLS' SIZES A retailing term for sizes 7, 8, 10, 12 and 14 for girls aged 7 to 11. Waistlines are slowly becoming defined and there is very little bust development.

G-LAMP An almost spherical or globular electric lamp. A round bulb available with a regular or candelabra base.

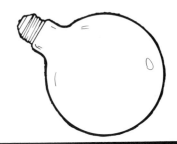

GLASS BASE PLATE A heavy piece of glass, equipped with a metal plate and extending rod, used to support a mannequin. The base plate can be round, square, hexagonal, etc., and is usually about 15″ to 18″ wide. See *butt rod* and *foot spike.*

GLASS BRICK, GLASS BLOCK A hollow block of molded soda-lime glass, which can be mortared together into walls.

GLASS CURTAINS Sheer, semi-sheer and/or semi-transparent, lightweight curtains. Not necessarily made of glass cloth.

GLASS EYES Large, artificial, but extremely realistic, eyes which fit into the hollow eye sockets of a mannequin. They are usually made so that the "eyes" can be repositioned i.e. look to the right, to the left, straight ahead or up or down, and appear to make contact with other mannequins in a grouping. Much more realistic than the painted eye.

GLAZED CHINTZ A chintz or plain-colored fabric that has been calendarized or paraffin-treated to make the fabric crisp of hand and shinier than it was. A glazed cotton fabric.

GLAZED DOOR A door made up of many panes of glass similar to a French door. The panes of glass are usually contained within a wooden framework.

GLAZED PAPER Printing paper finished with a high gloss or polish. A shiny, glossy paper. An enameled paper. See *flint paper.*

GLIDE A roller or attachment designed to facilitate movement back and forth, usually inside a channel or runner. Used on fixtures and furniture.

GLITZ A term used to describe a trendy or fad item, object or garment which is shiny, sparkly and obvious. The term may be derived from the words "glitter" and "sleaze."

GLOBE BULB, GLOBE LIGHTS See *eyeball lights* and *G-lamp.*

GLOBUS SYSTEM A modular construction system built with interrelating floors, ceilings and fixtures.

Named after the Globus Store in Zurich, Switzerland. It permits quick and inexpensive on-site changes, changing sizes of departments, adding or subtracting walls, etc. Panels can be suspended from the ceiling tracks (which may be electrified) and reinforced in the floor grids, which are parallel to ceiling tracks.

GLOVE HAND An accessory to a mannequin used to replace the regular hand that joins the arm at the wrist or a separate entity designed to wear gloves. The finger arrangement facilitates putting on and taking off of gloves, and yet present a graceful appearance.

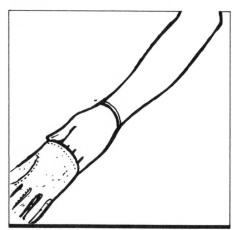

GLULAM A composite construction of glued and laminated wooden members used as girders and beams. Since they are man-made, of natural materials, they can be made almost in any size, are neither weakened by knots or checks nor subject to warping. Pieces can be produced in curved shapes for assembly in larger arcs and arches.

GODEY'S LADY'S BOOK The first American woman's magazine which dealt with fashion, etiquette and needlework. It was published from 1830–1898 in Philadelphia where it was started by Antoine Godey. The fashion plates became the "Bible of American Couture."

GOLD LEAF Very thin sheets of hammered and/or rolled gold used in decorative finishes. Also called Dutch gold. Commercially available as an amalgam of tin and copper, which can be adhered to surfaces that have been made tacky by the application of glue, shellac or "gold size."

GONDOLA A long, flat-bottomed merchandiser with straight upright sides. Usually designed to hold adjustable shelves and may be combined with cabinet or storage space below. The gondola may be designed with a center divider panel (perpendicular and equidistant to the end uprights) which would then make it two sided. Commonly used in groups on the selling floor and oriented into aisles or walkways.

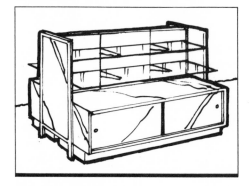

GOODS See *hard goods* and *soft goods*.

GOODWILL A retailing term to describe that special aspect of a store's image or reputation, which is built on the attitude of the store, its executives and its salespeople toward its customers and the community at large: the store's refund policy, cooperation with community plans and activities, willingness to let the "customer always be right."

GOOSENECK A flexible metal cable similar to a continuous closely twisted spiral band which can be turned in all directions without undoing its inherent spiral. The cable is hollow and can carry and protect electrical wiring such as in a gooseneck lamp, which is an electric socket and bulb shield attached to a length of this flexible cable. See *flex-arm displayer.*

GORE A tapering or triangular insert that adds greater width and flare without too much extra bulk. See *gored skirt.*

GORED SKIRT A skirt made of several triangular-shaped pieces of fabric similar to the sections of an umbrella. The gored skirt fits snugly at the waist and flares out toward the hemline.

GOTHIC TYPE A heavy, calligraphic typeface which is written with a thick, wedge-shaped nib. The dominant characteristics are the thick stems of the type and the angular extremities. Mainly used for headlines or banners of newspapers and in German script. Also a simple sans serif block letter.

GOUACHE An opaque watercolor technique for which pigments are mixed with white lead, bone ash or chalk. Used for the illumination of manuscripts during the 14th and 15th centuries.

GOUGE A type of chisel with a curved or arced cutting edge rather than a flat wedge. A scooper.

GOURMET SHOP A department or an area in "housewares" or an individual shop that specializes in the "fine art"

of food, food preparation, and prepared foods. The emphasis is on the unique and the unusual—on "delicacies" rather than "delicatessen"—on condiments, canisters and caddies. It is much more than a fancy grocery; the shop may also stock special appliances, recipe books, and exotic devices for preparing and serving exotic foods.

GRADATION The variations in tone from light to dark—from very strong to very weak—from palest pastel to deepest shade. The steps between the extremes.

GRADE The level of the ground around a building or structure. A basement is often said to be "below grade."

GRADES OF LUMBER See *common lumber* and *select lumber.*

GRADES OF PLYWOOD See *plywood grades.*

GRAFFITI From the Italian "graffito" which was a popular form of painted decoration on the stuccoed exteriors of Italian Renaissance buildings. It is also the term for drawing or writing scratched onto a wall. Today it refers to the drawings, writing and messages scrawled or sprayed on walls, fences, windows, trains and buses. Street Art.

GRAIN The directional structure of a natural material. In wood, the fiber lines of the wood determine the grain, as well as the relation to the direction of the vertical growth. It is the figure or pattern inherent in the material and it is obvious when the material is sectioned or sliced.

GRAINING The painted imitation of the grain of wood.

GRAPHIC ARTS An all inclusive term for artwork which use lines, marks, colors and forms on a surface, e.g., printing, painting, engraving, drawing, lettering and writing.

GRAPH PAPER Drawing paper which has been mechanically ruled or boxed off into precise squares. The boxes are usually scaled at so many boxes to the inch, e.g., eight boxes to the inch, five to the inch, four to the inch. Ideal for scale drawings, mechanicals, floor plans, etc. Also called quadrille ruled stock.

GRASS CLOTH Coarse vegetable fibers, loosely woven and/or glued onto a heavyweight wallpaper. Usually creates a nubby texture on the wall and, usually, a horizontal pattern. Grass cloth can be simulated as a printed or embossed paper.

GRASS MAT Shaggy, textured decorative cloth mats which resemble a lush, green lawn. The individual "blades of grass" are pulled through the canvas backing for a more realistic effect.

GRATICULATE Overlaying a drawing or a design with a scaled graph of boxes in order to draw the same design on another and larger surface, which has also been boxed off but in a larger scale. Whatever is drawn within an inch multiplied by an inch box will be visually blown up to fill a square of, maybe, one foot multiplied by one foot.

GRAVURE PRINTING A process for printing in which the impression is obtained from an etched or engraved intaglio plate. The image lies below the surface of the printing plate and the ink fills these depressions or wells. See *intaglio printing*.

GREENAWAY, KATE Popular illustrator of children's fashions published in England (1846–1901). The styling is basically "Empire" (see Empire style)

and the patterns and colors are gentle and muted.

GREENBELT A boundary or division in a community usually consisting of a belt or line of trees.

GRID In store floor plans, the term refers to the pattern created by the repetition of parallel spacing in a building structure. It also visually relates to the standardization of dimensions, lengths, widths, as well as heights.

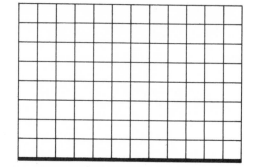

GRIDIRON PLAN See *grid*. A symmetrical store plan with parallel and perpendicular aisles and traffic patterns and formally arranged counters and departments. Also see *free flow store layout*.

GRISAILLE A monochromatic painting in grays or beiges that simulates a low or bas relief sculpture. It is "trompe l'oeil" in effect that it appears three dimensional. It may also be the original wash drawing for an oil painting.

GROMMET A metal ring or eyelet.

GROSGRAIN Silk, rayon or cotton fabric with ribs running crosswise. Used for millinery, neckwear and trimmings.

GROS POINT A coarse tapestry with the pattern created by heavy yarns on coarse linen, open mesh or canvas.

GROSS PROFIT The net sales after the cost of the goods being sold has been subtracted.

GROSS SALES The total dollar value of all merchandise sold.

GROUND COLOR The base or background color of a wallpaper, fabric, or other material which is printed or painted.

GROUND COVER A low, thick carpet of plants that do not require constant cutting and tending such as pachysandra, myrtle or ivy. It can also refer to marble chips, woodchips, etc.

GROUPING (OF MANNEQUINS) A term used to describe two or more mannequins designed, arranged or positioned to go together and to create a situation or a semblance of belonging in the same place at the same time. Mannequins that are proportioned and posed to be used together.

GROUP RELAMPING The periodic replacement of all lamps in an area at such a time when the lamps have passed their effective service life, and their output is less than that of the original expected output rating.

GROUT A filler and/or bonding agent which dries solid and hard, and cements tiles, mosaics, marble chips, etc. The filler and cement, mortar or concrete used to bond bricks and building units.

GUIMPE See *gimp*.

GUM WOOD A heavy, strong textured wood, which ranges from a pink to reddish brown color. Used for plywood as well as furniture carcases and architectural woodwork with a painted finish.

GUN METAL A bronze made of copper, tin and zinc, but usually descriptive of a metal with a dark blue-gray color.

GUSSET An expanding fold. A pleat of extra paper or other material which lies flat until needed to allow for expansion—like the folds of fabric on the sides of a pocket.

GYPSUM BOARD A wallboard and construction sheet which has a core of processed gypsum rock sandwiched between two, tough, heavyweight sheets of paper. The boards are commonly produced as 4′ × 8′ and ½″ thick. The paper surfaces can be primed and then painted or wallpapered. See *drywall* and *plasterboard*.

H

HACK SAW A carpentry tool consisting of a narrow cutting blade made of tempered steel with eighteen cutting teeth to the inch. It is attached to a metal, clamp-like frame with a wooden (or plastic) hand grip. Used to cut straight lines on metal, bolts, pipes, etc.

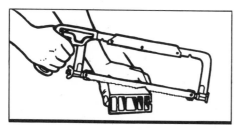

HAIRLINE The visible outline created by the mannequin's wig set against the face or neck. In the more realistic wigs, the fibers are hand-tied along the edges and the "hairline" is not sharply defined but naturally feathered.

HAIRLINE REGISTRATION A term used in printing to describe the precise matching of two or more designs, color plates, surfaces, etc.

HAIR LINES The fine or extra fine lines in Roman type. The Roman-type letter consists of two different strokes. The letter "E," for example, has a wide vertical stroke and the three horizontal bars are hair lines, by comparison.

HALF-CIRCLE RACK See *C-rack*.

HALF SHEET Half a standard poster card which is regularly 22″ × 28″. A showcard board which is 14″ × 22″. Used in signing.

HALF SIZES A retailing term for women's sizes 12½, 14½, 16½, 18½, 20½, 22½, 24½, 26½. A heavier, larger junior size with a shorter waistline.

HALFTONE The reproduction of a photograph, print or drawing which contains many gradations between highlights and shadows onto a printing plate, usually copper zinc. The designs are broken up into dots in a variety of sizes, uniformly placed, to create all the gradations required. It might also refer to the print or impression made from a halftone plate by the letterpress or intaglio process.

HALL TREE A hat or coat rack, or a more elaborate Victorian arrangement with shelves, seats and umbrella receptacles. See *bentwood costumer*.

HALTER, HALTER NECKLINE A triangular piece of fabric with a tie or drawstring at the apex. A halter ties high at the throat and secures around the neck leaving the shoulders bare and a very exposed back. Popular in the 1930s for beachwear and still popular for sunwear and formal wear.

HAND *1.* A technical term used in store planning and architecture to describe the direction in which a door swings open. If it swings to the right, it is referred to as a "right hand." *2.* The texture, feel or drapability of a fabric.

HAND BLOCKED A printing technique in which a design is carved or incised onto a block (wood, linoleum or composition). The dye or paint is rolled onto the surface of the block and pressure is exerted on the block, which is pressed against the fabric or paper. The gouged-out design appears in the background color on the fabric or paper.

HAND DRILL A hand carpentry tool consisting of a knobbed handle which rotates a wheel to turn the particular bit inserted into the adjustable clamp at the bottom. Resembles a hand egg beater. Various size bits can be accommodated in this simple device. Also see *power hand drill*.

HANDKERCHIEF HEMLINE An irregular pointed hemline appearing as though rectangular kerchiefs were tucked into the waistband and allowed to hang down.

HANDSCREEN See *silk screen*.

HAND-TIED The process of weaving, by hand, the individual fibers or westings into the wig cap on a mannequin to form a more natural looking hairline.

HAND-TO-MOUTH BUYING A retailing term for buying as little stock or merchandise as possible and only when necessary.

HANGER A wooden, metal, wire, or plastic triangle with the widest side at the base and a hooked attachment at the apex. Used to hold and show garments. Hangers vary in size and contour depending upon the type of merchandise to be shown. A hanger may be equipped with accessory clips, pants rod, etc.

HANG RAIL A horizontal bar of metal, wood, or Lucite upon which merchandise can be hung. The merchandise is usually draped over hangers which are then hooked over the hang rail. The bar may be round, square, or rectangular in cross section, and for some specialized uses, the bars or rails may be notched or perforated. Also called hang rod.

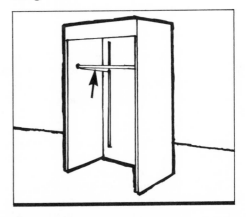

HANG ROD See *hang rail*.

HARDBOARD See *fiberboard*.

HARD-EDGE PAINTINGS Abstract, flat surface paintings or designs in which the bands or areas of colors are sharply and crisply separated from each other. The whole surface is treated as a complete unit and the designs usually flow from edge to edge. The paint is applied cleanly, evenly, and precisely to achieve the clear, sharp effect. A form of geometric abstract or emblematic art.

HARD GOODS A retailing term to describe merchandise such as major appliances, furniture, kitchen and bathroom equipment, lawn mowers, etc. The opposite of soft goods.

HARD SELL A retailing term to describe a strong, heavy, all out "push" to sell, such as big letters in bright, bold colors on strongly contrasted backgrounds to promote a sale. A forceful sales approach.

HARDWARE (COMPUTER) The electronic equipment that is necessary to receive and process the input material and produce the desired data.

HARD WIG The stiff, heavily lacquered and permanently styled mannequin wig, which is often made of horsehair. Also see *soft wig*.

HARDWOODS The wood of deciduous trees which lose their leaves in the fall. Hardwoods are usually more difficult to work, but are more durable, with attractive graining and take a better finish. They are used mainly where sturdiness and attractiveness are desired. Hardwoods include: alder, ash, aspen, basewood, beech, birch, butternut, cherry, elm, hickory, magnolia, maple, oak, sycamore, walnut, willow and yellow poplar. Also see *softwoods*.

HAREM PANTS Bloomer-type pants that are full and voluminous at the hip and drape into soft folds down to bands at the ankles.

HAREM SKIRT Full and draped skirt at the hips tapering to a gathered hemline. Similar in appearance to harem pants. Worn in the near East and popularized in the West during the 1910s by Paul Poiret. See *balloon skirt*.

HARRIS TWEED A soft tweed woven on the islands of the Outer Hebrides off the northwestern coast of Scotland (Harris, Lewis, Uist, etc., in this island group). Registered trademark of the Harris Tweed Association, London.

HEADER The top band or flat vertical surface at the top of a unit such as a cornice, fascia strip or cap. Used in architecture and interior design.

HEADLESS MANNEQUIN A full-size, full-scale lifelike mannequin which ends at the neck. The neck may be a straight, flat cut or it may end in a fanciful swirl. A nonpersonalized costumer.

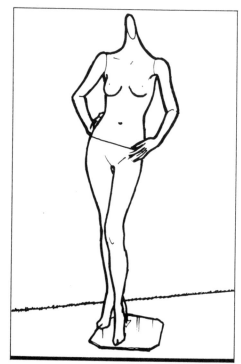

HEADROOM The vertical clearance on a stairway, in a passageway, a room, a low ceiling, etc. See *clearance*.

HEAT EMISSION The amount of heat generated by a lighting system and the effect of that heat on the surrounding atmosphere. The heat emission presents a problem where low ceilings are an architectural factor, or the lighting will be close to the merchandise.

HEAVY TRIM A term used in display to describe a full or "stocky" approach to the presentation of merchandise. A heavy window display would be a massive showing of merchandise. The opposite of a light trim.

HELVETICA TYPE A simple sans serif letter. It can be extended or condensed, thick or thin, bold or hairline thin. Adaptable, legible and contemporary. The most popular of the Gothic styles of type in use today.

ABCDEFGHIJKLMNOPQRSTUVWXYZ
abcdefghijklmnopqrstuvwxyz
$1234567890 :;&?!()%/—-''*

HEMLOCK A lightweight, light-colored wood, which resembles white pine. Strong and easy to work.

HEMP MATS Twelve-inch squares made of hemp in the color of natural rope or twine. The mats are tough and thick and servicable as a flooring or wall material where a tropical effect is desired.

HERRINGBONE Building or decorative materials (brick, wood strips,

stone, etc.) laid at angles so that the alternate courses point in opposite directions. A series of alternating "V's."

HEX WRENCH See *Allen wrench.*

H.F.C. (HOLD FOR CONFIRMATION) A memo that expresses an interest, an intent or a desire to make a purchase, but in itself is not binding on the customer or the manufacturer. It is not an order. To be valid, it should be confirmed with a properly signed and numbered store order form with quantities, prices, delivery dates, methods of shipping, etc., filled in.

H-FRAME A vertical side support which resembles an "H"; two vertical uprights reinforced with a cross stretcher or bar.

HICKORY A tough, heavy, hardwood of the walnut family which is especially effective where thinness of material and strength are required. Often used for molded or bent plywood construction.

H.I.D. LAMP A high intensity discharge light source. The term usually refers to mercury, metal halide and high-pressure sodium lamps. It provides illumination at reduced energy consumption by means of an electric current passing through any of several assorted gases. See *mercury halide lamp* and *sodium vapor lamp*.

HIEROGLYPHIC WRITING Ideographic symbols used by the Ancient Egyptians (as well as Mayans and Incas) as a form of communication or messages. The picture symbols were meant to be phonetic but never really approached the simplicity of an alphabet.

HIGH HAT A cylindrical lighting fixture, resembles an "opera hat," that houses an electric lamp. It usually directs the beam of light directly down onto the area below without much spread of light.

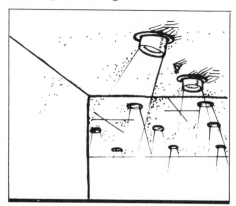

HIGH INTENSITY LAMPS See *H.I.D. lamp*.

HIGH OUTPUT FLUORESCENT LAMP A rapid-start fluorescent lamp

operating with a lamp current of 800 miliamperes.

HIGH-PRESSURE SODIUM LAMP See *sodium vapor lamp*.

HINGE A movable carpentry joint. See *butt hinge* and *folding screen hinge*.

HOBBLE SKIRT A tapered ankle-length skirt, rounded over the hips, which required a slit in the hemline to make any movement possible. Popular in the 1910s.

HOLD FOR CONFIRMATION See *H.F.C.*

HOLLOW WALL See *cavity wall*.

HOLOGRAPHS The end result of the passage of a beam of laser light through a hologram-wave interference photograph to reconstruct and present three-dimensional images. Also called stereo paintings.

HOMBURG A soft Tyrolean-type hat, often in dark, formal colors. Originally produced in Homburg, Prussia. See *fedora*. Popularized by Edward VIII in the 1900s.

HOME FASHIONS A retailing term to describe home furnishings and/or accessories, which include soft and hard goods.

HONE To sharpen with a fine, abrasive stone. A method of sharpening the cutting edges of tools, knives, razors, etc.

HONG KONG SHEATH See *cheongsam*.

HOOK An arm with a curved or bent return which keeps merchandise from sliding or slipping off from a vertical surface.

HOOKED RUG *1.* A rug made of fibers or threads pulled through a canvas backing and knotted to stay in place.

2. The term is applied to country-style braided rugs in which strips of wool or cotton fabric is braided and sewn into round or oval floor rugs.

HOOK STAND A counter unit equipped with hooks to hold bagged or carded merchandise; will also hold chains, necklaces, etc.

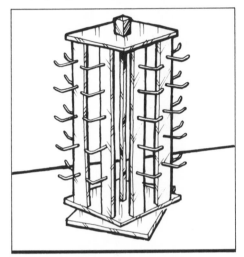

HORIZON, HORIZON LINE The eye level in a perspective drawing where earth and sky seem to meet. The line to which all parallel lines on any one receding plane appear to converge and meet. Also see *eye level, horizon, perspective* and *vanishing point.* (See illustration under *perspective.*)

HORSEHAIR Stiff fibers of rayon or nylon used in the manufacture of hard wigs. These wigs are heavily lacquered and permanently styled.

HORSEPOWER The power or energy required to lift 1000 pounds of mass, 33 feet in one minute is equal to one horsepower or 33,000 foot pounds of work in one minute. See *kilowatt.*

HOSTESS GOWN A formal "at home" costume or an informal dinner dress, usually long and flaring. Not necessarily a robe or item of lingerie.

HOT MELT GLUE A moderately strong and moderately durable synthetic resin adhesive, prepared in stick form for use in the electric glue gun. It sets quickly and the cemented parts cannot be adjusted after they are joined. It will work on wood, leather, metal and some plastics.

HOURGLASS SILHOUETTE See *wasp waist.*

HOUSEKEEPING See *maintenance.*

HOUSE ORGAN An internal publication or newsletter designed for, and usually by, the store personnel to keep the employees in tune with the store's activities and promotions, events, and personal social notes (weddings, births, deaths, retirements, promotions, etc.). An intra-store form of communication. A packaged bulletin board.

HOUSING *1.* A cladding or protective enclosure for a member that contains the electric wires such as the BX cable. *2.* A hollowed out area in one member which will accept and enclose a projection from another member. *3.* The envelope or enclosure for an electric lamp. See *eyeball light* and *high hat.*

HUE The particular tint or quality of a color. See *shades* and *tints.*

HUNG CEILING A dropped ceiling. A ceiling that is lowered from its regular height by means of creating a new, lower framework, which is then covered with acoustic tiles, plasterboard, plastic panels and/or special light units. Also called suspended ceiling.

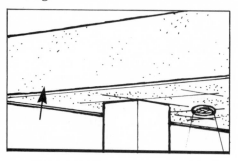

HUSKY SIZES A retailing term for boys' sizes 8 to 20, husky. The same relative age and proportions as Prep boy (ages 10–16) sizes 8 to 20, but a heavier or huskier boy. See *Prep Sizes.*

H.V.A.C. Abbreviation for *heating, ventilation and air-conditioning.* An architectural term to describe items to be included in the planning of most retail operations. A major item of expense in the "square-foot" cost of store planning.

I

ICON A sacred picture, often of a particular saint, used as a mini-altar in countries in which the Eastern Orthodox church is dominant.

ICONOGRAPH A book illustration or engraving.

ICONOGRAPHY The study of graphic representation.

I.C.S.C. International Council of Shopping Centers.

I.D. (INNER DIMENSION) A term used in architectural specifications and shop drawings to describe the measurement of the *(1)* size of the openings of tubes, hollow units, etc., and *(2)* the distance between two units or elements, but excluding any part of the units. See *O.D.*

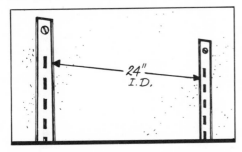

IDEOGRAPH A pictorial or symbolic representation of an idea or object. A trademark or logo.

ILLUMINATED LETTERS Highly ornate, decorated and/or brightly colored letters used to highlight a manuscript or a page. Often the first letter of the first word on a page at the start of a book or chapter of a book.

ILLUSTRATION BOARD A board which may have drawing paper pasted down onto one or both sides of a board. It is usually used for ink or watercolor work and should be relatively warp-proof. It is about 0.0325″ thick.

I.M. (INNER MEASUREMENT) A term used in architectural specifications and shop drawings to describe the measurement of the opening of a hollow pipe or tube, but does not include the thickness of the wall of the unit. Opposite of O.M. or outer measurement (please see).

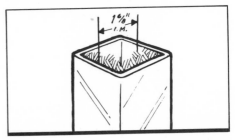

IMAGE All the stated and unstated, the visible and invisible facets of merchandising and policy that together create a special quality—a "oneness" —that sets this store apart from others. It is how the store shows, sells to and services its customers. A store's image can be created and enhanced by its window and interior displays, its architecture, the ambiance and the amenities provided, the type, style and price of the merchandise offered, the depth of stock maintained and how much of that stock is visible on the selling floor. The image is reflected in the lights, the signing, the feel and texture of the materials used in the construction and decoration of the store. It is the sales help; their selling approach—how they look, talk—how knowledgable they are—how proud they are of their store and the merchandise they sell. It is the store's graphics; the newspaper ads, the mailers, the posters, the shopping bags, the wrapping papers and the boxes. The image can be "seen" in the fresh plants and flowers, the paintings and sculpture on the floor, the size and fittings in the fitting rooms, the behind-the-scene operations that supply the service and satisfaction a customer has come to expect. Image is what a store appears to be and the appeal it presents to the customers it wishes to attract. It is what makes one retail operation seem different from another though both are selling the same merchandise at about the same price. A store can also project a negative image—and succeed with certain merchandise to a certain market.

IMBRICATE To layer in overlapping tiers, such as fish scales.

IMPORTS Merchandise brought in from abroad and sometimes collected and promoted as a group. An "Import Fair" might present a collection of gifts, housewares and gourmet supplies from a group of foreign countries, or it could be an all-China promotion and include ready-to-wear as well as gifts and housewares: cotton jackets, woks, rice cakes, and fortune cookies. The foreign origin is played up in the display of "import" merchandise rather than folded or tucked away in back when the "country of origin" is less than fashionable.

IMPULSE ITEM/MERCHANDISE An object or piece of merchandise that gets attention and is purchased on impulse rather than by plan. A spontaneous appeal created by seeing the merchandise, sometimes in relation to another piece of merchandise. See *point of purchase.*

IN & OUTERS Impulse merchandise purchased as the customer enters or exits the store. See *impulse item.*

INCANDESCENT FLUORESCENT A fluorescent light tube manufactured by GTE Sylvania which is supposed to emit a light similar in color to incandescent light.

INCANDESCENT LIGHT An electric filament light. The filament is enclosed in a glass bulb and a glow or light is produced when an electric current passes through the filament. Produces a warm, peach-toned light.

INDIA INK An especially black ink produced from carbon black and water. Used for drawing and writing. It is particularly suited for copy which is to be photoengraved.

INDIA PRINT (INDIENNE) Persian and/or Indian patterns printed on cotton fabrics. Usually in bright colors on a natural ground. Often produced by hand blocking.

INDIRECT LIGHTING Illumination of an area by any means other than direct overhead lighting or primary lighting. See *primary lighting, cove lighting* and *wall washing.*

INLAY A decorative technique of inserting contrasting materials or colors into pre-cut-out spaces. The inserts may be of wood veneer, metals, shells, ivory, etc.

INNER DIMENSION See *I.D.*

INNER MEASUREMENT See *I.M.*

IN SITU *1.* "On the spot." Work done on the premises rather than in another locale and brought in for installation. *2.* A British term for cast-in-place.

INSTITUTIONAL ADVERTISING/ DISPLAY Displays or ads which are used to promote the store's goodwill, and its involvement with the community, rather than to sell a product or particular line. An institutional display could be a salute to the Red Cross, sponsor a local community drive, recognize a hero or national statesperson, a cultural event, Christmas mechanical windows, flower shows, etc.

IN-STORE DEMONSTRATION Specialized selling, often enhanced by display, where a manufacturer's representative will show or explain the product; the application of a brand of cosmetics, sampling newly prepared foods, the use and special attributes of new equipment, etc.

INSULATION The use of special materials or techniques to keep in the warmth or the coolness, keep down the sound vibration and generally consider the "energy" problem. The insulating materials can be added to the exterior, used in the wall construction or added to the interior surfaces.

INSULATOR *1.* A non-conductor of electricity such as rubber, porcelain, asbestos, some plastics and fibers and used around electrical conductors (copper wire) as a protective coating. *2.* Materials used in insulation.

INTAGLIO An etching or carving impressed below the plane surface of the material. A design cut into and down below the face of an object such as a die or signet ring. See *engraving*.

INTAGLIO PRINTING A form of printing in which the images on the plates are sunk into or etched below the surface of the plate, as distinguished from letterpress in which the images are above the surface of the plate. See *gravure printing*.

INTENSITY The degree of pureness of a color. Also called chroma. The intensity of a hue is changed when it is raised or lowered in value; made lighter or darker by the addition of white or black.

INTERCHANGEABLE PARTS A term used in fixturing and store planning to describe parts that can be arranged, rearranged, added to or used in place of to create new configurations. The basis of construction systems and modules.

INTERIOR DISPLAY All merchandise presentation within the store: counters, cases, ledges, columns, fascias, platforms, islands, and floor fixtures. It can be the completely accessorized ensemble on an aisle liner such as a T-stand—a mannequin on a platform or on the floor with furniture and props, posters, floral sprays or a winter wonderland for Christmas. The enhancement of the selling floor and the presentation of the merchandise under the best possible conditions.

INTERSTORE TRANSFER The switching or exchanging of merchandise, fixtures or decorative props between branches of a store, between the main store and the branches, or between departments or areas within a store.

INTIMATE APPAREL Women's undergarments and sleepwear. See *lingerie.*

INVENTORY Material or merchandise on hand, on display, on the rack and in the storeroom. The total stock which has been paid for and thus belongs to the store or department.

INVENTORY CONTROL A system designed to keep track of all materials. How much, how many in use (on display), how many in stock, where in stock, and possibly rated as to age and/or condition.

INVERTED PLEAT See *box pleat.*

INVOICE A list of items or goods or services shipped or provided to a customer from the supplier; the itemized prices, special charges, freight costs and terms of payment including discounts, if any, are available.

IONIC ORDER One of the classic orders of architecture and recognizable by the volutes or spiral ends at the top of the Ionic capital.

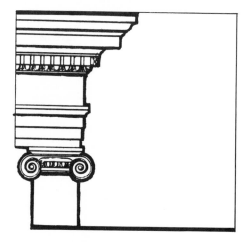

IRIDESCENT FABRICS Fabrics with changeable colors produced by using contrasting colors for the warp and filling yarns.

IRREGULARS Less than perfect merchandise. The defects may be slight and in some cases difficult to find. The irregularities may not affect the utility or wearability of the product: mismatched plaids, an offgrain piece of fabric, an off-print, an off-angle pocket, or a slub or pull in the weave, a smear or streak from a marking device, or just a dent in the packaging.

ISLAND DISPLAY A term used in store planning for an area completely separated from the conventional store display, yet accessible and viewable from all sides or directions. Usually given a special merchandising treatment and lighting. For example a rather large, raised platform with a grouping of several mannequins or a grouping of related merchandise such as chairs, tables, lamps and rugs.

ISLAND DISPLAYER A free-standing unit similar to an outpost.

ISLAND WINDOW A display window which can be viewed from all sides. A walk-around window which is usually part of an arcade front. A giant "fishbowl" with a removable panel or hinged glass door to facilitate changes.

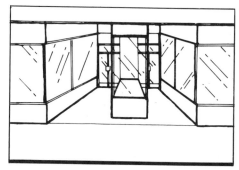

ISLON A trademark for a velvet-like, all nylon fabric with body, drapability qualities, soil resistance and color stability.

ISOMETRIC DRAWING, ISOMETRIC PROJECTION A schematic view of an object in which the lines are drawn at a 30°/60° angle to the horizontal and the vertical lines are projected from it. The entire drawing

is done in scale. It does not have the usual foreshortening one finds in a true perspective drawing, but the general appearance of the projection is more natural.

I.S.P. Institute of Store Planners.

ITALICS Letters that are inclined to the right from the absolute vertical, and are calligraphic in form, usually based on cursive script. They are used for emphasis and drama.

ITEM DISPLAY A promotional display of a coordinated group of special merchandise such as all running shoes, a designer's collection, a variety of dresses produced in a particular fabric, or fur-lined coats. Also see *assortment display*.

J

JABOT A cascade of ruffles. A soft fall of fabric that starts at the throat and covers the shirt front or bodice of a dress.

JACKET A term used to describe an insulating cover or wrap for exposed heating pipes.

JACK PLANE A 14″ general purpose plane used to smooth or level wooden surfaces.

JACQUARD, JACQUARD WEAVE Multicolored, intricate weaves used on fabrics such as damasks, brocades or tapestries.

JALOUSIES Louvered windows or window coverings similar to movable shuttered screens.

JAMAICA SHORTS Shorts that end at mid-thigh.

JAMB The interior side or the return plane of a door or window frame.

JAPANNING A method of finishing metal or wood units with enamel and/or colored shellacs. The decoration is raised in relief, in color and often touched with gilt. A pseudo-Japanese technique of work imported by the Dutch into Europe during the 17th century.

JARDINIERE A plant container or stand made of wood, marble, metal, porcelain, etc. Decorative in itself.

JASPE A streaked or mottled effect in a fabric produced by the uneven dyeing of warp threads.

JEAN A heavyweight, rugged, twilled cotton fabric used for work and play clothes. Available in solids and stripes and most recognizable as "blue jeans." Originally produced in Genoa, Italy—and thus the bastardized name—jean.

JERSEY *1.* An elastic or stretchy fabric in a tricot or stockinette stitch. *2.* Knitted shirts and tunics produced in the 15th century on the islands of Jersey and Guernsey, both located in the English Channel. The original "ganseys" or "jerseys" were tunics knitted for fishermen since it was able to absorb sea water without getting damp or clammy. The designer Chanel made it "respectable" and "dress-up" for fashion in 1918.

JET RAIL A steel hang bar with a transverse slot running the length of the bar. Specially designed hardware (brackets, waterfalls, rings, etc.) will catch and fit into the slot at any point along the bar. It is possible with a jet rail to operate a hang rod that extends out from a wall and rests on brackets, which are hooked into slotted wall standards.

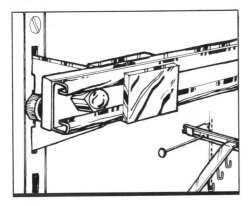

JEWEL NECKLINE A high, round, collarless neckline on a blouse or dress.

JIG A carefully constructed or cut-out device that maintains the proper position and relationship between the cutting end of the tool and the piece of work at hand. The jig is often made of wood or metal and is reusable for the same particular function, design, or relationship of parts.

JIG SAW An electrically powered hand-held cutting tool which is ideal for cutting curves, scrolls and irregular pat-

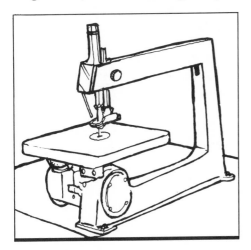

terns. The straight blade is removable and thus inside cuts and outside cuts are possible. The saber saw is a portable jig saw.

JIG-SAW DETAIL Cut-out or fret work made with a jig saw. The "gingerbread" or "steamboat Gothic" of the late Victorian period.

JOBBER A term used in retailing to describe the middleman between the manufacturer and the retailer. One who supplies the retailer. See *buy-out.*

JOB DESCRIPTION A term used in store planning to describe a written outline or statement listing and explaining the specific duties and responsibilities involved in a particular job. Also explains how that job relates to the department or organization as a whole.

JOB LOT A special purchase, usually at a drastically reduced price, which can be an indefinite assortment of sizes, styles, and colors—and even products. It is an "odds and ends" collection of not always related merchandise. Similar to a "close out" or an "odd lot."

JODHPURS Riding breeches, which originated in India and were adopted into Western fashion in the 1920s. The seat and "hips" are full and overly contoured, but the trouser leg is snug and fitted from the knee down to the ankle with a strap that passes under a shoe or low boot.

JOG An offset or a change in the direction in a surface. A set-back or step-up

from one plane to another. See *offset*.

JOGGING SHORTS Short shorts, trim and snug-fitted, with rounded slits up either leg to facilitate movement without extra fullness in the garment.

JOINTER A power-operated plane used to smooth and level wooden surfaces.

JULIET SLEEVE A puffed sleeve set into the armhole and cinched at the upper arm. The balance of the sleeve, down to the wrist, is close fitted and simple.

JUMPER A one-piece, sleeveless garment worn over a shirt, blouse, T-shirt or dickey. Similar to a pinafore. Sometimes with straps or bib front, wrapped and tied or buttoned or split at sides.

JUMPSUIT A one-piece coverall with or without sleeves, joined to pants and finished off with a belt, sash, etc. The garment is usually buttoned or zipped up the front.

JUNCTION BOX A term used in electrical work for a metal box which covers the joints between the ends of conductors, and also joins the ends in their metal cable covers.

JUNIOR DEPARTMENT STORE Smaller than the usual department store, upgraded or traded up fashion merchandise and more diversified than a specialty store.

JUNIOR MANNEQUIN A mannequin meant to wear a size 7 dress, but will usually carry off a size 5 or size 9 as well. Often posed and made up as a young, active type—more animated than the "Missy." The bust measurement is approximately 32A and the figure averages about 5'7" to 5'9" in height. Bust, waist and hip measurements will vary slightly depending upon the manufacturer and the country of manufacture. Depending upon pose and makeup, the figure can represent a college freshman, a young executive, or a sophisticated mature woman.

JUNIOR PETITE MANNEQUIN A mannequin meant to wear a size 5 to 7 dress. Often posed and made up as a super-animated, freckled and braided, saucy and perky teenager. The figure averages about 5'5" tall. Depending upon pose and makeup, figure can represent a small, mature woman.

JUNIOR PETITE SIZES A retailing term used to describe sizes 3, 5, 7, 9 and 11 for the smaller woman. Cut with a shorter waistline and generally shorter proportions.

JUNIOR SIZES A retailing term used for sizes 7, 9, 11 and 13 for the adult female. Cut with a higher bustline and a shorter waistline than the standard misses' figures.

JUNK SCULPTURE See *assemblage art*.

JUTE Long, tough, natural fibers from the stalks of plants native to India, Bangladesh and Pakistan. These fibers can be spun into strong, burlaplike yarns. Used to add weight and stiffness to carpet construction.

K

KALOGRAM A design incorporating all the letters of a name into a design rather than just the initials as in a monogram.

KANEKALON A man-made fiber, produced in the Orient, used in the manufacturing of soft, natural-looking wigs. The natural looking fiber is washable, but does not respond well to being reset with hot rollers. It is sometimes blended with Elura or other man-made fibers. See *wigs*.

K.D. See *knocked down*.

KERF The notch or slit made by a saw cutting across the grain of the wood, but not all the way through the wood. By making several kerfs or slits, one close to another, it is possible to bend the wood into an arc. This ability to bend is called "kerfing."

KEY COPY The catch phrase or simple direct statement that sums up the intent of a display and appears on a card or streamer in a window or case.

KEY CORNERED A rectangular frame whose four corners are broken by

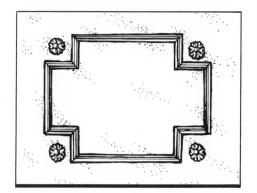

right angles. The cut-out corners are often filled in with rosettes. Popular in Adam and Neo Classic boiserie.

KEY DRAWING Copy consisting of guidelines only.

KEYHOLE An opening that is round and wider on top and tapers to a narrow, straight section. Used as a slot on standards into which brackets and attachments hook. The lower section keeps the bracket from slipping out of the slot.

KEYHOLE NECKLINE A high round neckline, usually collarless, with a pattern or diamond-shaped cut-out between the cleavage and the throat.

KEYHOLE SAW A hand carpentry tool with a long, thin cutting blade with about eight to ten teeth to the inch. It is designed for heavy, coarse and fast work. The narrow, tapered blade does allow for irregular cutting, often beyond the capabilities of a scroll saw. See *scroll saw*.

KEYSTONE The central stone of block, wedge-shaped, that forms the top of an arch in construction.

KHAKI See *chino*.

KICK PLATE A horizontal panel, usually 3 or 4 inches wide, at the base of case goods, counters or other units that continue down to the floor. This base is usually recessed slightly, or set back, from the front face of the unit. The kick plate takes the kicks and scuffs from the people standing in front of the case.

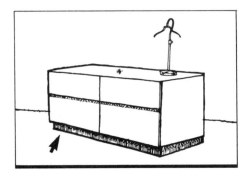

KICK PLEAT A short, inverted pleat extending about 4 or 5 inches from the hem and located at the sides or center back of a sheath or a close-fitting skirt. Used to allow for freer movement in walking or sitting down.

KICKER The advertised item in a sale that will probably attract the largest number of customers. The featured item in a sale or promotion.

KILOWATT A measure of power. Electric companies base their bills on the consumption or use of kilowatts. A kilowatt or 1,000 watts is equal to $\frac{1}{746}$ of an English horsepower. See *horsepower*.

KILT A pleated, plaid skirt that extends from the waist to the knee. Executed in Tartan plaids, it is worn by both sexes and usually with argyle knee socks.

KIMONO A Japanese garment, loose fitting, with full, square sleeves. The garment wraps around the man or woman and is secured with a sash or obi. Lengths may vary and the garment can be enhanced with embroideries and/or appliqués.

KIMONO SLEEVE A wide, full sleeve that is part of the body of the robe. It is not cuffed, cinched or fastened in any way at the wrist.

KINETIC ART Four-dimensional art in that it adds the dimension of time and/or movement to a three-dimensional expression. Examples of this art form are: mobiles, moving lights, machines that move or are caused to move by an action on the part of the viewer, or artworks that are manipulated and moved by the viewer. It is usually the combination of art with technical expertise (knowledge of lighting/engineering and/or physics). See *light art*.

KIOSK A self-standing booth or structure on the selling floor which may accommodate a salesperson as well as merchandise. A mini-boutique, outpost or an enclosed information desk. See *booth* and *gazebo*.

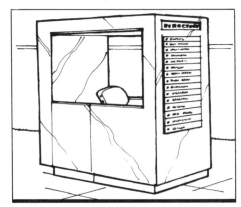

KIOSK WINDOW See *island window*.

KITSCH From the German to make cheap "verkitchen." Described as "artistic rubbish" which is mass produced for popular consumption and bastardizes past fine-art styles or forms. Cutesy and gadgety and usually associated with souvenirs and the tourist industry. "Art for the Millions," but reduced to the lowest taste level, sugar-coated, and garishly colored for popular acceptance.

KLEIG, KLEIGLIGHTS The many types of theatrical spotlights, light housings, striplights, etc., manufactured by the Kleigl Lighting Co. Generally a term applied to all theatrical and professional photographers' lighting equipment, or the super spotlights or arc lights associated with gala openings and premieres.

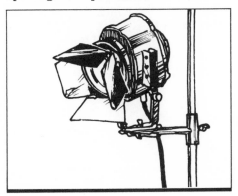

KLEM SYSTEM Trademark for a panel connector, which does not get screwed or nailed into the panels. The connector will hold panels, or most materials, at any angle from 90 to 270 degrees. The brushed chrome "jaws" accept interchangeable rubber inserts and will hold a variety of thicknesses of panels. The connector is secured with an Allen wrench. The "mini-klem" holds panels from $\frac{1}{16}''$ to $\frac{3}{4}''$ thick.

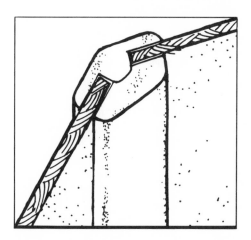

KNICKERBOCKERS Dutch-styled, loose, baggy breeches secured at the knee with a band, buckle or cuff. From this evolved the less voluminous knickers of the late 19th century and the "Plus Fours" of the 1920s golfing scene.

KNICKERS See *knickerbockers.*

KNIFE PLEATS Sharp folds in the fabric that are doubled over and only one clean crease shows. All folds go in the same direction.

KNOCKED DOWN (K.D.) A term used in fixturing, retailing and architecture to describe a unit sent in parts and not fully assembled. Usually assembling instructions are provided.

KNOCK OFF An illegal exact copy or reproduction of a higher priced design. A "line-for-line" copy in the fashion industry is based on the reproduction from an original which was purchased to serve as the model for the exact copies.

KNOTTED RUG A term used to describe an Oriental-type rug with the surface or pile formed by knotting the threads around the warp

KNOTTY PINE Pine planks in which the oval darkened knots make a definite statement. A very provincial or Early American look in wall linings or furniture.

KNUCKLE JOINT A hinged cabinetry joint that works much as a knuckle joint on the finger—movement back and forth in one plane only.

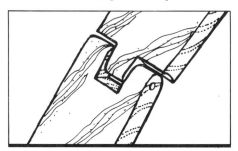

KNURLED SCREW A type of thumb-screw with the outer edge or rim of the head made up of a series of ridges similar to the edge of a newly minted coin. It permits a better finger or wrench grasp on the head of the screw. Used in fixturing and carpentry. See *thumb-screw bracket*.

KODEL Polyester fiber which when woven into fabric is quick drying, wrinkle and heat resistant. Kodel fibers are also used for stuffing pillows and soft sculptures. Trademark of Eastman Chemical Products, Inc.

KOROSEAL Vinyl fabric used for furniture upholstery and wall coverings. Trademark of The Goodrich Rubber Co. See *leatherette*.

KRAFT PAPER A coarse, comparatively light-brown paper made of wood pulp. Because of its strength, it is used primarily as a packing or wrapping paper.

KRYPTON LAMP An economical and efficient lamp which cuts power costs by 7½ to 15 percent. A 54, 90, or 135 Krypton lamp will produce light equal to an ordinary 60, 100 or 150 watt lamp.

L

LACQUER A hard, shiny, colored, sometimes clear and/or opaque finish made from shellac dissolved in alcohol. A varnish.

LADDER FIXTURE Two vertical straight sides connected by several equidistant horizontal hang rods or shelves. The unit is almost always conceived as adjustable in that the rods or shelves can be moved up or down on the "rungs." The ladder is sometimes applied perpendicular to a wall or column and used as a more decorative wall system.

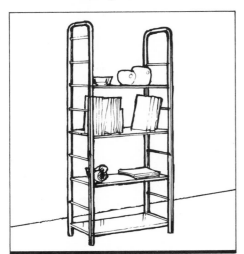

LAG SCREW A bolt-headed type of extra strong screw which requires a wrench to be turned. Used in carpentry and construction to attach lumber to lumber or hardware to lumber where bolting through is unfeasable or undesirable.

LALLY COLUMN A trade name for a steel pipe filled with concrete. Used as an added support under floors or platforms carrying extra heavy loads. It also works as a fireproof support in that the concrete within the column stores the heat of the fire.

LAMBREQUIN A valance board for draperies. See *valance*.

LAMÉ A shiny fabric woven or knitted with metallic threads or a combination of metallic and other fiber threads.

LAMINATED The end result of bonding or gluing together several layers of wood, paper and plastics and usually finished with a veneer or fine-surface design. Sometimes the layers are alternately cross grained to counteract warping. It can also refer to the bonding of a sheet of plastic film or acetate to a board.

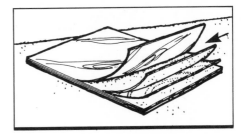

LAMP *1.* The complete light source unit, which consists of a light generating element (a filament or arc tube), the accessory hardware, the enclosure or envelope for the assorted parts and the base. *2.* An electric lightbulb in a variety of shapes and sizes. Larger watt bulbs require larger glass envelopes to dissipate the greater amount of heat emitted by them. Bulb sizes are expressed in numbers representing ⅛th inch, thus a 5″ diameter bulb would be a #40. Most standard household bulbs are designated "A" (arbitrary) or "PS" (pear shaped with straight sides). Other shapes are: "S" (straight sides); "T" (tubular); "PAR" (Parabolic Aluminized Reflector); "R" (reflector); "C" (cone shaped)" "G" (globe).

LAMP LUMEN DEPRECIATION See *L.L.D.*

LANAI An outdoor patio or veranda.

LANDSCAPE *1.* The arrangement, planning, plantings and decorations on the land or the area surrounding a building, structure or conglomeration of such units. A landscape architect would plan the locations and the clusters of trees, bushes, shrubs, ground cover, walkways, artificial waterways, bridges, gazebos, etc. The environment around a focal point. *2.* An outdoor scene of a horizontal frame or panel.

LANTERN LIGHT A raised skylight set above the roof of a structure. A small structure with openings for light placed at the very top of a dome, cupola or turret.

LANTERN SLEEVE A sleeve in two sections, narrow at the armhole and wrist, wider at mid-arm or at joining seam.

LAP JOINT Two pieces of wood are overlapped and joined at right angles to each other. Each piece of wood is grooved in exactly the same way, so that when they are laid one on top of the other they make a flush joint.

FULL   HALF

LAP REGISTRATION Colors overlap slightly when they are laid down one over the other. Where they print, a ridge or secondary color may result.

LATEX PAINT A quick-drying paint produced by synthetic resins, rubbers or polystyrenes dispersed in water. Paint becomes hard and dry by the evaporation of the water in the mixture. Less of a fire hazard than an oil-based paint.

LATHE A standing power machine consisting of a vertically fixed cutting or boring tool attached to a horizontal platform or bed. The wood or material

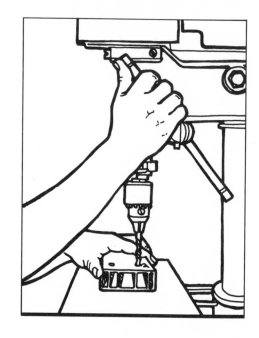

to be cut, shaped or drilled is moved around the vertical element while supported on the horizontal platform. It is possible to rotate a piece of wood while the various chisels are applied to remove the unwanted wood symmetrically about the axis of rotation. The lathe can be used to make spindles, balusters and turnings.

LATTICE A criss-crossing of strips of lath (thin wood) or metal. An open fretwork. A diamond pattern created by overlapping wood strips.

LAUAN A mahogany-like, reddish-brown hardwood native to the Philippine Islands.

LAWN A lightweight, semi-sheer fabric made of linen, cotton or man-made fiber yarns.

LAYAWAY A "buy-now, pay-as-you-go and collect-it-later" type of purchase. The layaway concept encourages early shopping while the selection and stock is best. The store will then "hold" the merchandise for a specified amount of time while the customer makes installment payments on that merchandise. When the payment is completed, the merchandise is delivered to the customer. As credit cards become more popular and accessible —the customer buys now, takes it now, and pays for the merchandise while it is being used. See *C.B.D.*

LAYLIGHT A glass or plastic panel laid flush into an opening in a roof to allow in natural (or artificial) light.

LAYOUT A term used in advertising for a working drawing of an advertisement with copy and artwork.

LAZY SUSAN A fixturing unit consisting of a stationary base with a horizontal rotating plane similar to a dish or tray. See *ball bearing*.

L.C.L. (LIGHT CENTER LENGTH) The average distance from the center of the light source to the bottom of the base contact. A factor in incandescent and high-intensity discharge lamps.

LEADED GLAZING Small (often diamond-shaped) pieces of glass set into a patterned fretwork made of lead strips soldered together to form a window or glass panel.

LEAD TIME The time period between when a confirmed purchase order is placed and the delivery, to the buyer, of that merchandise. The amount of time for advance planning that must be allowed for the purchasing and production of materials if an "opening" date is to be met.

LEASE A contract that specifies the terms of rental, and the duration of that contract. It permits a definite period for the use of land, space and fixtures without the outright purchase of those items. The lesser grants the lease to the lessee.

LEASED DEPARTMENT A particular department or area in a retail operation that is actually owned by the store, but is rented to an outside source, individual or chain operation. These operators sell a product that enhances the store's merchandise spread and its "image" and does not require any investment in stock. It can be a designer shoe salon (Charles Jourdan) which the store could not otherwise offer to its clientele—or a line of cosmetics, which is exclusive and sells only under its own name. The leased or rented department usually has to adhere to and contribute to the merchandise presentation and overall look of the store. The store may receive a set payment or a percentage of the lessees' sale.

LEATHERETTE A term formerly used to describe a plastic coating colored and embossed to simulate leather on a heavy cotton backing. Used as an upholstery fabric as well as for wall covering. Currently called leatherette fabric.

LEDGE The area raised above the storage units behind the selling counters on an open floor, or the area above the 4- to 5-foot shelf or bin unit next to a wall. Used for displays. The ledge displays will often dominate a main floor presentation by virtue of their elevation above the merchandise and the traffic.

LEFT WINDOW The mannequin's left-handed side as it faces the viewer outside the window.

LEG O'MUTTON SLEEVE A sleeve flared from the armhole to the elbow and then close fitting down to the wrist. Popular in the 1890s.

LENS A plastic or glass shield that covers the bottom, or the bottom and sides of a lamp. Used to control the direction and the brightness of the light as it comes from the lamp.

LENS PROJECTORS A spotlight lens to which is attached a lantern slide holder and an objective lens. Thus, it is possible to project clouds, rain, painted or photographed scenes, etc., onto a wall or screen with clarity of detail and sharpness of focus. See *projection*.

LEOTARDS Originally designed by the 19th-century trapeze artist, Jules Leotard. A one-piece, form-fitting, long- or short-sleeved, high- or low-neckline to crotch garment. In the mid 1950s, it became available in stretch nylon, and become all inclusive neck to toe. For many years, it was traditionally a black garment worn by dancers, acrobats and gymnasts. They are now available in a wide range of colors and textures and may be worn as an undergarment for a sports outfit.

LETRASET, LETRASIGN, LETRATONE See *dry transfer.*

LETTERPRESS The oldest and most commonly used method of printing. The area or design to be printed is raised above the surface of the plate. This raised or relief area is inked and then, by exerting pressure on the paper against the inked surface, the copy or design is reproduced on the paper.

LEVELER A fixturing attachment consisting of an adjustable screw and a pad. Used on the foot or base of a unit to accommodate any irregularities of the floor surface. By adjusting the levelers one can raise or lower one side or the other. Levelers can make racks or merchandisers more secure and less likely to rock or tilt.

LEVIS (BLUE JEANS) Work pants made of a sturdy blue denim fabric which were originally manufactured by Levi Strauss & Co. for the gold seekers in California in the 1850s. Sometimes, the wear areas are reinforced with copper rivets and heavy contrasting stitches. Also called jeans.

Today term is a trademark for work and sports clothes of this company.

LIEN A legal claim on a property, or a property used as a security for a debt.

LIGHT ART The use or the creation of art by means of light such as color organs, fireworks, neon tube designs and projected light. It may be part of a Kinetic Art design. Also called lumia or luminism. See *kinetic art* and *neon.*

LIGHTBULB See *lamp.*

LIGHT CENTER LENGTH See *L.C.L.*

LIGHTING LOUVERS Baffles or panels with geometric openings used to shield a lamp and cut down on excessive brightness or glare without cutting out too much of the light. See *egg crate.*

LIGHT TRIM A term used in display to describe a sparse and simple approach to the presentation of merchandise. A few, well-chosen pieces are shown with great care to detail. The opposite of a heavy trim.

LIMESTONE A gray or beige natural stone, mainly a carbonate of lime or of calcium. Used for facing buildings.

LINDEN A lime tree. A fine-grained, white wood from a lime tree. Excellent for carving.

LINE CUT A form of engraving in which the design is reproduced by lines as opposed to other methods using dots for half tones. Copper and steel engravings are made by direct incision of the burin into the surface of the plate.

LINE DRAWING A drawing made up of lines, dots and solid masses rather than soft, gray tonal variations as in a wash drawing. Shadings and gradations can be suggested by lines, crosshatching, stippling, etc., but always in the full intensity of the medium.

LINE ENGRAVING See *line cut.*

LINE-FOR-LINE COPY See *knock off.*

LINEN A natural fabric made from the smooth-surfaced flax fibers. Manmade fibers are often blended to improve characteristics.

LINEN FINISH The impression of woven linen or crash on the surface of paper or board. It can be obtained by compressing sheets of paper between alternate sheets of linen, or by embossing.

LINENS See *domestics.*

LINGERIE From the French word for "linge," linen fabric used for underwear from the Middle Ages to the 20th century. A collective term for women's underwear, including bras, panties, slips, nightgowns, robes, etc. A department or area selling these articles may use the term "intimate apparel."

LINING PAPER An inexpensive paper which is used as an undercoat for the more expensive and decorative paper or wallpaper that will finish the walls. It provides a clean, smooth and good adhering surface for the final paper.

LINOLEUM A manufactured floor covering supplied on a 6-foot roll and available in a variety of colors, textures and finishes. This sheet-type flooring is relatively thin, and requires a smooth floor underneath. The wearing surface is fairly resistant to oil and grease, but it will absorb moisture.

LINOTYPE A machine that sets type in slugs or solid lines. Various sizes of type, from 5 pt. to 14 pt., can be cast in a line up to 30 picas wide. Special machines will take larger type and set up to 36 picas.

LINTEL A horizontal piece of wood or stone over a door, window or other opening to support the weight above. The lintel rests on uprights or vertical elements called posts.

LIP A term used in fixturing to describe a raised edge or short return to prevent slippage.

LISLE A hard-twisted, two-ply cotton or wool thread often used in the manufacture of hosiery and underwear. Named for the city, Lisle, in France, where it originated.

LIST PRICE The full price "listed" by the merchant without any discounts or reductions.

LITHOGRAPHY A planographic process of printing from a flat stone or metal plate. Also the process of reproducing designs executed with a grease pencil or crayon on a special ground. The end result—the lithograph—is usually produced in limited and numbered quantities. An art form.

L.L.D. (LAMP LUMEN DEPRECIATION) The gradual decrease in the output of a lamp during its life span. The mean or average lumen of a lamp.

LOAD The total weight or total downward pressure exerted on a particular area or weight-supporting element. The "dead load" would be the weight and pressure existing in the structure itself, while the "live load" refers to the temporary weights added. For example, the "dead load" of an elevator compared to the "live load" of the passengers using the elevator at a particular time.

LOBBY WINDOW Often an all glass enclosed or mostly glassed-in window in front of the main entrance to a store in an arcaded or angled store front. See *angled front, arcaded front,* and *island window.*

LOFT An upper floor space, an attic or loft, sometimes left raw and unfinished. Today, the term refers to whole buildings composed or large, open, high-ceilinged floors which are not predivided or sectioned off into special areas, and thus free for many uses, including manufacturing, art studios, performing art studios and selling or living spaces that are different and untraditional.

LOGGIA An arcaded gallery or a room or corridor that is open to the outdoors on one side, and that open side is arcaded. An Italian term. See *arcade.*

LOGO, LOGOTYPE A trademark, emblem or insignia which represents an individual, business, product, service, etc. It may be a decorative grouping of letters (monograms) which are part of the name of the company or product, or an ideograph or stylized drawing which represents the company or item.

LOOK-THRU WINDOW A look-through window that permits an open

exposure of the store interior beyond. There may be a railing, low partition, half wall, screen or divider which only semi-obstructs the interior view in favor of the window display presentation. An open-back or see-through window.

LOOP PLAN A single wide aisle that makes a complete circuit around a selling floor. A ring or loop that circles around a central core, atrium or well and provides greater visibility of the entire floor as well as access to the assorted departments or divisions that are just off the aisle.

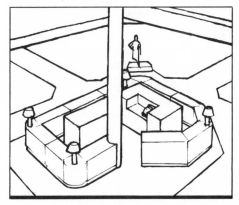

LOOSE REGISTRATION Colors can be printed one over the other without affecting the finished product. See *hairline registration, lap registration,* and *registration.*

LOSS LEADER The merchandise that is offered for sale at cost, or below cost to obtain the customer's attention and entice them into the store or department. The lure.

LOUVER A panel made up of slats placed at an angle and used over an opening on a wall or ceiling. The slats are usually adjustable to allow in air and/or light. See *lighting louvers.*

LOWBOY A low cabinet or drawer unit. Not as tall as the standard counter (36″–42″).

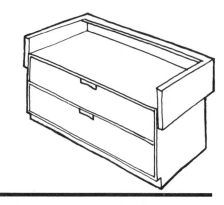

LOWER CASE The small letters of a type font as distinguished from the upper case or capital letters.

LOW PRESSURE SODIUM LAMP An efficient and economic lamp producing 183 lumens per watt. See *sodium vapor lamp.*

LUCITE See *acrylics.*

LUCITE AR A specially treated acrylic, which is more abrasion resistant than standard Lucite.

LUG A small lip or projecting surface on a building or surfacing material. It is an extra surface to cement into place and thus an extra surface for adhesion.

LUMBER CORE A laminated panel board, usually ⅜″ or thicker, which is constructed of strips of wood glued together between a pair of outer veneer boards whose grain crosses the core strip. It is supposed to be more rigid than plywood. Called coreboard in Europe.

LUMEN The measure of the quantity of light produced by any source, but compared to the amount of light produced by a single candle. The time rate of the flow of light. Luminosity is the quality of being capable of giving or reflecting light.

LUMEN HOUR The unit of light quantity. Used to compute the "cost of light" and the result is given in "dollars per lumen hours." It is analogous to "kilowatt hours."

LUMIA See *light art.*

LUMINAIRE A complete lighting unit including lamp, socket, housing, frame, holder, reflector, shield and if necessary ballast. From the French word for "light" or "lamp."

LUMINISM See *light art.*

LUNETTE A semicircular window or a crescent-shaped unit.

LUREX Trademark of Dow Badische Company for their metallic fiber and yarn.

LUSTRAGRAY A trademark for a gray tinted plateglass which can reduce glare from the sun by up to 50%. The transparency of the glass is not affected and the neutral color does not affect the store or interior design, but more light is required in the display window to counteract the gray glass.

LUSTRE FABRICS, LUSTRE RUGS Cut pile fabric with a silky sheen similar to handwoven Oriental carpets.

M

MACHINE BOLT A connecting piece of hardware consisting of a threaded shaft with a square or hexagonal head.

MACHINED A metal surface which has been finished or polished on a lathe or planer.

MACQUETTE See *dummy*.

MADRAS A cotton fabric made in Madras, India in brightly colored ginghams, plaids, checks and stripes. Madras fabrics bleed, when washed, and eventually a soft blending of the colors occurs.

MAGNETIC TACK HAMMER A thin-headed hammer on a tapered wood handle. The striking surface is smaller than the standard hammer and magnetized to hold the tack which is to be struck. The clawed end is also less angled and slighter in appearance than the standard hammer.

MAHOGANY A reddish wood with a handsome grain that works well and takes a beautiful finish. A fine furniture wood. The veneers are effective for lining walls.

MAILLOT A one-piece, form-fitting, swimsuit with a low cut neckline and narrow shoulder straps. From the French word for "tight garment."

MAIL-ORDER HOUSE A retail operation that shows and sells through their own catalogs or magazine ads. Orders are received by mail, processed and then shipped by mail. Usually, there is no retail store from which a prospective customer can shop.

MAINTENANCE A retailing term used to describe provision for the upkeep of the store such as cleaning, repairs, lighting and water and sewer repairs.

MAKEUP As used on mannequins: The skin tone of the body and face; the coloring and artwork used on the lips, cheeks, around the eyes; the subtle or dramatic use of rouge, mascara, etc.; the brushwork and the blending or sharpness of line and color. The mannequins' type or image as personalized by artwork.

MALL An indoor park, garden, and walkway filled with fountains, sculptures, plantings. Sometimes covered and surrounded by stores, shops, restaurants, etc. Shopping malls are often anchored at either end by a branch of a major department, specialty or chain store with specialty shops and restaurants between them.

MALLEABLE The quality in a metal or plastic material that makes it possible to form, bend, shape or extend that material by means of beating, hammering or exerting pressure upon that material.

MALLET A hammer with a striking head of wood, rubber or hard plastic. Used to put together and take apart modular systems or to strike metal or plastic without denting or scratching the finished surface.

MANDARIN COLLAR A standing collar vertically slit at the throat, and attached to the close-fitting neckline of a dress, coat, jacket, etc. Also called a Nehru collar and Chinese collar.

MANIFEST A shipping form listing who is sending what to whom, how much in how many pieces or packages, when it is sent and how it is being sent, and sometimes the cost for the transfer and the transaction. Used by carriers, and also for interstore transfers.

MAN-MADE FIBERS Fibers created in laboratories and produced by means of machines, vats, etc., from combinations of chemicals, coal, tar, wood pulp, etc., rather than fibers grown in nature. It is possible to develop fibers that are more resistant to heat, certain stains, sun-fading, and have greater strength and resiliency. Man-made fibers can be woven or blended with natural fibers (cotton, silk, wool, linen) to reinforce and strengthen them.

MANNEQUIN A three-dimensional representation of the human form—somewhat idealized and stylized. Used to show apparel. It can be a realistic interpretation, semi-realistic, or abstract. Mannequins vary in sizes and proportions depending upon type and age group, and are also available in various ethnic groupings. Also spelled mannekin and manikin. For specific types of mannequins see *abstract mannequin, semi-abstract manniquin, semi-realistic mannequin, realistic mannequin, ethnic mannequin, junior mannequin, petite mannequin, junior petite mannequin, full-figured mannequin.*

MANSARD ROOF A hipped roof with a slope in two planes; the lower plane steeper than the higher plane. Popularized by François Mansart in the 17th-century, French Renaissance Architecture. See *gambrel roof.*

MANTILLA A lace scarf or shawl in black or white, sometimes worn over a tall comb, by Spanish women.

MANUFACTURER The producer of specific goods and not necessarily the vendor of these products. The person or company responsible for designing, making and/or assembling a product.

MANZANITA BRANCHES Twisted, gnarled branches from the manzanita shrub of the western U.S. Used for interesting displayers of small hanging pieces such as chains and jewelry.

MAPLE A light-colored wood, similar to birch, that is hard, strong and usually straight-grained. Bird's eye maple has a swirled or blistered grain.

MARABOU The soft, fluffy feathers from the wings and tail of a species of stork. May be dyed in a variety of colors. Used as a trimming on dresses, negligees, etc., or as a complete garment. See *boa.*

MARGIN 1. *In retailing* The excess of sales over the cost involved in making these sales. 2. *In printing and graphics* The blank border or edge around printed material on a page. May contain a design, a line or box of copy.

MARKDOWN A term used in retailing to describe a reduction from the originally stated retail price. Used to encourage buying.

MARKET A term used in retailing to describe a group or particular portion of the buying public a store is appealing to. Based on the purchasing power, taste level and life style of the group.

MARKET RESEARCH A term used in retailing to describe the results of studies and statistics of the public's buying habits and preferences regarding design, color, price, function, etc., of products. Often researchers will sample a community and record the answers and attitudes of the individuals on a new or established product, and evaluate the answers according to age, sex, level of education, etc.

MARQUEE A projection or canopy that extends out from or over an entrance to a building. It is often decorative and usually made of metal and/or glass. It can also be made of canvas set into a metal frame. A marquee may also be a cantilevered projection out from the wall and just above the entrance to a public building, and designed to carry a message or sign, such as over a theater entrance. See *awning* and *canopy*. Also spelled marquise and marquess.

MARQUESS, MARQUISE See *marquee.*

MARQUISETTE A lightweight open-mesh fabric. Used for curtains.

MASK *1. In merchandise presentation* Any device (such as screen, flat, border, valance or proscenium) used to hide the lighting or construction paraphernalia in a display window from the viewer outside. A means of focusing the eye on the merchandise pre-

sentation rather than on the how, what and where the display was done. See *teaser* and *tormentor. 2. In printing* An opaque frame or bar of material used to protect open or selected areas of printing plates during photoexposure. Strips of tape used to prevent bleeding or printing over into a finished area.

MASONITE A rigid building board compressed and tempered for extra strength. It is difficult to nail into. Usually available in 4′ × 8′ sheets and in various thicknesses. See *fiberboard.*

MASONRY That part of the building industry dealing with plaster, concrete construction, and the laying of stone, brick, tile, etc. The mason is the workman doing the masonry work.

MASS MERCHANDISING STORE A self-service store which displays and stocks a wide variety of merchandise.

MASTIC *1.* A caulking compound or form of cement which retains a certain degree of elasticity. *2.* A quick drying, waterproof pointing or plastering material. *3.* A sealer. *4.* A substance in glue.

MATELASSÉ A fabric which has a raised, embossed or quilted design. From the French word for "padded" or "cushioned." Used for clothing and upholstery.

MAT KNIFE A cutting tool consisting of gripping handle with a single-edge blade, in some cases retractable, between the two sides of the handle. It is possible to adjust the exposed length or depth of the cutting blade or to retract the blade completely when not

in use. Particularly suited for cutting cardboard, paper and where straight or beveled cut lines are desired.

MATRIX BOARD See *particle board.*

MATTE FINISH A dull, flat, no-shine finish.

MECHANICAL The finished layout or artwork ready for reproduction. See *layout* and *working drawing.*

MECHANICAL DISPLAYS See *animated displays.*

MEDIA *1.* The means of communication such as radio, television, newspapers, magazines, books, posters and billboards, and verbal reports; the variety of ways to communicate a message. *2.* The particular material used to express fine and graphic arts such as oil, watercolor, gouache, tempera, and crayon. *3.* The vehicle in which pigments are mixed such as oil, water, wax and egg.

MEDIUM The singular form of media.

MEDIUM SCREW BASE The standard, common screw base found on most lamps and bulbs. It is made of copper, though aluminum is used where smaller wattages are involved. The medium screw base is 1″ in diameter and is used on most lamps of under 300 watts.

MELAMINE FORMALDEHYDES A generic term for a plastic sheeting material, which is hard, tough, waterproof, resistant to most household chemicals and to normal stains; able to stand up to daily wear and use such as scuffing and rubbing; easy to wash and maintain. Available in a variety of colors, textural patterns and surfaces, densities, gauges, and in imitations of wood, marble and other natural materials. Often available laminated onto a wood fiber substrata. Produced by many companies under such trademarks as Formica, Micarta, Nevamar, Parkwood, Pionite and Textolite. Used on counters, walls, fixtures, tables, cabinets, etc.

MELTON A closely woven, sturdy, dull-finished fabric, resembling felt. Used for pea jackets.

MEN'S LONG SIZES A retailing term for men's sizes 34 to 46 and sizes 35 to 45. For the taller man (over 6′ tall) with an otherwise average build. The size indicates the chest circumference measurement.

MEN'S REGULAR SIZES A retailing term for men's sizes 34 to 46 and sizes 35 to 45. For men 5′7″ to 5′10″. The size indicates the chest circumference measurement.

MEN'S SHORT SIZES A retailing term for men's sizes 34 to 44 and sizes 35 to 45. For men 5′3″ to 5′7″ tall with an average build. The size indicates the chest circumference measurement.

MERCHANDISE MIX The variety, type and price of merchandise being offered to create a balanced sales picture, or to present a particular store character or image.

MERCHANDISER A unit, rack, column or wall attachment, container, table, cabinet, etc., that holds and shows a selection and stock of merchandise. The better the design, the more merchandise is contained in the least amount of floor space, with the greatest flexibility in use and ease of self-selection for the customer. A basic concept in fixturing. For types of merchandisers see *A-rack, C-rack, quad rack, round rack, star rack, 2-rack,* etc.

MERCHANDISING REQUISITION BOOK See *book out.*

MERCURY VAPOR LAMP A light source in a tubular form that depends upon mercury vapor for its light ability. The latter is made luminous and emits light when electricity passes across a gap between the wires inside the tube. A high intensity discharge light source often used for outdoor illumination where its bluish tint is not

a great disadvantage. See *warm deluxe mercury lamp.*

MERGER The coming together or blending of two businesses or departments. Where one business buys out the other, the purchaser becomes the dominant factor in the new operation.

MERINO *1.* A sheep raised in the U.S. and Australia. *2.* The wool obtained from the merino sheep.

MESSALINE A satin-weave fabric; soft, lustrous and lightweight. Used for lingerie and women's wear.

METAL BASE The flat base found on mannequins with a perpendicular flange into which the butt rod or ankle rod can be fitted. It is heavy enough to sit on the floor and support the mannequin in an erect position. See *base flange* and *butt rod.*

METAL HALIDE LAMP A high intensity discharge light source. Light is produced by the radiation from mercury combined with the halides of metals such as sodium, thalium and indium. It is more efficient than the mercury lamp and has generally acceptable color properties. The lamp has a life range from 7,500 to 15,000 hours.

METAL SCULPTURE Three-dimensional art produced from shaped sheet metal. Sometimes combined with metal rods and tubes. Often designed into multileveled friezes or panels or pierced, hammered, cut, bent, formed or shaped strips and pieces of sheet metal.

METER A linear measurement equal to 39.37 inches.

METRIC SYSTEM A decimal system of weights and measures. The basic units are: the meter (39.37 inches) to measure length, and the gram (15.432 grains) for weight. A centimeter is 0.01 of a meter. 2.54 centimeters are equal to an inch. A decimeter is 0.1 of a meter. A decameter is 10 meters. A hecometer is 100 meters. A kilometer is 1000 meters or just over $\frac{6}{10}$ths of a mile.

MEZZANINE A low-ceilinged story usually just above the ground floor, when that main story has an especially high ceiling. A half-floor between the ground level of the main story and the next story over it.

MEZZORILIEVO See *anagylph.*

MICARTA See *melamine formaldehydes.*

MIDDY BLOUSE A fashion adaptation of the U.S. Navy's blouse, often done in white fabric and trimmed with navy blue or black piping. Sailor collar hangs square down the back and tapers to a "V" in front. A sailor's neckerchief ties under the collar and the ends hang down the front. Also called sailor collar.

MILLWORK Finished woodwork, doors, windows, frames, trim, which has been machined and partly assembled at the mill.

MIRROR BALL A decorative sphere whose multifaceted surface is completely covered with small pieces of mirror. Surface catches and throws off myriad flecks of light. A popular concept of the big ballrooms of the 1920s and 1930s, and now is in great use in displays and discotheques.

MISSES' MANNEQUIN A mannequin meant to wear a size 8 dress in a variety of heights, from 5'8" to 6' tall. There is a variety of interpretations in the Missy group of mannequins and, depending upon the manufacturer, pose, makeup, and wig, it can represent a young college type, an active sports woman, a career woman or a supersophisticate. The Missy mannequin can be personalized to represent the store image.

MISSES' SIZES A retailing term for women's sizes 6, 8, 10, 12, 14, 16, and 18.

MITER The angled, corner junction of two units with diagonal cuts at an end, which form a right angle when joined. The corner of a picture frame.

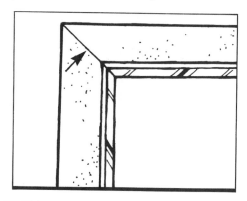

MITER BOX A device or form that guides a hand saw, at the proper angle, for cutting miters or angles to be used in a mitered joint. See *back saw.*

MITER GAUGE A graduated tool used to set a saw to cut at a desired angle.

MIXED MEDIA *1.* Art composed of different materials or techniques such as oil paints, fabric or paper. See *assemblage art, collage* and *montage. 2.* A presentation that combines dance, film, sound and lights. Also referred to as multimedia.

MOBILE A three-dimensional sculpture composed of movable elements. A series of objects or forms suspended at various planes and connected to each other or suspended from a skeletal form. The shapes are connected in such a manner so that the air currents will cause them to move about and change their special relationships to each other. It is movement in space. See *kinetic art.*

MOCK-UP See *dummy.*

MODEL A three-dimensional, scaled representation of a design, structure, piece of sculpture, etc.

MODEL FORM See *dressmaker form.*

MODULATION The repetition of uniform sizes or shapes which can be interrelated and organized within the building grid. Lighting units, fixtures, partitions, etc., can be designed to conform within a grid pattern thus making mass-production feasable and economical. See *globus system, grid,* and *module.*

MODULE *1.* A measuring unit used in architecture. *2. (As illustrated)* Basic, interchangeable, same-sized units; they can be added to or subtracted from. In floor planning, this system makes for greater flexibility and mobility. It is possible to make adjustments and changes as new needs arise. Modules of lighting units can be of the same basic size and thus rearrangeable. Most important in a modular system is the strict adherence to the dimensions, the detailing of the connections and connectors, the availability of accessories and the ability to rearrange parts visually and simply.

MOGUL SCREW BASE A 1½″ diameter, copper screw base used on the larger watt (over 200) bulbs. Used for stage and window display lighting. The larger bulbs need the stability of greater physical support and the heavier currents require larger electrical contacts.

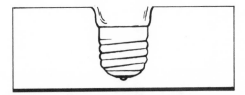

MOHAIR A pile fabric with cut or uncut loops, resembling frieze. Obtained from the hair of the angora goat, combined with other fibers to produce a durable and resilient fabric.

MOIRÉ A lustrous fabric with a watered or wavy-patterned surface. The "watered" effect is produced by embossing the grain by means of engraved rollers or cylinders.

MOLDING Shaped strips of wood, metal or plastic with interesting profiles or silhouettes used to add interest, dimension or relief to flat surfaces. The decorative-shaped bands around the bases of columns or on top of classic capitals. Also spelled moulding.

MOM & POP STORE A family owned and operated unit, usually small, independent and located in a "neighborhood" rather than a shopping center. It can evolve into a chain of small stores, still under "family" ownership or supervision, but no longer supervised by the close, watchful eye of "mom" or "pop." Originally, the neighborhood dry-goods store, the candy store, the corner grocery, the home bakery, etc.

MONDRIAN A pattern of rectangular shapes in various sizes that form an interesting arrangement. Used in display presentations. Influenced by the 20th-century abstract artist, Piet Mondrian, and his designs of rectangles and geometric division of space.

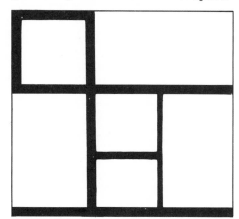

MONEL METAL A trademark for an alloy of nickel and copper, with a high resistance to corrosion. Used in fixturing and decoration.

MONK'S CLOTH A heavy, coarse, woven fabric. May be made from cotton, jute, flax and man-made fibers.

MONOCHROMATIC One color; the shades and tints of a single color. A monochromatic color scheme would include the many variations from the palest pastel of a color to the darkest, deepest shade of the *same* color.

MONOGRAM The first initial or initials of a name used as part of a graphic design—as a logo—or for quick identification. For example the letters "A" and "S"—in a specific typeface would stand for "Abraham and Strauss"; the script "L" and "T" for "Lord and Taylor."

MONTAGE A superimposed composition of bits and pieces made from assorted sources into one design. A coordinated and harmonious patchwork that makes a new statement based on the many and varied parts overlapped and superimposed. See *assemblage art, collage,* and *mixed media.*

MORTAR A bonding material used in masonry. Usually a mixture of cement (or lime) mixed with sand and water, which dries hard and firm. Used to fill in the spaces between the building blocks, but also holds them together.

MORTGAGE A piece of property (something of value) pledged as a security for a loan. The mortgage usually has a specified time limit in which the loan must be repaid, and the interest payments for the use of the money is also indicated.

MORTISE A slot, hole or groove, usually of a special size, dimension or shape, into which some other shaped member will fit. See *mortise and tenon joint.*

MORTISE & TENON JOINT A form of cabinet joinery in which the projecting element in one member (the tenon) fits into the groove or slot in the other (the mortise). The joint is then glued together.

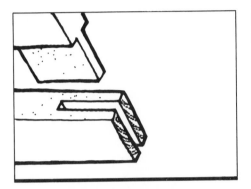

MOSAIC A pattern or design composed of small, often irregular-shaped pieces of glass, tile, marble or wood glued or cemented into place.

MOTIF A dominant design or single element that can be embellished or elaborated upon.

MOUNTING PLATE The flat metal, wood or plastic panel onto which some perpendicular or angled device has been attached or welded, which, in turn, can be applied to a wall, column, counter, floor, etc. The intermediary between a projection and the flat-bearing surface which will carry that

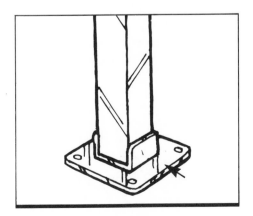

projection. The mounting plate usually has pre-drilled screw holes or similar means for attaching.

MOUSSELINE A fairly sheer, soft, lightweight fabric made of cotton, wool, silk, or man-made fibers.

MOUSSELINE DE SOIE A sheer, lightweight plain woven silk fabric. Fabric is crisp and firm.

MRA Menswear Retailer's Association.

MUKLUKS An above-the-ankle boot with the fur side in and the skin side out. Worn by Eskimos. The authentic mukluks are made of seal or walrus skins.

MULLION The thin, vertical or horizontal, strips that separate the panes of glass in a leaded glass window, door or panel.

MULTIMEDIA See *mixed media.*

MULTI VAPOR II A metal-halide lamp which has been greatly improved in color rendition (see *CR*). Produced by General Electric. Most metal-halide lamps produce a *too blue light,* but Multi Vapor II has a color much like a standard cool white fluorescent lamp, but it is still somewhat bluer and cooler than the incandescent lamp. See *metal halide lamp.*

MUNSELL'S COLOR NOTATION SYSTEM A three-dimensional system of color notation developed by Albert Munsell, (1858–1918), that is accepted by the U.S. Bureau of Standards. Munsell's three dimensions of color are: *hue*—a method of separating one color from another; *value*—the lightness or darkness of a color; *chroma*—the strength or weakness of a color. The color wheel is broken up into ten basic hues: red, yellow-red, yellow, green-yellow, green, blue-green, blue, purple-blue, purple and red-purple. See *Ostwald's Color Notation System.*

MURAL A kind of wall painting—either painted directly onto the wall or printed on paper or canvas and then applied to the wall surface. It is not the same as a fresco which becomes an integral part of the wall, ceiling, arch, etc. See *fresco.*

MUSEUM CASE A security, glass or plastic case raised on a riser, platform or pedestal. The sixth side of the glass or plastic cube is the bottom and it is omitted so that the merchandise which rests on the pedestal base can be protected by the glass sides and the glass (see-through) top. The merchandise can be viewed from all sides. See *security case.*

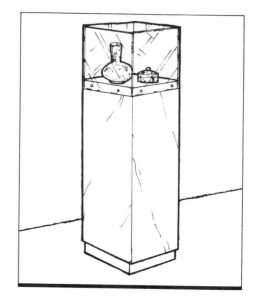

MUSLIN A plain weave fabric, available bleached or unbleached. A sturdy, utilitarian fabric which can be dyed or printed. Muslin is available in widths ranging from 36 inches up to 108 inches. The wider widths make excellent background fabric for theatrical display drops, cycloramas, etc. The muslin used in theatrical displays is usually available in white, light blue, or in the natural color.

MYLAR A polyester film coated with aluminum particles and made into fiber yarns, which have a silvery sheen, are nontarnishable and soft in hand. A mirror-like film. Used in decorative merchandise display. Produced by E.I. du Pont de Nemours.

N

NACRE The iridescent, lustrous material lining some seashells.

N.A.D.I. National Association of Display Industries.

NAIL SIZES In woodworking/carpentry, nail sizes are based on the "penny system"—the number of nails, or a particular size, in one pound or penny. A thousand ten-penny nails weigh ten pounds. The "penny" is abbreviated to "d" the English symbol for "pence." A 2d nail is 1″ long, 3d is 1¼″ long, 4d is 1½″ long, 5d is 1¾″ long, 10d is 3″ long and 20d is 4″ long.

N.A.S.F.M. National Association of Store Fixture Manufacturers.

NATIONAL BRANDS A term used in retailing for products that are manufactured, and often promoted, nationwide, by the manufacturers in the various media under the special brand names. Products that are recognized by a particular name throughout the country.

NAUGAHYDE Trademark of The United States Rubber Co. for a vinyl fabric. Used for upholstery and wall coverings. See *leatherette*.

NECKBLOCK The hollow top filler or plug for a shirt, dress, or suit form. The neckblock may be painted, chrome-plated, fabric-covered, etc., and/or have decorative details such as finials, hoops or moldings.

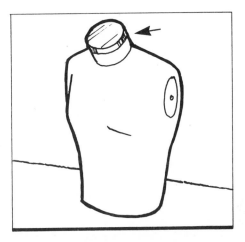

NEON Luminous tube lighting in which neon gas, helium, argon and mercury vapors supply the source of illumination. A special color-glow available in reds, blues, greens, blue-violets and yellows. Used for signs and decorative devices. See *light art*.

NET PRICE The wholesale price to the retailer.

NET SELLING AREA A term used in store planning for all the space designated for the actual selling operation including the forward display and merchandising areas, the adjacent stockrooms, fitting and dressing rooms and cash and wrap counters.

NEVAMAR See *melamine formaldehydes*.

NEWEL A vertical post or turning at the head and end of a handrail or a stairway. Originally, the central pillar of a spiral staircase.

NEWSPRINTS A generic term for the kind of paper used in the printing of newspapers. It is composed primarily of mechanical wood pulp with some chemical wood pulp, machine-finished and slack-sized. An inexpensive paper.

NICKEL-PLATED An electroplating process by which a piece of metal is covered with a fine film or layer of nickel. It imparts a chrome-like finish to the metal that is being plated, but it does not wear as well or look as slick as the chrome plating.

NINON A lightweight, transparent, open weave fabric.

NIPPERS A small hand tool with diagonal cutters. Used for clipping wire and pin heads.

NIPPLE A short pipe coupling with threaded ends. A projection or protub-

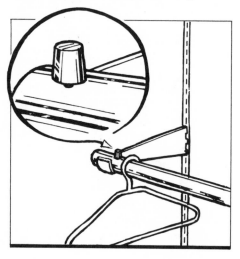

erance from a surface into which something may be fitted or attached. Used in fixturing and construction.

NONCONDUCTOR An insulator. A material that does not readily conduct electrical current.

NONSELLING AREAS A term used in store planning to describe those areas reserved for the store operation that do not directly involve the customer. Areas other than the net selling areas, such as receiving, warehousing, personnel and employees' facilities.

NONUNIFORM LIGHTING Lighting that is brighter or more intense in some areas and not so bright or intense in others. Usually the "task" or "object" or special selling and/or display areas get more concentrated lighting than the "walk areas" or mass-merchandising locales.

NO SEAM PAPER Extra wide paper available in a wide variety of colors. Usually available in 9' widths and in 36' or 50' lengths. Used for backgrounds. Also called seamless paper.

NOSING A short valance, return or baffle.

NOTCHED COLLAR, NOTCHED LAPEL A V-shaped cutout on the front opening of a garment formed where the collar meets an extension of a shirt, dress, jacket or coat.

NOTCHED JOINT A joining technique similar to a dado joint with this exception: the notch is cut out on the edge of the piece of lumber rather than across the face of the unit. See *dado joint*.

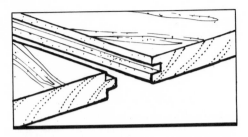

NOTIONS Merchandise often associated with sewing, such as threads, buttons, trimmings, small cases and boxes and chalk. Also, fashion and beauty merchandise such as bobby pins, barettes, hair nets and lace collars.

NOVA PLY See *particle board.*

N.R.M.A. National Retail Merchants Association.

NYLON A thermoplastic man-made fiber, which can be made into a yarn or in a sheet form. The material produced is tough, strong, and elastic, dries quickly and is easy to care. Can be combined with other fibers or yarns to make fabrics or carpets.

O

OAK A hard, tough and durable, but porous, wood that requires being treated with a filler before it can be finished.

OBI A wide, colorful silk sash worn with the traditional Japanese kimono.

OBLIQUE DRAWING A pictorial representation in which all vertical and horizontal lines are drawn vertically and horizontally and parallel to each other. The lines drawn to indicate depth may be drawn at an angle, however, they are drawn parallel to each other. It is possible, in an oblique drawing to draw the height and width of an object in scale or in actual size—the depth lines can also be drawn in scale. It is not a true perspective drawing, but it is particularly effective in drawing circular or irregular-shaped forms. The irregular face is drawn, in scale, parallel to the picture plane. Used for shop drawings. Also called cabinet perspective. See *isometric*.

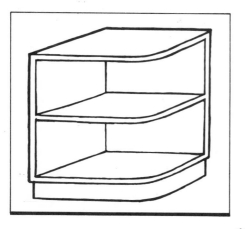

OBSCURE GLASS A translucent glass. It permits the light to pass through but does not afford a clear view.

O.C. (ON CENTER) A term used in construction and fixturing to indicate the distance from the center of one object to the center of another object.

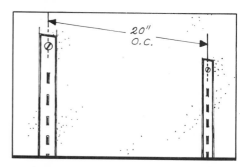

O.D. (OUTSIDE DIMENSION) A term used in construction and fixturing to describe the overall or outer measurement of a unit, including the thickness of the wall of the unit. See *I.D.*

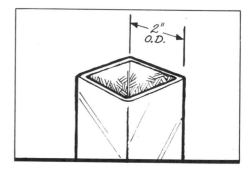

ODD LOT An unequal, and sometimes irrational, collection of merchandise in a variety of colors, sizes, fabrics and quality. Not an in-depth or complete line of merchandise.

OFF BRAND A manufacturer or label not easily recognized by the average customer.

OFFSET *1.* A term used in architecture to describe that part of a facade or body of a building that is recessed. At a certain height the construction of a building may recede back from the building line established at street level. The set-back or step-back appearance of the pre-1960s skyscrapers. *2.* A term used in construction or fixturing to describe a jog or set-back or change of planes. See *jog.*

OFFSET LITHOGRAPHY The newest and most popular printing process in which the printing area is level with the nonprinting surface surrounding it. This process is based on the lithographic principle that grease and water do not mix and the ink is first offset from the plate to a rubber blanket and from the rubber blanket to the paper. It also, as a technique, makes the use of illustrations feasable and economical.

"OFF THE RACK" Ready-to-wear. Garment which are presewn and presized according to trade standards and available for immediate delivery. The customer selects the merchandise right "off the rack" on the selling.

OHM'S LAW A term used in electricity to describe the relationship between current (given in amperes), resistance (given in ohms), and the electromotive force (given in volts). The product of the current and resistance equals the voltage. Volts = amperes $\times$ ohms.

OIL-BASE PAINT A paint that contains a drying oil or oil varnish as the basic vehicle for the spreading of the pigment. See *vehicle.*

OIL CLOTH A term used to describe any fabric that is treated with oil making it waterproof. Usually stiff and shiny. Used for decoratives and kitchen accessories.

OILED FINISH A wood-finishing process in which the surface is treated with several coats of boiled linseed oil, which is rubbed and polished into the surface. A low, satin-luster finish, which is more "natural" and is also fairly resistant to heat and water stains.

OILED SILK A type of oilcloth, which is soaked in oil and then dried for a special kind of look and use. Used for shower curtains and other uses requiring waterproof fabrics.

OIL PAINTING An art technique in which the pigment is ground in oil and applied to a canvas or other slightly absorbent surface.

OILSKIN A term used to describe fabrics that are impregnated with oil and gum and thus rendered waterproof. Used for rainwear, slickers, etc.

OLD ENGLISH TYPE A style of black letter closely associated with the first typefaces used in English printing.

O.M. (OUTSIDE MEASUREMENT) A term used in architectural specifications and shop drawings to indicate the distance from one outer surface across to the other outer surface including the thickness of the unit. See *I.M.* For example when measuring a hollow tube or pipe the O.M. would be the distance of the outer surfaces including the thickness of the walls of the tube or pipe.

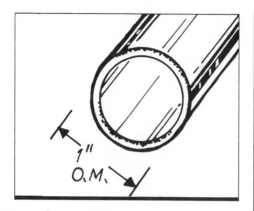

OMBRÉ A shaded or graduated pattern in which a color goes through a range of shades and/or tints to create a blend or subtle, irregular-striped design.

ON CENTER See *O.C.*

100 PERCENT LOCATION A term used in store planning for heavily trafficked areas on the sales floor near entrances, elevators or escalators. These locations are valuable because of the heavy traffic and are thus expected to render greater volume returns per square foot.

ONE-ITEM DISPLAY A merchandise presentation of a single-featured item in a window such as a special gown, a piece of jewelry, or a single pair of shoes.

ONE-STOP SHOPPING An expression used in retailing for department stores that carry everything a customer may require.

OPAQUE Not transparent. A dense covering that does not permit the passage of light.

OP ART Abbreviation for *Optical Art.* Abstract paintings or designs using parallel lines or patterns or circles and squares painted with sharp delineation, and in contrasting colors to create shimmering or "moving" patterns or violent after-images. Dazzling patterns tend to create three-dimensional or moving effects. Op Art is sometimes considered as a form of Kinetic Art since movement by the viewer will seem to create new patterns or images.

OPEN-BACK WINDOWS Display windows without back walls that allow a free, unobstructed view of the selling floor from the street or mall.

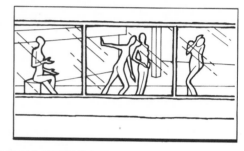

OPEN DISPLAY A merchandise display that welcomes handling and examination of items by customers, such as one might find on a feature table or on a counter.

OPEN FRONT FACADE The non-enclosed fronts of shops or stores in an enclosed shopping mall or shopping center. The complete exposure to the common mall is desirable and often required by the developer. It allows the customers freedom to circulate in and out of stores. There is no psychological barrier to prevent the customer from entering into a shop.

OPEN PLANNING A concept in store planning that avoids the use of definite dividing walls or partitions or the creation of smaller shops in favor of an open, flexible selling area.

OPEN STOCK A retailing term used for patterns of china and glass that are always available. Pieces can be ordered to replace ones that have broken or have been chipped.

OPEN-TO-BUY Money to spend. A budget allowance or a need that must be satisfied (fixtures for a new store with a definite opening date). A buyer in the market who has the money to spend on merchandise, props, or whatever is needed for the retail operation.

OPTICAL ART See *Op Art.*

OPTO SYSTEM Trademark for a tube and clamp system. The tubes are a high carbon Swedish steel, available in brass or chrome plating and protected with a clear coating. The new approach is "color tube" which is metal tubing covered with a thick polyvinyl "skin" and available in a variety of seven colors. Tubing is sold in precut lengths of 16′ × 16′. The clamps are symmetrical and three-lobed. The clamp halves are tightened together by a single nut and bolt (using an Allen key or wrench) to grasp the tubes in three planes and align them into perfect right angles. Used to construct shops, displayers, merchandisers and "walls." Produced by Opto, Inc., Pittsburgh, Pa.

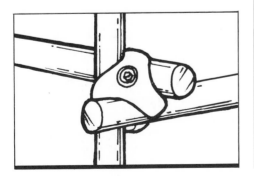

ORDERS OF ARCHITECTURE The classic order consists of a pedestal (base), column and entablature. The Greek orders were Doric, Ionic and Corinthian. The Roman orders include the three Greek orders and the Tuscan and the Composite. The column capital is usually simplest to recognize as to the order it represents.

ORGANDY, ORGANDIE A sheer, translucent, rather stiff cotton or man-made fiber fabric.

ORGANZA A sheer man-made fiber fabric which is stiffened slightly. Usually associated with romantic ball gowns and bridal wear.

ORIENTATION A term used in store planning to describe a sense of direction based on some established point such as the aisles or the layout of a department in relation to escalators, traffic flow, and doors. The established relationship between a fixed object or point of reference and variables.

ORIGAMI The Japanese art form of creating three-dimensional objects by scoring, folding and twisting paper into decorative designs. See *paper sculpture.*

ORLON Trademark of E. I. Du Pont de Nemours and Company for their acrylic fiber used to produce fabrics and carpets. It adds warmth without weight, and resists sun-fading.

ORTHOGRAPHIC PROJECTION A method of presenting a three-dimensional item or object on a two-dimensional surface. It presents the object as seen from the front (front elevation), from the side (profile or side elevation), and from the top (plan view). See *elevations* and *plans.*

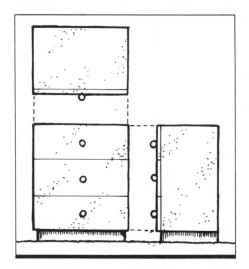

OSTWALD'S COLOR NOTATION SYSTEM Based on principles similar to the Munsell's Color Notation System, and the concept that all colors seen by the eye are composed of assorted combinations of hue, black and white. The circumference of his scale consists of twenty-four chromatic hues. See *Munsell's Color Notation System.*

OTTOMAN *1.* A heavy corded fabric, similar to faille, made in silk, wool and man-made fibers. *2.* A long footstool.

OUTLET A distribution source of electrical current such as a socket in the wall into which portable electric units (lamps, vacuum cleaners, etc.) can be plugged into to draw the current necessary to run that unit. A receptacle through which electrical power may be drawn.

OUTLET STORE A discount, retail operation through which a manufacturer or a group of manufacturers can unload overruns, returns, seconds or out-of-date merchandise. Also called clearance centers.

OUTPOST A free-standing, self-contained, selling unit containing a stock of a given type of merchandise plus display and signing relevant to that merchandise. An island displayer. An independent, single unit such as a gondola, étagère, armoire, kiosk. Often located in another selling area, e.g., a cosmetic outpost in a junior ready-to-wear department.

OUTRIGGERS Horizontal members attached, bolted or screwed into a wall or column, which serve to reinforce, support and keep the horizontal element out and away from the bearing surface. The outrigger also spaces a vertical element away from the supporting vertical surface. Used in fixturing and construction.

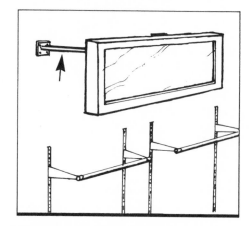

OUTSIDE DIMENSION See *O.D.*

OUTSIDE MEASUREMENT See *O.M.*

OVEREXPOSURE An expression used for merchandise on the selling floor that is not being watched or guarded sufficiently by the store personnel. Merchandise is vulnerable to pilferage.

OVERHANG An element projecting out beyond the supporting structure below such as a balcony, mezzanine or architectural shelf. A cantilevered construction. See *cantilever*.

OVERHEAD All the indirect expenses and costs that cannot be applied directly to the buying or selling of merchandise such as rent, heat and light, pilferage, replacement of rugs, and wallcoverings.

OVERHEAD TRACK LIGHTING See *track lighting*.

OVERLAY A transparent or translucent sheet such as acetate or tracing paper placed over a drawing, plan, perspective, etc. Used to indicate corrections, additions, details, crop marks, color separations, etc. A method of making reference to an original

piece of art without actually harming or marring it.

OVERRUN A manufacturer producing more merchandise than required or than on order; a retailer selling more of an item than was anticipated.

OXYHYDROGEN WELDING TECHNIQUE See *welding*.

OZALID A reproduction technique, similar to blueprinting, but the end result is black, blue or brown lines, depending upon the chemical makeup of the printing paper on a white ground. A positive print rather than a negative, as in the blueprint. A negative is made from the original line artwork and then the positive ozalid is printed. Many copies can be made from the same negative. Also possible to blow up the artwork to panels measuring 42″ by 8′ or more.

P

PACKAGE OR SELF-CONTAINED UNITS Compact heating/cooling units for store temperature control, usually placed on the roof of the building.

PAD *1.* A board covered in fabric or a decorative material used as the flooring for a case or bottom of a counter. *2.* A flat pillow, often in velvet or jersey fabric, used to present jewelry and fine silver pieces. *3.* A quilted or lightly stuffed pillow used to "flesh-out" such as a sleeve pad.

PADDLE HAND See *pocket hand* and *wooden jointed arm*.

PAILLETTES Small shiny disks of metal or plastic, in gold, silver or metallic colors, sometimes with faceted edges, that are sewn or glued onto fabric for decorative effects. Also called sequins and spangles.

PAISLEY Amoeba- or paramecia-shaped patterns that create an allover design similar to the woolen fabrics originally woven in Paisley, Scotland. The original fabrics were used for shawls produced in the 18th and 19th centuries.

PALETTE *1.* The complete range of colors; the colors in which papers, fabrics, carpets, etc., are available. *2.* The board, tray or surface used for mixing paints.

PANAMA HAT A summer hat, usually with a wide, sun-shielding brim, delicately woven from leaves of the jipijapa plant. Though mainly produced in Peru, Columbia and Equa-

dor, this design discovered and popularized by the American soldiers in Panama in 1895.

PANEL RETAINER CLIP A clip specifically designed to hold a removable panel inside a slot or channel. It makes it possible to lift out and replace panels without destroying or taking apart the basic frame.

PANEL WALL A non-bearing wall built between the columns and piers in the skeletal construction of a building. The wall is completely supported on each floor.

PANNE VELVET A shiny velvet with pile pressed down in one direction.

PANTOGRAPH A machine that makes it possible to mechanically trace, cut or copy a design. The design can be executed in its original size or it can be enlarged or reduced. A most useful "blow-up" device. See *blowup*.

PANTS FORM A three-dimensional sculptured form (male or female) starting at the waistline and ending at the toes. Men's forms will usually wear a size 30 with a 32″ length; boys' forms will wear a 28″ waist with a 30″ length. Female pants forms are designed to properly show off a size 8. See *slacks form.*

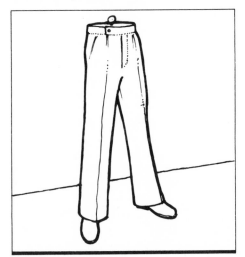

PANTY (PANTIE) FORM A three-dimensional form extending from the knees to above-the-waist. Used for a counter or ledge display of panties, girdles and/or bikini bottoms. The long-leg girdle form will show a longer leg and will average 25″ to 26″ in over-

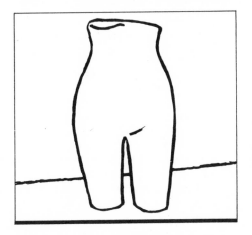

all length compared to the panty form's 22″ to 23″ length.

PANTYHOSE (PANTIEHOSE) FORM A lightweight, three-dimensional flesh-colored, plastic female form extending from the waist to the toes. It may be used with the waist as the base and the toes up or with the toes set onto the base. The same form can also display stretch tights and slacks.

PAPER SCULPTURE A technique for creating full-round or bas relief decorative designs and objects by means of scoring, folding, cutting, curling and applying papers of assorted colors, textures and weights. See *origami.*

PAPER STUCCO See *papier mâché.*

PAPIER-MÂCHÉ, PAPER MÂCHÉ A technique for producing three-dimensional objects such as some mannequins and decorative display figures by means of pulped paper. Pulped paper is mixed with glue and, sometimes, with whiting. This "mushy" material can then be shaped, filled into molds, or formed around shapes or forms. As the mâché dries, it becomes harder, stronger and more durable. Strips of paper can also be moistened with paste and layered over and over in a mold or around a form to make a papier-mâché reproduction of a unit. Sometimes referred to as "paper stucco" when used to create architectural details such as moldings and frames. See *anaglypta.*

PAR (PARABOLIC ALUMINIZED REFLECTOR) LAMPS Incandescent lamps with wide, convex-headed hard glass envelops with built-in reflecting surfaces, available in wattage from 75 to 500. Made of molded, heat-resisting glass, are heavier than the R- or reflector lamps, which they are similar to. PAR lamps are available as "spots" or "floods." Can be used outdoors. The "spots" are preferable for long, intense throws of concentrated light. The "floods" have smoother fields of light and much wider spreads than the spots. Pressed glass reflector lamps.

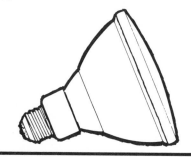

PARAFFIN PAPER A wax-coated waterproof paper useful for stencils and pouncing outlines.

PARALLELOGRAM A four-sided figure with opposite sides equal. The area of a parallelogram is the base multiplied by the height. When the four sides are equal and all four angles are 90-degrees, the shape is a square. When the opposite sides are parallel, but the two pairs are not equal in length, and all four angles are 90-degrees, the unit is a rectangle.

PARAPET WALL The section of an outside or facade wall that extends up above the roof line.

PARKA A hooded, hip-length fur jacket worn as an Arctic outer garment.

PARKWOOD See *melamine formaldehydes*.

PARQUET, PARQUETRY Strips or blocks of wood laid in a specific geometric pattern; inlay work using assorted colors and grains of wood. Used in woodworking, flooring and decorative fixtures.

PARTICLE BOARD A synthetic "wood" panel made of wood waste such as chips or sawdust and compressed with synthetic resins (which act as binders). It is rather heavy and is formed into sheets, usually $4' \times 8'$. Used for light construction work or for cabinets or furniture which will be veneered. Also called flakeboard, chip board and matrix board. Not as heavy or dense as fiberboard. See *fiberboard*.

PARTY WALL A mutually shared wall between two buildings. Each structure is a separate entity, but they are joined by the party wall.

PASSEMENTERIE A strip of lace, or any trimming material such as gimp, braid or cording.

PASTEBOARD A stiff board or cardboard of medium thickness. Often a cardboard lined with cover stock of a better grade.

PASTEL DRAWING A drawing executed with pastel chalks or crayons.

PASTELS *1.* Light tones of a color or hue. The addition of white to a color to reduce the intensity of a color. *2.* A drawing medium of dry-powdered colors mixed with gum and formed into sticks. When the sticks are rubbed against a textured paper, the chalk will rub onto the paper. However, a fixative spray is required to adhere the colored particles to the paper.

PATENT LEATHER A highly lacquered soft, shiny leather; used for shoes, handbags and fashion accessories. Also produced as a man-made material.

PATENTS Documents which formally grant the exclusive rights to make, use, reproduce or sell a specific item for a specific period.

PATINA, PATINE The coating formed on an item which has been exposed to light, to oxidation, and to a great deal of waxing. The "mellowing of age." The greenish coating on a piece of bronze or copper. The low luster on fine, old, well-cared-for wood.

PATIO See *atrium.*

PATIO PANTS Women's sports or dress-up pants which end approximately at the ankle bone. The classic pant length.

PATTENS See *clogs.*

PAVEMENT The flooring of a building or the area around a structure made of stone, marble, tile, poured concrete, or asphalt. Outdoor ground surfacing.

PAVEMENT LIGHT Heavy glass insets in the pavement which allow light to filter down into a basement or to a below-grade area.

PAVILION Derived from the Latin word for "butterfly." Originally a tent with the roof spread out like butterfly wings. Today, the term refers to any light, airy, garden-type structure.

PEA JACKET A hip-length, outer coat made of a closely woven wool fabric. A double-breasted design with two rows of buttons that close high on the chest, vertically slashed pockets and a notched collar that can be secured across the neck. The Pea Jacket was worn by sailors as far back as 1850 and is traditionally a dark blue or black color.

PEAKED LAPEL A lapel that forms a sharp point as it approaches the collar and leaves a triangular space between it and the collar. See *notched lapel.*

PEARLIZED FINISH A lustrous, milky finish on a mannequin or form; reminiscent of the sheen of a pearl.

PEASANT SLEEVE A long, full sleeve, shirred and gathered at the dropped shoulderline and also at the tight-fitting wrist cuff.

PEAU DE SOIE A firm, but soft fabric of plain weave with a matte finish on both sides. Made of silk or man-made fibers. Used for formal wear and accessories as well as wedding gowns.

PECKY CYPRESS A texturally attractive, but structurally weak, wall lining material that is scarred, pitted and crumbly looking. This look is reproduced in vinyl wall coverings and on laminates.

PEDAL PUSHERS Pants that end at mid calf.

PEDESTAL A base, foundation or support. A device for elevating an object or element to a better height for viewing. It is often a decorative rectangle or cylinder with a molded base and a flat top surface. A pedestal base could be a single, solid, center element upon which an entire superstructure can rest, such as a pedestal table.

PEDIMENT In classic architecture, the triangular space at the roof line which was embellished with moldings of the entablature. Often this area was filled with sculpted figures. Today, the triangular top of a piece of furniture or an architectural design.

PEDIMENT

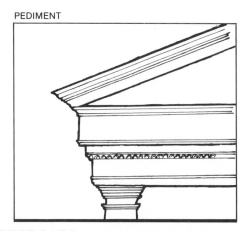

PEGBOARD A masonite panel board, usually 4′ × 8′, with predrilled equidistant circular holes over the entire surface. Used for construction as well as wall surfacing. Special pins and attachments have been designed to hook into the holes and hold shelves or to hang merchandise, tools, etc. Also called perforated board. See *fiberboard* and *masonite*.

PEGGED GARMENTS Skirts or pants that are voluminous or full from the waist to the hips, tapering to the hemline.

PEIGNOIR A loose-fitting robe, often matched with a nightgown, in soft, transparent fabrics.

PELLON® Registered trademark for all nonwoven interfacing fabrics produced by Pellon Corporation. Used to stiffen and shaped constructed garments from the inside.

PENDANT LIGHT FIXTURES See *droplights.*

PENETRATING SEALERS See *sealers.*

PEPLUM A short overskirt or hip-length flounce that usually starts at the waist or beltline.

PERCALE A plain weave fabric with a smooth finish and made of cotton or man-made fibers.

PERFORATED BOARD See *pegboard.*

PERFORATED METAL Sheet metal pierced with holes or with an allover pattern of decorative geometric openings. A flat grill or cane-like pattern stamped out of metal.

PERIMETER LIGHTING Lighting, usually indirect, around the perimeter or enclosing walls of an area. See *cove lighting* and *wall washing.*

PERIMETER PARTITION A wall separating the direct selling areas from the dressing rooms, adjacent stock areas, and the non-selling areas of the store. An enclosing device separating the forward selling area from the "behind the scenes" operation. Also called peripheral partition.

PERIOD FURNITURE See charts on pages 224–243.

PERIPHERAL PARTITION See *perimeter partition.*

PERSPECTIVE A wide, deep view of an object. A three-dimensional representation of an object with height, width and depth on a two-dimensional surface. A drawing in spatial recession based on the thesis that parallel lines never meet but appear to a "vanishing point" which is located at the viewer's eye level—on the horizon. See *axo-*

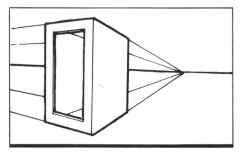

nometric. (Illustration also applies to *eye level, horizon* and *vanishing point.*)

PERSPEX See *acrylics.*

PERUKE From the French "perruque" which became the English "perwyke" or "periwig." A wig.

PETER PAN COLLAR A turned-down, rounded collar with a front center opening.

PETITE MANNEQUIN A smaller, slighter mannequin that usually wears a size 5 and presents the clothes for the shorter proportioned Missy or Miss type.

PETTICOAT An underskirt, sometimes ruffled, flounced or stiffened as in a crinoline.

PEWTER A metal alloy of tin and lead with a dull gray appearance, which would approximate an antiqued, brushed steel. A rather specialized finish which might appear dull or too dark on the selling floor. The metal itself is too soft to use for counter stands or merchandisers.

PHENOLICS Dark-colored, heat-resistant, non-burning plastics which are not decorative but are stable and possess good insulating qualities.

PHILLIPS HEAD SCREW A screw with a slightly dome-shaped head and a cross incised in the middle of the head instead of the usual single slot. Requires a Phillips screwdriver to fit the cross on the head. See *Phillips head screwdriver.*

PHILLIPS HEAD SCREWDRIVER A screwdriver with a round shaft ending in a point, which is formed by four arcs or chamfers cut out of the end of the metal shaft. The point fits into the center of the "X" on the Phillips head

screw for a better bite and grasp. It is possible to tighten the screw without the screwdriver slipping out of the slots. See *Phillips head screw.*

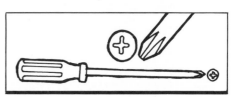

PHOTO BLOWUP A photographic enlargement of a piece of artwork, a small photograph, a line engraving, etc. The blow up can be quite large and serve as a wall mural. See *mural* and *ozalid.*

PHOTOELECTRIC EYE A device consisting of a fixed beam of light extending between sending and receiving ends of the device. When that stream of light is broken or interrupted, it may sound an alarm, trigger a door to open or close, start or stop a machine or electrical procedure. Used in store security systems. Also called photo-electric-cell-operated-relay.

PHOTOENGRAVING A process for producing a design on a sensitized metal plate. A transparent negative is placed between that plate and a source of light. Those areas which are not made water insoluble by the passage of light are washed and etched with acid solutions.

PHOTOGRAVURE A process for making prints from photomechanically prepared etched (intaglio) plates.

PHOTOMURAL An enlarged photograph, or a series or montage of photos used to line a wall, to create depth, the illusion of space or as a purely decorative design. See *mural* and *ozalid.*

PHOTOSTAT A photographic negative made directly onto a sensitized bromide paper. The negative has a black ground with white lines and images. It is possible to make many "positives" from this "negative" and the positives will resemble the original drawing or document.

PICA A printer's unit of measurement. There are six picas to the inch.

PICKLED PINE Pine wood with a mellow, antique-like finish, used for walls and furniture. Pine is rubbed with white paint and the excess paint is then wiped off. The paint that remains enhances the grain and accentuates the knots.

PICOT A small, decorative loop along the edge of fabric or ribbon.

PICTORIAL DRAWING A method of representing an object of three dimensions (width, height, and length) on a two-dimensional surface. See *oblique drawing, orthographic projection* and *perspective.*

PIECE DYED Fabric that is dyed after it has been woven rather than fabric woven from predyed fibers or yarns.

PIECE GOODS Fabrics sold by the yard.

PIER A heavy, vertical supporting member in architecture, such as a column or pilaster but without the proportions or finish of the latter. The pier is incorporated into a wall where extra strength is needed to sustain the weight or thrust of arches, beams or lintels.

PIGGYBACK A combination rail and truck set-up used for shipping merchandise.

PIGMENT A powder that can be used to endow color to a paint, ink or dye when mixed with an extender. See *extender.*

PILASTER An engaged pier or a structural unit which is part of a wall and also extends out from that wall. Usually proportioned and detailed with a base and capital. A support for a cornice or an entablature. See *engaged column.*

PILFERAGE Theft and/or shoplifting. Part of the shrinkage problem of retail operations. See *shrinkage.*

PILLAR A shaft, column or vertical member which may or may not serve as a support.

PILOTIS A structure raised up on stilts. A technique of erecting a multistoried building by raising it on reinforced concrete columns, thus allowing the area beneath the structure to be open and uncluttered. A concept favored by the architect, Le Corbusier.

PIN BEAM See *pin spot*.

PINE A soft, inexpensive wood, rather light in color and easy to work.

PINKING Sawtoothed, jagged edge on fabric to prevent raveling by using a pinking shears (shears with V-notched blades).

PINNING A display technique for shaping and smoothing out a garment on a form, figure or hanger by the use of simple, straight pins.

PIN SPOT A high intensity, pinpoint spotlight beam. A 30-watt pin spot can achieve a light output equal to a 300-watt PAR-56. The Pin Beam (produced by Fostoria Industries, Inc.) has a built-in, step-down transformer, which is regulated for 1000 hours of lamp life and permits use of a 6-volt lamp on standard 120-volt circuits.

PIN TICKET A tag attached by pin or staple to a garment with information on price, size, color and style.

PINWALE Narrow ridges running vertically on fabric, as in pinwale corduroy. See *corduroy*.

PIONITE See *melamine formaldehydes*.

PIPE RACK The round metal tube forerunner of floor racks. Usually associated with "work-horse" duties in a factory of holding and moving par-

tially finished garments in, around and out of the plant. It is a simple construction of two upright pipes connected by a hand rail with knobby elbows (the joining area). The rectangular base is equipped with wheels or casters. Sometimes a skeletal construction with four uprights and two connecting rods above. See *rectangular rack*.

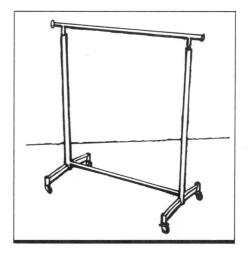

PIPING A decorative tubing made with pliable cord wrapped in fabric. Used on upholstery and garments.

PIRAYO A large square of fabric, usually 4' × 4', and often patterned. The oversized scarf can be tied or draped in many ways to become a long or short overskirt (over a swimsuit), a sarong or a cape. A popular "cover-up" beachwear accessory.

PITCH *1.* The angle of inclination or slope in a roof, a ramp, a flight of stairs, etc. The degree of rake of a floor or platform. See *raked floor. 2.* A coal tar product used in covering certain roofing materials and in paving streets and roads.

PLACARD A notice or announcement printed on a cardboard; a poster.

PLAN (FLOOR PLAN) The horizontal projection of any object. A drawing showing the arrangement and floor or base measurements of a room, building or object. A scaled, detailed drawing which shows the width and depth of an object. For heights, one must refer to an elevation drawing. Also see *bird's eye view*.

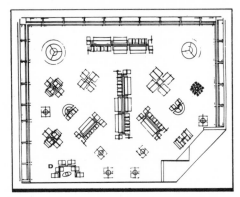

PLANTER'S HAT Wide-brimmed natural-colored or white straw hat with high dented crown and dark-colored ribbon band.

PLASTER A surfacing material made of lime, sand and water and sometimes, plaster of Paris. Used to coat and finish walls and ceilings.

PLASTERBOARD A building material composed of several pieces of thin, ground-wood pulpboard bound together with silicate of soda or a pre-cast, veneered paper, used in dry wall construction. *Sheetrock* is a trademark for plasterboard. Also see *dry wall* and *gypsum board*.

PLASTER OF PARIS A quick-setting composition used for making casts and molds. A white powdery compound of ground and calcined gypsum is mixed with water; swells and sets and dries quickly.

PLASTIC A generic term for a man-made resinous material which can be formed, shaped, extruded, heat- or pressure-shaped.

PLASTICINE A modeling clay which can be molded and shaped without the addition of water. Used by sculptors for initial studies and models.

PLASTIC RESIN GLUE A urea-resin adhesive prepared in dry powder form to be mixed with water. It produced a light-colored glue line with a good resistance to heat and water. It is strong, but brittle, and not recommended for oily woods or poorly fitted joints. Good on large wooden surfaces.

PLAT An engineered drawing for the plan of a site for a development, building, etc.

PLATEGLASS A generic term for large sheets of flat glass that have been cast from selected materials and are usually clearer and less textured than drawn glass. A quality glass with minimal distortion or imperfection, often used for display windows.

PLATEN PRESS Any press which creates an impression by bringing together two flat surfaces: the platen and the bed; usually, a small printing press. See *letterpress*.

PLATFORM A raised section of flooring; an elevated stage or dais. Used for special displays or performances.

PLATING A metallic film or skin surface added on by electrolytic means. See *anodizing* and *chrome plating*.

PLATOK See *babushka*.

PLEATS Folds, usually equal, set in a pattern and stitched down or pressed into a fabric. See *box pleat, knife pleat, kick pleat* and *sunburst pleat.*

PLENUM The space between a hung ceiling and the floor (or roof) above, usually 3 to 5 feet, into which are gathered electrical conduits, utility lines, air ducts, as well as other mechanical devices needed to service the floor below.

PLEXIGLASS BASE A heavyweight, heavy duty, nonbreakable plastic material used with mannequins to support the upright figure. Similar in design and function to the glass base plate.

PLIERS A hand vise or clamp consisting of two gouged or etched surfaces that can be brought and held together by means of hand pressure on the two "legs" of the tool. Used to hold objects firmly or to bend and cut wires. See *nippers.*

PLISSÉ A plain weave cotton or manmade fiber fabric with a crinkled-striped texture.

PLOTTING PAPER See *graph paper.*

PLUMB LINE, PLUMB BOB A string with a weight at one end that hangs straight down and used to find the vertical or true vertical line. Also used with dye on a cord for ceiling or horizontal planes.

PLUME A long, fluffy curling feather like an ostrich plume.

PLUS FOURS From the British Army term for breeches that reach to the knees plus four inches. See *knicker-bockers.*

PLUSH A long cut pile used in some rugs and outerwear.

PLYWOOD A man-made wood panel made of plies or layers of wood. The layers are glued together, under great pressure, and are laid so that the grain of one ply is perpendicular to the one above, etc., thus "cross-banding" each other for greater strength and resistance to warping. A think veneer finish is glued onto either face of the panel.

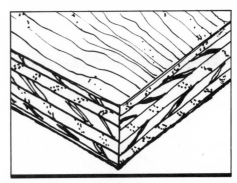

PLYWOOD GRADES For *hardwood plywood,* "type" indicates the glue-bond durability and the ability of the various plies to adhere under the varying conditions of weather.
Type I—suitable for outdoor work.
Type II—water resistant but not waterproof.

Type III—not commonly made, but used for general construction and containers.

Premium Grade (A)—high quality face veneer, few small curls, pin knots, etc.

Good Grade (1), Sound Grade (2), Utility Grade (3), Backing Grade (4) An "A3" grade would indicate a panel with a premium veneer on one side and a utility veneer on the other.

Most "types" of *softwood plywoods* are made of Douglas Fir and are graded "EXT" (external use) or "INT" (interior use). They, too, are graded from A to D depending upon the finish and slickness of the veneer and the face of the plywood. "A-A" would be prime veneer on face and back, while an "A-D" rating would indicate an excellent face finish with an inferior back finish.

POCKET HAND A non-detailed hand (no separated fingers) on a mannequin which fits into a pocket and presents a smooth outline of that hand rather than assorted fingers and knuckles— much like a hand encased in a mitten. It is also flatter and more tapered to slide into and out of pockets. Also called a paddle hand. Also see *wooden jointed arm*.

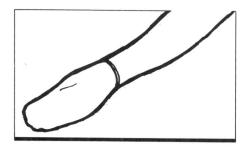

PODIUM A platform or pedestal or an elevated area, used for a speaker or performer, sometimes includes a speaker's stand.

POINT-OF-PURCHASE Merchandise presentation at a location where the sale is usually completed: counters, cash/wrap desks, check-out counters, bars, etc. Suggested and auxiliary sales can be made at this point by having the merchandise on display or available where the customer is momentarily "captive."

POINT-OF-PURCHASE DISPLAYS Displays supplied to the retailer by the manufacturer or dealer to promote the sale of their merchandise. Displays are usually self-contained and will sometimes be designed to carry a certain amount of stock along with promotional information. Also called *dealer displays*.

POINT OF SALES A term used by architects and store planners to define counters, self-selection fixtures, racks, bins or tables where the potential customer selects and makes a purchase. See *point-of-purchase*.

POINTS *1.* One thousandth of an inch in paper and board calibration. *2.* Seventy-two points equal one inch, in printing.

POLISHED CHROME A high, mirror-like, silvery finish on metal, often on steel. It is accomplished by means of an electrode plating process which uses nickel and chromium to create the fine, silvery coating on the metal to be plated.

POLISHED EDGE An extra grinding, sanding and/or polishing of the edges of plastics or glass panels for a smooth, clear, more reflective surface. It obliterates any saw or abrasion marks that might occur during the cutting or shaping of the plastic or glass.

POLO COAT A 20th-century, all-around, belted coat, usually made of polo cloth (napped camel's hair and wool mixture), and in the traditional beige-camel color. The true "polo coat" is double-breasted, peak-lapelled, and has outside patched pockets. In the 1920s and 1930s it was worn casually, thrown over the shoulders—as a warming coat used by polo players while waiting to get back into the play.

POLYCARBONATES A thermoplastic material with high impact strength (will not smash too easily), good heat resistance, low water absorbsion, good electrical properties and good optical properties (about 87% light transmission). Available in sheets, in many colors, (transparent and opaque). Can be cold-formed and retain its shape once it has been bent. A polycarbonate can be vacuum formed and is effective for use in outdoor displays, or as a glass substitute in some fixturing.

POLYCHROMATIC Multicolored.

POLYESTER A generic term for a man-made fiber composed of dihydric alcohol and terephthalic acid. It is popular as a wash-and-wear fiber alone or combined with natural and other man-made fibers. A widely used thermosetting material available as a tough, clear or vacuum-metallized film (under trademarks: Mylar or Videne). It is also available as a liquid resin which, when catalyzed, will cure (harden or set) at room temperature. The material can be reinforced with burlap, jute, glass fibers, or decorative fabrics to create rigid, fabric-like drapes, swags, headdresses, garments, etc. Polyesters can also be used to encapsule objects, or to produce stained-glass effects.

POLYSTYRENE, POLYSTYRENE-EXTRUDED FOAMS Generic terms for polymers of styrene that have excellent electrical properties, good thermal stability and are resistant to staining. They can be used for extrusion, and injection or compression molding. Polystyrene-extruded foams are made by injecting a volatile liquid into polystyrene in an extruder. As it emerges from the extruder die, it expands into a "log" of low density (under trademark, Styrofoam). A blowing agent may be incorporated with the polystyrene beads and then the beads may be molded in a closed mold. They may expand up to 45% of their original volume, or they can be pre-expanded by heating and then molded. When combined with nucleating agents it is possible to extrude the expanded material in sheet form. Used in decorative and point-of-purchase displays.

POLYVINYL WHITE RESINS A milky, white liquid adhesive which bonds as it dries, or loses water, and produces a clear, colorless glue line. It has moderate strength and moisture resistance and is somewhat flexible. Used to bond wood, cardboard, textiles and paper. Commercially sold as "Elmer's Glue" and "Sobo."

PONCHO A square-shaped blanket with a slit in the middle for the head. Originated by the South American Indians, and is traditionally woven in brightly colored stripes. An "over-the-head" raincover when made of a waterproof fabric.

PONGEE A fabric, originally woven from wild silk, with a slight slub yarn. Today, produced from natural as well as man-made fibers.

P.O.P.A.I. Point of Purchase Advertising Institute.

POP ART Originally the popular arts of mass culture, and later applied to the fine arts based on themes which extol the affluent consumer society, such as movie actresses, sport heroes, film strips, commercial packaging, advertising, photography and automobiles. Andy Warhol and James Rosenquist were leading exponents of this style as were Roy Lichtenstein, Claes Oldenburg and Robert Indiana. Pop Art peaked in the late 1950s and early 1960s in the United States.

POPLIN A plain weave fabric with a decided cross rib, made of cotton or blends of cotton and man-made fabrics.

PORCELAIN FINISH A shiny, white-enamelled or pastel-lacquered finish on mannequins and forms.

PORTE-COCHÈRE An overhead extension over a driveway used to protect those getting out of vehicles from inclement weather. Originally, a gateway for carriages into a Renaissance manor.

PORTICO A porch-like device; a roof supported by columns or a run of arches, but basically open-sided.

PORTRAIT FINISH The matte, lightly stippled texture or "brush stroke" finish of a mannequin's face and body. The "skin" appears more porous and thus more real; the flat finish adds depth to the skin color which may, and does, vary as per the customer's specifications.

P.O.S. See *point-of-sale*.

POSE The position or line of the mannequin's or form's body. The relationship of the arms and legs to the body; the angle of the head to the shoulders; the swing, movement, suggested animation of the body.

POST An upright or vertical element. A supporting, bearing or framing member in a construction. See *lintel*.

POSTER A large outdoor advertising sheet. "One-sheet" poster is 28″ × 42″; "two sheet" poster is 56″ × 84″. This type of poster is associated with theater, special events such as notices on station billboards or advertisements of an event or product. In retail stores, 22″ × 28″ is the popular poster size.

POSTER BOARD A smooth, mat board for artists, designers, etc., available in a variety of colors. An unglazed coated paper board with a smooth, eggshell finish.

POUNCE A method of transferring a design from a stencil onto another surface by means of rubbing powder through holes that have been pricked through the lines of the stencil. A powdered, dotted line indicates the design on the surface on which the design is to be transferred.

POWER HAND DRILL A high speed, lightweight and portable drill with an adjustable clamp to receive and hold bits in assorted diameters. The bit used will depend upon the type of material, desired diameter and depth of the hole, as well as the kind of hole

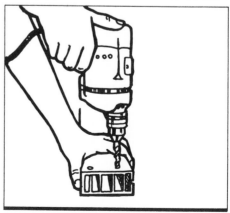

(clean bore, taper, ream, etc.). Also see *hand drill*.

POWER SAW Electrically powered saw for straight line cutting which may be fitted with special blades to rip or crosscut, or do a combination of cuts. See *pullover saw, skilsaw* and *table saw*.

PREFAB, PREFABRICATED Pre-formed, constructed, shaped or finished units brought to the site of construction or place of use in a comp-leted or ready-to-use form.

PREFOCUS BASE LAMP A lamp base with a locking device designed to hold the filament of the lamp in a precise relationship with some optical feature of the instrument in which it is meant to burn. Depending upon the size of the lamp, the prefocus base may be "medium" or "mogul."

PRE-PACKAGING Merchandise that is packed and sealed at the manufac-turer and sold in the retail operation to the customer in this sealed pack-age. See *blister packaging*.

PREP BOYS' SIZES A retailing term for teenage boys' sizes 8 to 20. The growing boy and young man who has not grown to his full adult size. The sizes usually correspond to the boys' ages (10–16).

PRE-SOLD MERCHANDISE Goods with wide customer acceptance and demand due to manufacturers' adver-tising campaigns such as in newspa-pers, magazines or on television.

PRESTYPE See *dry transfer*.

PRÊT-À-PORTER French term for "ready-to-wear" apparel. See *ready-to-wear*.

PRETEEN MANNEQUIN A retailing term for the ten- to twelve-year old mannequin. Figure is still childlike, but has the beginnings of a young woman's body. The preteen manne-quin is often proportioned to wear girls' sizes 8 to 10.

PRE-WRAP Wrapped and packaged merchandise for the customer to "take-with." This technique is espe-cially popular for holidays when one item is on display and the pre-wrapped and gift-tied units can be picked up and paid for without delay.

PRICE FIXED The retail or selling price determined by and insisted upon by the manufacturer.

PRICE TAG See *pin ticket*.

PRIMARY COLORS The basic colors from which all other colors can be created. Red, yellow and blue are the primary colors in paints and dyes, while red, green and blue are the pri-mary colors in lighting. Bright, full-intensity, basic colors.

PRIMARY LIGHTING The basic, most elemental lighting of a store or selling area. Usually it is devoid of special lighting effects such as spots, filters, floods or washers, and it lacks any sort of atmosphere or mood shading. See *atmosphere lighting* and *general illumination*.

PRIME COAT, PRIMING The under-coat or preparation layer on a surface, usually a coating of white lead and linseed oil which is applied over the sizing. Other primers are casein and whiting, or whiting and sizing. See *size coat, sizing* and *undercoat*.

PRIMITIVE ART Simple, naive, unso-phisticated art either by design or lack of training and background. Re-fers to Native Art, prehistoric art, African art, or the art of Grandma Moses and early 19th-century Ameri-can barn or traveling artists.

PRINCESS LINE SILHOUETTE A fitted or semi-fitted garment with vertical seams and with no special horizontal break at the waist or bustline, and that flares gently at the hemline.

PRIVATE BRANDS Merchandise developed and sold under the name of the store or retailer that is selling the product—not the name of the manufacturer or prime packager.

PROFILE A side elevation or cross-section view of an object or construction.

PRO FORMA According to form. Most often, a sale that is dependent upon a partial or full payment, more than a deposit, before delivery will be made. It is usually required when the customer has not established a credit rating with the seller.

PROGRAM A set of instructions that tells a machine or computer how to work. A plan of action with time schedules.

PROJECTION A technique or process used in decorative merchandise presentations. The process or technique of projection consists of a light source, objects or slides to be projected, and a surface or screen upon which the images will be projected. The projector is the light source and the image may be projected by the use of a lens for a sharper effect, or by the less complicated use of shadows. *Front projection* places the projector *in front* of an opaque screen (downstage), while *rear projection* places the projector *behind* a translucent screen (backstage). In either case, a certain amount of space is required between the projector and the screen—depending upon the lens and the size of the image desired. See *lens projectors.*

PROMOTION The stimulation of sales on a particular product through displays, advertising, signing, stocking, or presentation and location of the product. An "extra push."

PROMOTIONAL DEPARTMENT STORE A retail operation that advertises and advances the concepts of price and value. See *promotion.*

PROMOTIONAL DISPLAY A display set-up designed to sell a particular product, color, idea, etc.

PROMOTIONAL TABLE A variation of the dump table. Special merchandise is quickly set out on the selling floor, often on collapsible tables which may be treated with decorative covers, cloths, signs, etc. See *dump table* and *promotion.*

PROMOTIONAL WINDOW A display window to influence a *sale* or to advance a particular look, trend, or designer.

PROOF A sample or test of an ad or advertisement before it is printed to check the various details and to make any corrections that might be necessary to produce a correct copy. Also see *artist's proof.*

PROP Abbreviation for property. A term used in display to designate the decorative, and sometimes functional, elements—not necessarily merchandise—that are used to enhance and promote the garments or objects being promoted. For example: chairs, tables, plants, risers, urns and statues, papier-mâché Santas.

PROPORTION The relative size of one part to another or to the whole. The relationship between one object to another based on mass, form, color and line. The relative harmony.

PROSCENIUM The masking wall, valance or frame around the window glass of a display window. The proscenium usually frames the top and two sides of the window, and depending upon the size of the masking panels, the window opening can be reduced to shadow-box dimensions, especially with the addition of another panel on the bottom. See *mask, teaser,* and *tormentor.*

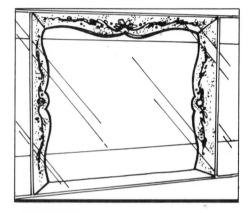

PROTOTYPE A standard for comparison or measurement. A correct or accurate example which is the standard for all future reproductions.

PROTOTYPE STORE An experimental store or one that may be the mold or design from which other stores may be fashioned in the future.

PROTRACTOR A drafting instrument for laying out and drawing angles at

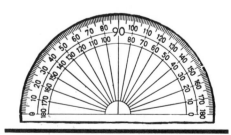

their proper pitch. A protractor square will also measure an angle in degrees.

PS BULB A pear-shaped lampbulb with a screw base.

PSYCHOGRAPHICS The study of the lifestyle, motivations, needs, etc., of the target market for a particular store. See *target market.*

PULL *1.* To dismantle or remove a display set-up or store trim; to remove merchandise temporarily from stock for use in a display presentation or in a fashion show. *2.* In advertising to pull an advertisement is to cancel it from being presented or run.

PULLOVER SAW Electrically powered saw (one horsepower) with a 10- to 12-inch cutting blade. Used to cut heavy lumber. It is accurate for cross cutting because of the pullover action and the long table, but limited as a mitering tool. The guide fence may become inaccurate over a period of repeated cross cutting.

PUNKAH A ceiling fan used in India and other exotic and warm climates.

PURCHASE ORDER An official numbered form authorizing a manufacturer or vendor to supply a stated amount of specific items at designated prices. The form usually contains shipping information, required date for delivery, and specific store terms. It is signed by someone with the authority to approve such purchases or countersigned by an official in the organization.

PURCHASE REQUISITION A request for permission to buy certain specified materials, sometimes indicating the vendor or manufacturer, the stock number of the desired items, the price, and the date the materials are needed in the store.

PUSH-BUTTON CATCH A button-like, retractable projection used to make hang rods, Tee-stands, racks and counter units adjustable without unnecessary screws, bolts, winged nuts, etc. This button-like projection is used on a hollow tube. The tube is placed within another hollow tube, of a slightly larger diameter and designed with predrilled holes along its length. The button will extend and catch through one of the aforementioned holes and hold the inner tube at a set height. To raise or lower the inner unit, the button-like projection is pushed in passed the hole and the inner unit is raised or lowered as desired. The button then snaps out of a new hole, and holds the tube at the desired length. Also see *button catch*.

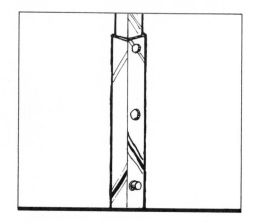

PYRAMID BUILD-UP Merchandise built-up from a wide base to an apex; a triangular build-up.

Q

QIANA Trademark of E. I. Du Pont de Nemours and Company which is licensed for identification of this nylon filament fiber. Fabrics must meet Dupont's standards. Fabric falls and drapes gracefully and is lustrous.

QUAD RACK A four-armed merchandiser which makes possible a full, round presentation of merchandise. In most cases, the four arms are arranged so that there is a "face-out" or "front-forward" viewing of all the garments. Where the unit is designed to be adjustable, it is possible to show coordinates at assorted levels. A variation of the quad or four-arm rack consists of each arm turned out at

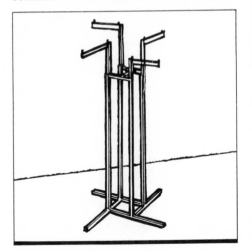

right angles from the central core or upright—a swastika configuration. This angled presentation makes for four different front-on views, and uses less floor space in the store layout. Racks can be constructed of assorted metals, woods and plastics as well as combinations of the above. Also called quadruple arm floor stand. Also see *four-way rack.*

QUADRILLE RULED STOCK See *graph paper.*

QUADRUPLE ARM FLOOR STAND See *quad rack.*

QUANTITY DISCOUNT Specified discounts or reductions in price available to quantity purchasers; "X" discount for ten or more units purchased, "Y" for twenty-four or more, "Z" for fifty or more, etc.

QUARREL See *quarry.*

QUARRY *1.* A diamond-shaped piece of glass usually used in leaded windows. Also called quarrel. *2.* A square paving tile or a natural deposit of stone, marble, etc.

QUARTER SHEET A cardboard measuring 11″ × 14″ and is one quarter of the size of a standard 22″ × 28″ poster card. Used in signing.

QUARTZ IODINE LAMP See *tungsten halogen lamp.*

R

RABBET A channel or groove cut out of a face or an edge. Often used to make a lap joint.

RABBET JOINT See *dado joint.*

RADIAL ARM SAW A standing, power-operated saw with the cutting mechanism mounted on an arm set above the table surface.

RADIANT HEATING A heating system that makes use of heat coils set into the floor, walls or both. When these coils are heated by means of electricity, hot water or other energy sources, they emit the heat that warms the area.

RAGLAN A loose topcoat with sleeves set in at an angle from the underarm up to the neckline, rather than the traditional set-in sleeve, which is fitted at the shoulder. A soft, sloping shoulderline. Designed by Lord Raglan, during the Crimean Wars (1850s).

RAIL The horizontal strip of wood in a framed unit, used in woodworking and paneling. There is usually a top

and bottom rail and sometimes a toggle rail, which is the middle bar or reinforcement of the framed panel. The vertical members are called stiles or styles. See *stile.*

RAINCAPE A tropical foliage "covering" or panel, usually 3' to 4' long, made from the saber-like Pandama leaves and gathered to hang loose—like a hula skirt. Used for valances, awnings, or wall coverings in a decorative merchandise presentation to create a tropical or jungle effect.

RAKED WINDOW A term to describe a display window with an inclined floor that is slanted from the window line to the back wall or partition. Also called a ramped window.

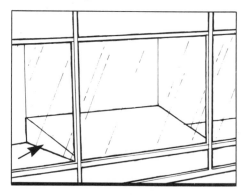

RAMP *1.* An inclined surface used to join two levels without the use of steps, especially effective for moving dollys or weighted loads from street level to a raised entrance level. *2.* An elevated surface, usually available in units that can be used individually or assembled in a variety of shapes, widths and lengths. Used for fashion shows.

RAMPED WINDOW See *raked window.*

RANDOM RUBBLE A technique in masonry in which roughly surfaced stones in varying shapes and sizes are used with no clearly defined courses or rows. Used for walls, fireplaces, fences, etc.

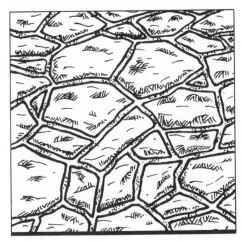

RANDOM WIDTH The use of planks, in assorted widths, vertically or horizontally to sheath a wall or floor to create an interesting pattern.

RAPID-START FLUORESCENT LAMP A fluorescent lamp designed to operate on a ballast circuit, which will provide a low voltage winding for preheating the cathodes. It eliminates the need for rather high voltage being applied to the lamp. All "high output" and "1500 milliampere" lamps are rapid start.

RASP A hand tool consisting of a metal rod, with row after row of teeth, set into a wooden hand grip. Used for crossgrain smoothing and shaping. The teeth tear into fibers and leave a rather rough, unfinished appearance.

Piece usually requires a further smoothing or finishing operation with a fine rasp or sandpaper.

RATCHET A tooth or detent used in conjunction with a ratchet wheel. The ratchet wheel consists of many inclined teeth around an outer rim and a catch. When the ratchet catch is released, it may then catch on to one of the other angled teeth, secure itself and thus keep the wheel from turning any further. The ratchet catch sets the amount of turns of a ratchet wheel.

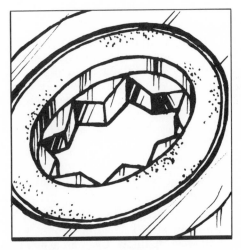

RATCHET SCREWDRIVER A screwdriver with a ratchet device set below the handle. The ratchet device can be set to turn the spiral-grooved spindle to either secure a screw or to release a screw. The ratchet responds to pressure applied to the handle, and may be worked with one hand and kept steady by holding the revolving chuck sleeve (that part that receives and holds the assorted screwdriver blades) with the other hand. Used in difficult and/or extensive screwing operations.

RATTAN Long, solid stems of a palm found in India and in the Far East.

These unbranched stems are tough, but pliable. Used in wickerwork furniture and basketry. The material can be lacquered, but does not stain well.

RAYON A generic term for a man-made fiber of regenerated cellulose. Lustrous, high absorbency, affinity for dyes and crisp hand. Can be used in combination with natural and other man-made fibers.

READY-TO-WEAR Apparel that is presented in a finished state, in specific sizes, styles and colors. Garments are not "made-to-order." Abbreviated form is RTW. See *prêt-à-porter*.

REALISTIC MANNEQUIN A full round, sculpted form that resembles in face, pose and proportions a particular type or "image." Form may be a young, animated "junior"—a sophisticated or swinging "missy"—a teenager—a sporty, young male—a classic man—a portly, middle-aged man, etc. Not abstract.

REBATE *1.* A return of part of a payment. A discount or deduction. *2.* See *rabbet*.

REBOZO, REBOSA, REBOSO A long narrow shawl in a dark color, woven in wool or linen. Used as a head and shoulder cover or as a sling to carry children when it is wound about the shoulders and hips. A Mexican and South American costume accessory.

RECEIVABLES Money owed to a business and has yet to be collected.

RECESSED LIGHTING See *cove lighting*.

RECONSTRUCTED STONE See *cast stone*.

RECTANGLE A four-sided figure with pairs of equal sides and four right angles. To determine the *length of a di-*

agonal through a rectangle, use the Pythagorean theory, as used in finding the hypoteneuse of a right triangle—one leg or side^2 + the adjacent leg or side^2 = the hypoteneuse^2. The *area* of a rectangle is the result of the length multiplied by the width. See *square*.

RECTANGULAR RACK A traditional fixture consisting of two vertical sides connected by one or two hang rods and cross-braced at the base or near the base. When the sides are narrower than 20″ there is usually one hang rod connecting the center of one upright to the center of the other. If the sides are wider than 20″, it is possible to have two hang rods connecting both ends and, thus, the merchandise can be hung from either side. A more decorative version of the skeletal pipe rack.

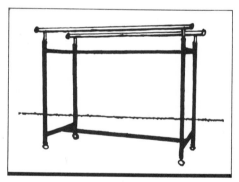

RED GUM A reddish brown, fine-grained wood that is used for veneering doors and interior walls. It can be stained to simulate maple, walnut or mahogany—depending upon the graining of the piece of wood.

REDINGOTE French for "riding coat." *1.* An 18th-century man's outercoat—double-breasted, large collar with a tiered capelet over the shoulders and wide lapels or revers. *2.* A 19th-century woman's fitted outercoat—flared out from the waist, double-breasted with a wide collar and leg o'mutton sleeves.

REDWOOD A handsome, reddish-colored wood, native to the western part of the United States. It stains well and is easy to paint.

REEDED TUBING A round tubing with fine vertical channels running the length of the tube. A miniature fluted effect.

REFLECTOR *1.* A polished or mirrored surface. Used to redirect light in a desired direction or onto a specific area. *2.* A baffle or screen to reflect heated air.

REFLECTOR LAMP See *R-lamp.*

REGISTRATION The precise alignment of plates or screens that are to be printed or reproduced in a series on the same surface. When the various plates, screens or stencils are not aligned or registered perfectly, they are said to be "out of register."

REHAB, REHABILITATION The reconditioning, remodeling and refixturing of an existing retail store or department. A renovation.

REINFORCED CONCRETE A term used in construction to describe concrete that has been reinforced or strengthened by the use of metal rods or mesh. The rods or mesh are embedded in the poured concrete. Also called ferroconcrete.

RELATED ITEM An expression used in retailing for a coordinated piece of merchandise, such as ties with shirts, belts with pants or slippers with robes. See *accessory.*

RELATED MERCHANDISE DISPLAY A presentation of a variety of items that are related by color, use, theme or place of origin. For example, a "red" promotional display showing dresses, shoes, bags, hats—all red.

RELIEF A carved or applied ornament or design that is raised above the general surface level of the panel or sustaining surface. See *bas relief.*

RELIEF LETTERPRESS Printing from raised surfaces as opposed to etched or intaglio plates. Examples of raised or relief plates would be: type, woodcuts, zinc and copper halftone plates and line cuts.

REMOTE STOCKROOM Storage space or stock area that is quite apart from the actual selling area such as on another floor or in a separate warehouse.

RENDERING A pictorial representation of a proposed development, building or interior. Usually done in perspective, in full color, sometimes photographic, and often with figures drawn in to give a sense of scale or proportion.

REP, REPP A heavy plain weave fabric with a distinctive crosswise *rib.* Used for men's ties and for draperies.

REPLICA An exact copy or reproduction. A line-for-line copy.

REPOUSSÉ A raised design on the face of a metal surface, produced by hammering or pressing the design on the reverse side of the metal.

REPRODUCTION A faithful and careful copy, however, not an attempt to "fake" or counterfeit.

RESERVE STOCK Merchandise that is not on the selling floor, but is easily available.

RESIDENT BUYING OFFICE See *buying group or office.*

RESORCINOL A high-strength adhesive; a dark red or purple liquid which has to be combined with a curing agent to be effective. It produces a dark glue line. Resists water, oil, most solvents and mold. Used outdoors or under severe service conditions.

RETAIL The business of selling merchandise directly to the customer.

RETAIL PRICE Price at which goods are sold to consumer; reflects markup to cover expenses, costs and profit. See *wholesale price.*

RETROFIT A term for an energy-saving device or technique requiring the use of more efficient lamps and/or lighting techniques. It can sometimes be accomplished by using the same fixtures, but changing the type of tube or lamp used in that fixture.

RETRO, RETROSPECTIVE A survey of the past looks, events, etc.

RETURN The right angled turn away from the normal face of a unit. The side of a structure. The side end of a projecting element.

REVERSE LETTERING Negative lettering. The image or design printed in white or a lighter color onto the deeper background.

REVOLVING RACKS Round fixturing racks designed to rotate a full 360 degrees so that the merchandise passes in front of the customer. A turning wheel on a vertical shaft.

RHEOSTAT A mechanism for regulating the flow of electric current.

RICE PAPER A very thin, soft paper produced from the bark of the bamboo plant. It is usually a pale ocher color. Particularly used for wood engravings, and sometimes for proofs of steel plate engravings.

RIGGING, RIG An expression used in connection with dressing a mannequin or especially for dressing a man's coat or suit form. Padding, pinning and plumping out of merchandise on the inanimate form to make the merchandise look attractive, exciting, and as perfectly fitted as possible.

RIGHT WINDOW The mannequin's right hand or side as it faces the viewer outside the window.

RIPPING Cutting lumber parallel to the grain.

RIP SAW A hand saw principally designed to cut efficiently in the direction of the wood's grain. The cutting teeth are angled and flat-edged, like a chisel, to chip away at the wood *with* the grain. There are usually six to eight teeth to the inch.

RISER *1. In merchandise presentation (as illustrated)* A small platform; an elevation; a block, cube, cylinder or

decorative form or device used to raise a piece of merchandise (a piece of china, a bottle of perfume, a small sculpture, etc.) from the counter surface, window or shadow box floor. A riser is especially effective in bringing attention to one or two pieces of merchandise in an otherwise mass presentation such as a shoe stand in a popular-priced shoe display. Also see *build up. 2. In architecture* The vertical member of a stair set between two treads—the horizontal components.

R-LAMP An incandescent lamp, sort of mushroom-shaped, with a convex-rounded head, and a built-in reflector surface. Available in wattages from 30 to 1000, but the 150 and 300 wattages are most commonly used. The R-lamp is blown in one piece, lightweight, relatively fragile and not recommended for outdoor use without a housing or shield. Compared to the PAR lamp, it has a wider spread and smoother field, but it is not as powerful as the PAR spot. R-lamps as well as PAR lamps are available in some colors as well as clear, and the frosting on the face of the lamp determines the beam spread. Also called a reflector lamp.

ROCKER-LOK SYSTEM Trademark for a 1″ chrome-on-steel tubing system, which combines vertical and horizontal lengths of tubing by means of seven different fittings. Each fitting is basically a cube with assorted projections (two to form a right angle, three

to form a "T," four to form a cross or "X," etc.). The Rocker design on each projection assures a firm joining when the hollow tube slides over it to meet the cube element. The steel tubing is also available slotted in assorted patterns on one, two, three or all four sides. The system is available in assorted metallic and enamelled finishes. Produced by Kason Fixture Ware.

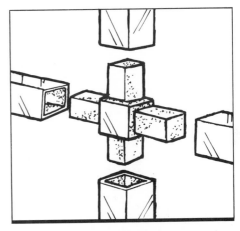

ROLL (OF WALLPAPER) A term used with wallpaper to denote 36 square feet of paper. The length will vary depending upon the width of the paper (18–36 inches). A double roll is twice as long as the single roll, the triple is three times as long, etc. Several rolls together are called a bundle or stick.

ROLL SLEEVE, ROLL-UP SLEEVE A sleeve that is designed to be turned up.

ROMAN TYPE A family of typeface characterized by the vertical emphasis and based on early humanistic handwritings. In the older Roman examples (Old Style) there is greater strength and boldness in the strokes and a comparatively uniform thickness with an absence of the fine hairlines. The serifs are rounded and the general appearance of the letter is legible and clear. Caslon is an example of Old Style Roman. Modern Roman (see *Bodoni*) is characterized by heavier shadings, thinner hairlines and straight, thin serifs.

ABCDEFGHIJKLMNOPQRSTUVWXYZ
abcdefghijklmnopqrstuvwxyz
$1234567890c :;&?!()%`

ROPE DISPLAYER A counter unit designed to show various longer lengths of necklaces, chains, pearls, beads, etc. Usually the unit is tiered so that more merchandise can be shown. Sometimes the unit is made adjustable to accommodate the variety of lengths and styles.

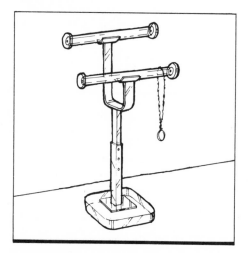

ROSETTES Little roses. Decorative ornaments like petals in a circle, elliptical or square. Often found in the corners of key-cornered moldings or on decorative bands. See *key cornered*.

ROSEWOOD A heavy, deep-colored wood, often purple-brown with black streaks, that is hard and durable.

ROTARY PRESS A printing machine associated with the preparation of newspapers and magazines with large circulation. It is a high-speed press which passes a long stretch of paper between an impression cylinder and the curved printing form on the plate cylinder.

ROTUNDA A round building; a round, central enclosure in a building, usually surmounted with a dome.

ROUGH A quick sketch or study. An approximation of a design or concept, without any real attempt at details or specifics. A preliminary sketch, usually one of several, to be developed.

ROUGH CAST A surfacing plaster which contains pebbles, gravel, or cement. Used on exterior walls.

ROUGH LUMBER Rough, splintery and furry wood which is then dressed, planed and smoothed down in the large factories that purchase this type of lumber. Can be used in woodworking and construction where the lack of finish is not obvious or visible.

ROUNDELS Colored glass, circular filters that are used with spotlights and floodlights to achieve specific color changes or effects.

ROUND RACK A circular rack, in plan, usually 3 feet in diameter. The round hang rod may be supported by a single pedestal upright or a series of legs and, depending upon the construction, the unit may be adjustable in height. Some round racks are constructed with two or three tiers of hang rods, while others may have a central platform or shelf on top to display a form, a softly draped arrangement or a sign. Available in many types of finishes and materials and are especially economical in the amount of "shoulder-out" garments they can hold in a limited area of floor space. See *shoulder out* and *three-part rack*.

ROUND WIRE CARPET See *Brussels carpet*.

ROUTER A small power tool designed to make inside cuts and shapes of pieces. The motor is in a cylindrical housing, the cutting blade or bit extends down through the opening in the circular plastic disk, which is the base of the unit, and a pair of knobs, one at either side, guides the cutting blade. The tool can also cut rabbets, tenons, and dados. Special bits can be attached to do specific cuts or functions such as V-grooves, veinings and moldings.

RTW Abbreviation for *ready-to-wear*. See *prêt-à-porter* and *ready-to-wear*.

R-20 (LAMP) An economic, low voltage lamp. A 25- or 50-watt R-20 can replace a 75- or 100-watt standard reflec-

tor lamp. Available in a full color range.

RUBBER COMPOSITION See *rubber mâché*.

RUBBER MÂCHÉ A rubber, latex-like compound poured into a specially made hollow mold and allowed to dry or set (or force dried through heat in an oven). The excess material, which did not set or harden, is poured off and the "rubber" unit is allowed to cure and become rigid. It usually requires a minimum of smoothing or rasping to finish the surface that formed next to the mold. When finished, it will be firm and fairly resistant to breakage. The rubber-mâché piece can be painted, gilded or appliquéd and made to resemble wood, stone or other structural materials. Used in mannequin construction and decorative props.

RUBBER TILE A nonporous, resilient, man-made floor covering material, which remains flexible over a wide range of temperature changes. It is adversely affected by oil, grease and other solvents. Available in numerous colors, patterns and simulated textures.

RUCHING Trimming of pleated lace or fabric, used on collars, necklines, cuffs, hemlines, etc.

RUNNER A channel or track within which a unit moves, slides or glides. For example, a track under a drawer to keep the drawer in line while it is slid in and out. A guide.

RUNNING LIGHTS See *chasing lights*.

RUNWAY A raised platform or aisle for fashion shows. Space for audience is usually available on either side or in the surrounding area of runway.

RUSH A beige-colored long grass, which is dried, twisted and then woven or plaited into seats or backs for provincial-styled chairs or into mats or tiles.

RUSTIC STONEWORK A technique in masonry in which the exposed face of a rectangular stone is purposely textured while the edges and sides are smoothed out for greater contrast. Stones are laid in straight, even courses. Popular in the Italian Renaissance.

S

SABER SAW A portable, electric jig saw. See *jig saw*.

SACK COAT A man's short, plain jacket without a waist seam. A single or double-breasted, loose-fitting jacket.

SADDLE *1.* An inverted U-shaped riser or platform with the edge of the "U" flattened out and elongated. A bench with rounded corners. A unit to elevate merchandise, a form or a mannequin. *2.* See *sill*.

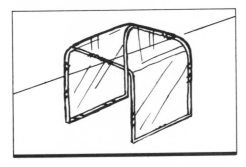

SAFARI JACKET See *bush jacket*.

SAILCLOTH A closely woven, firm, strong and durable cotton canvas. Man-made fibers are also used.

SAILOR COLLAR A broad, square collar hanging in the back, which tapers, over the shoulders, to end in a deep "V" in the front at the chest. A take-off on the collar of a sailor's blouse.

SALES PRODUCTION The annual volume of earnings divided by the gross sales area of a department or store.

SALES PROMOTION Advertising, display and other media used to stimulate the sales of a particular item or group of merchandise. Techniques used to stimulate the consumer's purchasing response to a given product.

SAMPLE DISPLAY A specialized and dramatized presentation on the selling floor of a single unit such as a fur coat, a gown or a pair of shoes. The back-up stock on that unit is kept in a forward stockroom and not necessarily on the selling floor.

SANDBLASTING A technique for cleaning the stone surfaces of a structure by means of bombarding that surface with a stream of sand particles, jet propelled by steam or air pressure. The sand abrades the stone surface and wears away the stains or discolorations.

SAND COAT A texture paint combining sand particles with an oil- or latex-base paint, gives a rough, sandpaper-like texture to the treated surface. It can cover blemishes, nailheads, small cracks and other small imperfections on the area to be painted while imparting a new color and texture.

SAND FINISH A final plaster coat, usually of lime and sand, which leaves the surface smooth but sandy to the touch. A sandpaper-like finish.

SANDPAPER A paper to which abrasive particles have been cemented, giving the whole surface a rough, sandy coating. The degree of abrasiveness can be controlled. Used for smoothing and for polishing. The paper may be coated with silicon carbide, aluminum oxide, garnet, etc.

SANDSTONE A natural building and surfacing stone, usually a warm beige color. It is composed of sand particles compressed together with silicic acid, and may also contain some carbonate of lime or oxide or lime.

SANFORIZED® Registered trademark of The Sanforized Company, a division of Cluett, Peabody & Co., Inc., appearing on fabrics with a residual shrinkage of not more than one percent, despite repeated launderings, according to the U.S.'s standard wash test.

SANGUINE A chalk or drawing that is terra-cotta in color. From the French for "bloody." A soft pastel technique.

SANS SERIF Typeface without slashes or strokes (see *serif*) at the start and end of the vertical strokes. The letters are constructed of strokes of equal thickness. It is the updated version of the oldest Roman inscriptional letters. See *block letters*.

ABCDEFGHIJKLMNOPQRSTUVWXYZ
abcdefghijklmnopqrstuvwxyz
$1234567890 :;&?!()%

SARAN A generic name for a stiff, sunlight- and weather-resistant vinyl filament. It makes a tough, heavy-duty fabric for furniture and floor coverings. Not used in apparel.

SARAPE See *serape*.

SARI *1.* A woman's outer garment consisting of a long length of fabric worn over a short blouse (choli), shirred at the waist and draped over one shoulder; worn mostly in India and Pakistan. *2.* Fabric made of fine cotton, silk, or a combination of fibers; often brightly colored, printed or embroidered. Usually with an ornamental border around the entire length and width of the fabric.

SARONG A draped skirt consisting of a wide, rectangular piece of fabric that wraps around the hips and tucks into the waistband or sash with a central opening or slit. Used by natives of both sexes in the South Sea Islands. Popularized by Dorothy Lamour in the movies of the 1930s and 1940s.

SASH WINDOW A double hung window—one behind the other—either can be raised or lowered. Each fills only half of the window frame.

SATEEN, SATINE A satin weave fabric made of cotton fibers, with a lustrous face and a dull back.

SATIN *1.* One of the basic weaves. *2.* A soft, lustrous fabric made from silk fibers and named after the Chinese seaport of "Zaytoun," now Canton. Also, produced in many fibers.

SATIN FINISH A matte, rubbed or brushed finish on metal, which is achieved by rough grinding the metal surface before the plating or coating process.

SAUSAGE LAMP See *showcase lamp*.

SAVONNERIE A classic French, high pile carpet often done in pastel floral and scroll designs. Most popular in 18th-century room settings. Used with furniture of that period.

SAWDUST COAT A technique for texturing a wall or ceiling surface in theatrical painting. Small wood chips or sawdust are mixed into the paint and then applied with a brush or roller. The small flakes or particles will adhere to the painted surface, add texture, and cover blemishes and scars.

SCAFFOLDING A skeletal framework constructed around a building, wall, etc., used as a work surface for that structure while it is being repaired or worked on. A means of working on a surface that cannot be reached or treated directly from the ground.

SCAGLIOLA Imitation marble composed of marble chips and coloring materials in a compound of gypsum or plaster of Paris.

SCALE The relationship or proportion of elements to one another in height, width and depth. The proportion of a fixture or counter to a particular area—in relation to the size of the department and the unit to be employed.

SCALE DRAWING The drawing of an object in proportion. One inch of the drawing will represent one foot of the actual object. The reduction or enlargement of that proportion is given in scale: ¼″ = 1″, ⅛″ = 1″, etc.

SCARF JOINT An overlapping joint in cabinetry. Two beveled edges are laid one over the other for a continuous level surface.

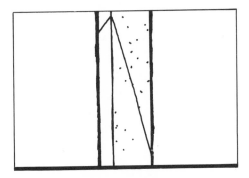

SCARF WHEEL A circular, spinning attachment on a counter, ledge, or floor unit with rings, loops or cutout holes through which scarfs or ties may be looped and draped.

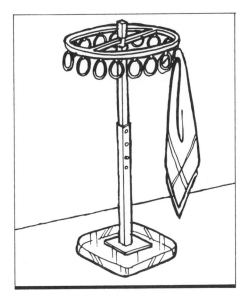

SCATTER Small shreds, shavings, or granules of plastic, paper, cork or wood. Used for floor cover to create "islands" or patterns on which merchandise can be displayed. See *scatter grass*.

SCATTER GRASS Plastic snips or "blades" of grass that can be scattered, spread or piled to create grassy knolls or lawn-like effects. Usually available in green, but also produced in neutral beige tones for autumn displays.

SCENIC WALLPAPER A wallpaper mural of three or four (or more) panels covering from 9′ to 11′ and presenting a view, panorama or decorative design, often with depth and distance. Available on various grounds, in assorted colorways and an infinite range of designs and subject matter.

SCHOOL OF A group of creative people (artists, designers, architects, etc.) who work in a similar tradition with similar values, theories and concepts. See *Bauhaus*.

SCIOPTICON An instrument that produces moving effects by means of light projection onto a wall, cyclorama or screen. Used in decorative displays for theatrical effects. Within the drum of the sciopticon is a plastic or mica disk upon which the effect to be produced is painted such as rain, snow or moving clouds. The disk is turned or rotated by a clock mechanism or by a motor.

SCONCE A wall bracket to hold a source of light such as candles or bulbs. Originally designed with a shield to cover the candle flame, and sometimes with a mirrored background to enhance the light produced by the flame.

SCOOP NECKLINE A deep, U-shaped neckline.

SCOTCHGARD® A fluorochemical process applied to fabrics to make them more resistant to dirt and stains without affecting the feel or color of the fabric. Trademark of Minnesota Mining and Manufacturing

SCRATCH COAT A rough, first coat of plaster applied to a wall, and then further roughed, scratched or scored before it is thoroughly dry. The second or finishing coat of plaster will adhere better to this rough surface.

SCREW HOLE A predrilled hole into which a screw can be inserted and secured. It is often countersunk.

SCREWS Metal fasteners consisting of a slotted head and a spiral-like turned or threaded root, with a smooth shaft between the head and root. Screws vary in length, shape and diameter; heads may be flat, oval, round, etc. Most screw heads are slotted to receive the standard screwdriver, however, the Phillips head screw requires a different screwdriver to fit the cross on the top of the head. Wood screws have pointed root ends, while most metal screws have flat root ends. Screws usually have better holding power than other fasteners; can be tightened to draw parts closer together; when properly driven or secured are neater than nails; can be withdrawn without damaging the material. See *lag screw* and *Phillips head screw*.

SCREW STAIR A spiral staircase that rotates around a vertical upright pole. See *spiral staircase*.

SCRIBE To mark or outline by cutting or scratching a line.

SCRIM An open weave, coarse fabric, usually white or ecru, with various sized openings. Made of cotton and man-made fibers. Used for needlework and hooking. A lighter weight, marquisette-type scrim is used in the theater and also as a filler between plasterboards.

SCRIPT TYPE Typeface that imitates handwriting. Usually flowing, rounded and connected letters. See *cursive type.*

SCROLL SAW A lightweight hand tool consisting of a thin blade, with twelve teeth to the inch, contained within a deep metal clamp-like frame with a wooden grip. It is capable of being turned to follow an irregular shape, profile, curve or scroll. The blade is removable to make interior cuts. See *coping saw.*

SCULPTURE The art of the end product of three-dimensional forming, carving or molding. Carving cuts into the material, while modeling builds up the clay, wax or plasteline into a relief form and then cast in plaster or metal (usually bronze).

SEA GRASS MATS Similar to hemp mats but lighter and lacier in appearance. Available in squares, 6″ or 12″, and can be woven, sewn or stapled together into wall or floor coverings.

SEALER A liquid finishing material used in woodworking and cabinetry as a first coat on close-grained wood or over the filler on coarse-grained wood. Sometimes used as the coat between the stain and the finish, and prevents the former from reacting with the latter. There are also penetrating sealers which are used as final finishing coats on an object to supply a natural, hard coat to the wood. Penetrating sealers resist alcohol, chemicals, moisture, heat, cold, scratches, burns and grease, and are made from either synthetic resins or tung oil. Penetrating sealers are invisible and impart no sheen unless many coats are applied. The sealer sinks into the pores and becomes an integral part of the surface. It is easy to repair with a quick, additional coat.

SEAM The line or joint formed when two materials are joined.

SEAMLESS PAPER See *no seam paper.*

SEASONAL DEPARTMENT A department that carries merchandise of limited time or seasonal appeal such as swimsuits, ski-wear and heavy winter outerwear or "Trim-a-Tree" shops.

SEASONAL DISCOUNTS Discounts offered to customers on seasonal merchandise when the "season" is past. Such as swimsuits in August or Christmas cards after Christmas. See *clearance.*

SEASONED LUMBER Newly cut or "green" wood which is air- or kiln-dried to improve the durability of the lumber, to control checking and warping. Treated and "aged" wood.

SECOND An irregular or less than perfect piece of merchandise. See *irregular.*

SECONDARY LIGHTING The lighting beyond the basic or primary lighting plan such as spots, floods, filters and washers. Used to add depth, dimension and atmosphere to the lighting plan. See *ceiling washer, cove lighting* and *indirect lighting.*

SECTION A side view, a profile view, a vertical slice of an object which can give dimensional information as well as structural details. A silhouette. Used in shop drawing.

SECTIONAL DRAWING A drawing of a vertical cut through an object showing the interior construction. A cross section.

SECTIONAL DRAWING

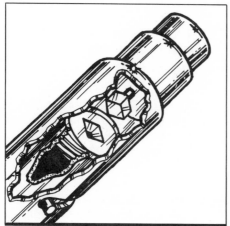

SECURITY CASES Cabinets, bins and other enclosures used to display and store merchandise, but also to control the accessibility to the merchandise. The merchandise may be kept under lock, fastened down, attached or bolted onto the case. A pilfer-proof case. See *museum case.*

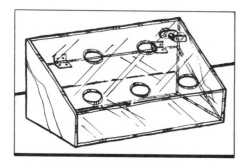

SECURITY DEPARTMENT The department of an establishment responsible for the protection of the store's property, merchandise, customers and personnel. Usually created to counteract pilferage. Department may include guards (both in and out of uniform), electronic devices, closed circuit television, alarm systems, or security devices such as special tabs or tags on merchandise.

SEERSUCKER A crinkled or puckered fabric made of cotton, silk, man-made fibers or combinations. Crinkled stripe created by varying the tension of the warp yarns. Associated with summer clothing.

SELECT LUMBER A grade of softwood. The lumber is generally clear with only minor defects which can be covered with paint. It is further graded A, B, C and D. Also see *common lumber.*

SELF-SELECTION DISPLAY The merchandise is presented on fixtures which are designed to show, coordinate and sell the merchandise. Garments can be conveniently removed from and replaced onto these fixtures. Sales personnel may only be required to write up the sale. See *merchandiser.*

SELF-SELLING, SELF-SERVICE A discount or check-out type of selling technique in which the customer picks out merchandise from price- and size-marked racks and counters, and presents it at the checkout counter for payment.

SELVAGE, SELVEDGE *1.* The reinforced outer edge of a piece of fabric parallel to the warp to prevent ravelling. *2.* The unprinted border or edge of a width of wallpaper.

SEMI-ABSTRACT MANNEQUIN An abstract or highly stylized mannequin which may suggest, either in the sculpting or in the minimal artwork, features or a suggestion of a type of individual. More realistic than an abstract mannequin—more abstract than a semi-realistic mannequin. See *abstract mannequin* and *semi-realistic mannequin.*

SEMI-CLOSED BACK WINDOW A display window with a partial back or partition that does not extend above the viewer's eye level. The divider contains the view of the merchandise on the floor and builds up in front of it, but permits a look into the selling floor beyond.

SEMI-REALISTIC MANNEQUIN A fairly realistic sculpted mannequin which is made more stylized by the lack of clarity of the facial features or the look of realism in the artwork or makeup. Makeup may be omitted from the realistically sculpted face and stylized artwork may replace the natural look. Wigs may be forsaken for painted hair styles and the "hair" may be sculpted in, but not detailed. See *semi-abstract mannequin.*

SEPARATES The various components of an outfit such as skirts, pants, shirts, blouses, sweaters and vests designed to be worn together, but not to be sold together. They are designed in coordinated fabrics, patterns and colors.

SERAPE A long, rather wide, woolen blanket, folded lengthwise and worn wrapped around the body or over the shoulder by Mexicans, Central and South American Indians. Also spelled sarape.

SERGE A suiting fabric with a diagonal twill on both face and back.

SERIF The stroke or slash lines perpendicular to the principle stroke of a letter. The serifs on straight stems may be slab (heavy or fine), wedge-shaped, bracketed or unbracketed. Gothic letters are "sans serif" (without serifs).

ABCDEFGHIJKLMNOPQRSTUVWXYZ
abcdefghijklmnopqrstuvwxyz
$1234567890c :;&?!()%"

SERIGRAPHY A method of producing original, multicolored prints that have a real paint quality. Paint or ink is forced through specially prepared stencils of fine silk (or synthetic fabric). It usually requires a different stencil or silk screen for each color laid down on the surface being printed. A fine art form of silk screen printing. See *silk screen.*

SHADE *1.* The darker gradations of a color obtained by the addition of black to that color. *2.* The darker tone produced when an object is turned away from the source of light.

SHADOWBOX WINDOWS Small, shallow windows, usually at eye level, either inside or outside of the selling area. Used to display small merchan-

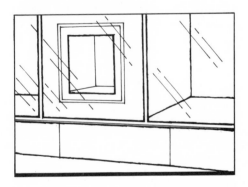

dise, accessories or "precious" objects. Sometimes a larger window can be masked to make a shadow box window. The shadow box requires sharper, more pinpoint lighting, and can accommodate smaller spotlights.

SHAKE Rough, split-wood shingles. Used for building exteriors or for achieving certain effects on interiors.

SHANTUNG A plain weave silk fabric made with uneven yarns to achieve a textured effect. Made of cotton, silk, man-made fibers and/ or combinations. Originally manufactured in the Shantung Province of China.

SHARK'S TOOTH SCRIM A strong, semi-transparent, rectangular- or ladder-patterned net fabric made in 30-foot widths for use in theater design and display. Dense enough to be painted with dyes; appears semiopaque when lit from the front and semi-transparent when lit from behind. See *bobbinet*.

SHAWL COLLAR A narrow or wide collar that usually ends below the bustline, cut in one piece or seamed in back; without lapels.

SHEATH A narrow, close-fitting garment. See *shift*.

SHELF A horizontal surface, usually parallel to the floor, to hold and/or display merchandise. It may be permanently attached or affixed to a unit or wall surface, or may be adjustable. See *bracket* and *standards*.

SHELF GUARD An edging or rim attached to the end of a shelf to keep merchandise from sliding off; a guard rail. It also protects the edge of the shelf from damage.

SHELF PACK Prepackaged merchandise that can be displayed as it is on a shelf or in a bin.

SHELF PIN A pin consisting of a round stem and a flattened disk surface—similar to a ping pong paddle. The stem is inserted into a snug-fitting, predrilled hole and the disk is placed parallel to the ground and underneath a shelf or plate. Almost always used in groups of four and inserted into drilled uprights of bookcases, casegoods, bins and cabinets. It makes adjustable shelving possible without the use of large exposed brackets or hardware.

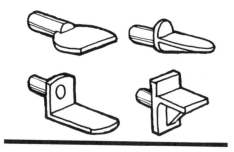

SHELF SUPPORT Any clip, bracket, pin or brace that is used to keep a shelf level and steady. See *bracket* and *slant bracket*.

SHELL *1.* The skeletal structure or bare framework of a building; exterior walls, roof, beams, girders, columns, basic floors. *2.* A sleeveless overblouse.

SHELLAC A quick-drying, varnish-like substance that is fairly impervious to water. It is a natural resin which is soluble in alcohol. When applied to wood, it produces a shiny surface. Often used as a prime coat on unfinished wood, since it acts as a sealer.

SHELL & ALLOWANCE LEASE The leasing of space or a building which is basically an empty shell within which the merchant will decorate and finish, such as to add flooring, wall finishes, lighting, fixtures and furniture. There is an allowance for that construction and the financial outlay has been agreed to by the developer or builder. *Shell and no allowance* lease, however, means that the developer does not give any allowance or financial discount for the specific completion of the shell or skeletal store.

SHELL BASE A metal base cut, stamped and compressed into a flat, rectangular or pillbox-like cylinder; plated and decoratively surfaced. Used as a cover over the actual weighted non-decorative base of a t-stand, costumer, counter, ledge or floor unit. Heavy enough to keep the unit upright and prevent tipping.

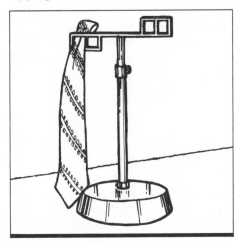

SHELL FORM A lightweight plastic bra, blouse, sweater or dress form with fully sculpted bust and shoulders and a *scooped out* or *concave back*

rather than an anatomically sculpted back.

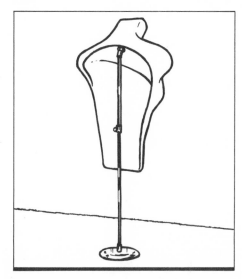

SHELL & NO ALLOWANCE LEASE See *shell & allowance lease.*

SHIFT A simple straight, close-fitting garment, beltless and often sleeveless. Also called chemise or sheath.

SHIKI A heavy silk or rayon fabric with a slubbed or irregular horizontal rep running across the width. Used for draperies or as wallcoverings, by means of either irregular yarns glued onto a paper backing or graphically reproduced with artwork and embossing.

SHIM A thin, wedge-shaped filler. Used to align or to straighten irregularities resulting when two surfaces or planes do not meet exactly as they should and an open space or gap is evident, or to increase slightly the height of an object such as a table or chair leg. The filler is usually a piece of wood, but depending upon the problem at hand and the materials available it can be anything from a coin to a matchbook cover.

SHINGLES Thin wood, asbestos, slate, etc., tiles used to face a wall or surface. Asbestos shingles are used to cover roofs. See *shake*.

SHIRT COLLAR The traditional man's collar which buttons at the neck with two pointed or slightly rounded ends. Sometimes the collar ends are "buttoned-down."

SHIRT DRESS See *shirtwaist*.

SHIRT FORM The male version of the blouse form. See *blouse form*.

SHIRTWAIST The feminine adaptation of a man's shirt with a buttoned-down front (to the waist, hips or hemline), tailored collar worn with a bow or tie, in a variety of sleeve lengths (often cuffed and buttoned) and a variety of fabrics. Can be formal or informal. Originated in the 1890s and popularized by Charles Dana Gibson and his "Gibson Girl." Also called *shirt dress*.

"SHMATAH" BUSINESS "The Rag Business." The garment trade; any part of the industry involved in making or selling ready-to-wear.

SHOE CARRIER An angled wire or plastic shelf used to hold and show shoes. It may be equipped with a heel stop to keep the shoes from sliding off the raked shelf.

SHOJI A Japanese style frame divided into smaller rectangles by means of rails and stiles. The openings are filled with translucent materials such as rice paper, fabric or plastics. The traditional shoji screen or panel is used to divide areas or rooms without permanent construction.

SHOP *1.* A specifically subdivided, designed and fixtured area, used to present one special type of merchandise. For example, a bath shop, sleep shop, maternity shop, or infants' wear shop. *2.* A free-standing independent store.

SHOP DRAWING A detailed drawing, usually in scale, with all the specifics and requirements of construction indicated. A working drawing.

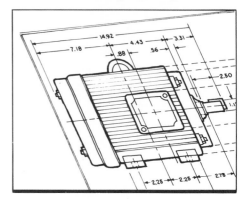

SHOPPING CENTER A large group of stores usually gathered together in a suburban setting, usually near a main road or highway, and equipped with a large parking area. Often, there will be branches of one or more noteworthy department or specialty stores, plus many small shops and boutiques, restaurants, possibly cinemas, commercial enterprises, etc. The larger stores or branches of major stores are called the "anchor stores." Shopping centers are also appearing in urban or "downtown" sections and often the street or streets are closed to vehicular traffic and made into promenades. See *mall*.

SHOPPING GOODS Usually the big ticket (more expensive) items that a customer will shop around for to compare prices, styles and guarantees.

SHORING Temporary framework constructed around a structure used to support that structure while it is being repaired or worked upon.

SHORT SHORTS Abbreviated sport shorts that end just below the crotch or high on the thigh.

SHOULDER OUT Merchandise that is stocked, stacked or shown with the shoulder and sleeve side forward as opposed to a "face out" or full front view presentation. For example, garments hung on a round rack or in a closet on the traditional hang rail. See *face out* and *round rack*.

SHOWCARD BOARD Cardboard that is coated on one side and lined on the other with a "book" paper; available in a variety of thicknesses or plys (4, 6, 14), colors and finishes. Used for counter display, easel and window signs.

SHOWCASE A cabinet, vitrine or see-through-contained unit that makes it possible for merchandise to be shown, but not necessarily handled. A showcase often allows for a full round presentation whereas the glass-topped or glass-fronted counters limit viewing. Also see *case* and *museum case*.

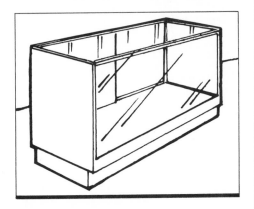

SHOWCASE LAMPS Long, thin, sausage-shaped incandescent lamps; available in 25, 40, and 60 watt strengths. Also called t-lamps.

SHOWING A fashion show or a merchandise presentation. A public viewing of new or special merchandise under optimum conditions.

SHOWPIECE BUYING Purchasing very limited quantities of a prestige item—mainly for display and image projection—not intended to be stocked.

SHRINKAGE The loss of inventory caused by employee pilferage, shoplifting, inefficient help, damaged merchandise, or administrative errors in markups, markdowns, or inventory control.

SHUTTER A wood, metal or plastic panel; often designed to control the amount of light and air that passes through the area that is shuttered. Used as a window screen or cover. See *louver*.

SHUTTERING The temporary walls or supports used to enclose poured concrete. When the concrete hardens, the walls are removed.

SIDEWALK SALE Merchandise shown and sold outside of and in front of a store. A popular technique in some major European cities.

SIG The signature or identifying logo of a store, designer, manufacturer, etc. See *logo*.

SIGNAGE A visual and graphic form of communication by means of type and/or recognizable symbols; the illustrated or illuminated message. The outdoor and indoor signs, posters, card toppers, department, shop and merchandise identifiers, directories and floor listing necessary to a commercial or public-oriented venture. The impact and effect of signage may depend upon the size and style of type used (or not used), color, contrasts, scale and proportion. It may be all symbol—devoid of lettering or words. Signs are produced on all types of materials such as neon tubes, electric bulbs, paper, plastics, wood, fabric banners and metals.

SIGN HOLDER See *card holder* and easel.

SIGN PAINTING ART See *emblematic art.*

SILHOUETTE *1.* An outline drawing, completely filled in and usually in black, against a white- or light-colored background. *2.* A fashion line or look.

SILICONES Resins with good electrical properties and strength at high temperatures. Used for encapsulating electrical components and reinforcing laminates; making molds for other plastic materials. Solvent solutions of the silicones are also used in coatings and varnishes.

SILK A fine delicate, drapable fabric produced from the natural fiber extruded by the silkworm as it spins its cocoon. The fibers can be used alone or combined with other natural or man-made fibers to enhance the strength and durability of fabric woven.

SILK SCREEN A printing process in which designs are printed by means of paint or dye forced through screens, which are covered with a fine silk (or synthetic) mesh. The areas that are not to be printed are masked off. The paint is passed over and through the screen with a squeegee. A separate stencil or screen is required for each

color to be laid down. It is a popular technique used in producing displays, posters, wallpapers, fabrics, and in applying logos and designs on special surfaces. Also see *serigraphy.*

SILL The bottom horizontal strip or member on a frame or construction. A door sill is referred to as a "saddle."

SISAL A stiff, hard natural fiber, used to weave floor mats or to produce twine.

SIZE COAT Surfacing with a sizing agent. See *sizing.*

SIZING *1.* A generic term for a gelatin-like substance made from materials such as glue, resin, starch and latex used to prime coat a wall. The sizing fills the spaces between the pores and creates a smooth surface ready for painting, printing, papering, etc. In some cases, waterproofs the surface. A new paper or coat of paint will adhere better to a wall that has been treated with sizing. See *size coat* and *undercoat.* *2.* A finishing process on fabrics to make them appear smoother, stiffer, denser and stronger.

SKELETON CONSTRUCTION *1.* Any "Jungle-Gym" sort of merchandising device consisting of horizontal

and vertical bars and joints or connectors and not necessarily covered or sheathed in any way. Used in fixturing. See *Apton* and *Abstracta Systems.* *2. (As illustrated)* The assembly of posts and beams—the framework of a construction—before adding the finishing and bearing walls and partitions.

SKETCH A rough draft or quick drawing; a preliminary visualization of a composition, construction or layout.

SKILSAW A portable lightweight circular saw equipped with a small blade. It is limited as to the depth of the cut and its accuracy, but it can be used anyplace, within the area of an electric outlet for ripping or cross cutting. A way of bringing the "shop" to the construction.

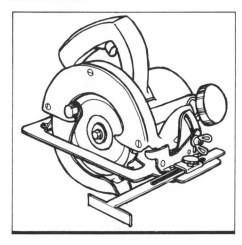

SKIN The surface treatment or envelop of a building; the outer facing.

SKIRT/SLACKS BAR ATTACHMENT An attachment to a costumer, similar to an oversized "bobby pin," to hold, grip or clamp onto skirts or slacks and hold it *out* from the vertical upright of the unit and in relation to the jacket or balance of the costume.

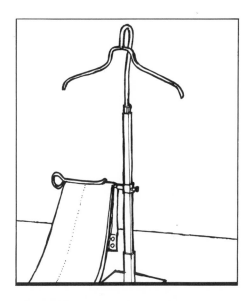

SKYLIGHT A window or glazed surface that is angled up towards the sky or is parallel with the roof and thus completely oriented skyward. A covered opening in a roof that allows in the light and keeps out the elements.

SLACKS DRAPER An arm or horizontal attachment to the vertical element

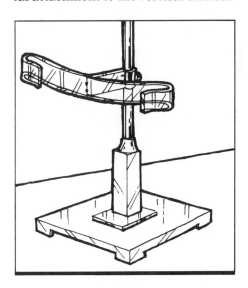

of a costumer, draper or valet through which a pair of slacks can be hooked and shown. It may also refer to a serpentine wire or plastic counter or ledge unit which will display slacks in a wavy, semi-fluted manner.

SLACKS FORM A three-dimensional sculptured form (male or female) of a pair of legs and hips that ends at the waistline or slightly above it. If the legs are crossed over—one leg will be removable to facilitate dressing the form. The form often is provided with a foot spike that will hold the form in an erect or standing position. See *pants form.*

SLANT BRACKET A bracket that is secured to a vertical surface at a 45- or 60-degree angle; it is *not perpendicular* to the vertical surface. The shelf that rests on this type of bracket must have a rim, lip, or shelf guard to prevent merchandise from sliding off; also called sloped shelf. Bracket and shelf are used to display and/or hold merchandise such as shoes, papergoods, magazines and placemats.

SLANT SHELF See *slant bracket.*

SLANT TOP STAND A t-stand with two descending waterfall arms. Similar in silhouette to an arrowhead.

SLAT A horizontal connecting bar or strip between two upright members such as the "slats" in a ladderback chair. Also, thin strips of wood or metal such as those used in Venetian blinds or "lath" wood.

SLATTED WALL, SLATTED FIXTURE Walls or fixtures faced

with horizontal strip or panels (2½ inches to approximately 4 inches wide) which are spaced a specific distance from each other. Especially designed Z-shaped hooks are attached to a wide range of available accessories to make it possible to snap brackets, shelves, hang rods, hangers or hooks in any desired arrangement onto the slatted area. It is simple to rearrange the attachments on the wall or fixture. The slats are made of wood, sometimes stained or varnished, but they can also be covered with vinyl fabrics or laminates.

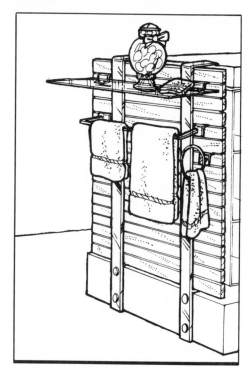

SLATE A clayish stone that splits into fairly flat tiles or plates. Used for paving or insets into floors or outdoor walks; also for roofing.

SLEEPER A surprise hit! An unexpected and often unpublicized item that "takes off" and becomes very popular—and profitable.

SLEEPERS The shallow wood strips placed over a concrete floor and then covered with a finished wood floor. This "bed" between the finished floor and the concrete base "gives" and makes standing or walking on the wood floor more comfortable.

SLEEVE PADS Flattened, sausage-shaped cushions used to pad out or fill in the sleeves of coats and jackets shown on armless coat or suit forms. They add dimension and form to what would otherwise be limp appendages. Usually associated with the rigging of men's wear. See *rigging*.

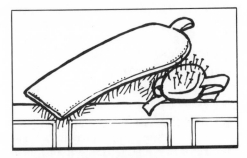

SLIDING ATTACHMENT An attachment that can be raised or lowered on the vertical shaft of a displayer. Usually equipped with a set screw or simi-

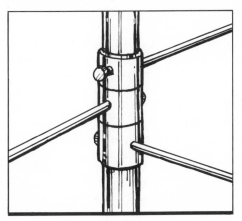

lar tightening device to secure the attachment at a given level once it has been set.

SLIMLINE FLUORESCENT LAMP An instant-start, hot-cathode fluorescent lamp with a ballast circuit which supplies from 400 to 1000 volts to start the lamp. It usually has a single pin base and requires only one connection at each end of the lamp.

SLOPED SHELF See *slant bracket*.

SLOTTED A pattern of regularly spaced vertical cuts or slots. Often tubes or channels are slotted and brackets are designed to fit into the slots. See *Garcy* and *standards*.

SMALL SCREW BASE See *candelabra base bulb*.

SMOCK A garment used to protect clothes while individual is working.

SMOCKING Rows of stitching to hold fabric together in a decorative pattern and to give fabric stretch.

SMOOTH PLANE A plane, usually about 9 inches long, used for planing short pieces of lumber parallel to the grain of the wood. It can shave or pare down a surface to an accurate dimension.

SNOOD A coarse hairnet designed to hold a person's hair in place at the nape of the neck. Often made of decorative fibers or ornamented with jewels, ribbons, flowers, etc.

SOBO See *polyvinyl white resins*.

SOCKET *1*. A hollow receptacle with spiral ridged sides that is meant to receive and hold an electric lightbulb mechanically and connect it electrically to circuit wires. *2*. An opening, cavity, or receptacle into which another element can be attached, bolted or screwed. A hollow depression.

SOCLE A square pedestal or base, usually untrimmed and unmolded, designed to hold a piece of artwork, a mannequin or form or a cabinet or drawer unit.

SODIUM VAPOR LAMP A light source mostly used in street lighting. It is based on an electric discharge into the sodium vapor to produce a yellow light. It approximates the maximum luminosity in the spectrum. The sodium vapor lamp is very efficient and can have a lamp life of up to 20,000 hours, but at present, is not good for merchandise presentation since it changes the color of the object it lights.

SOFFIT The finished underpart of an arch, lintel, overhead ducting system, cornice or other spanning unit. The side most often seen by anyone looking up.

SOFT ART SCULPTURE Designs and forms created from "soft" materials such as vinyl, rubber, fabrics, plastics, string, yarn and fiberglass. It is often soft and limp, pliable and/or reshapable.

SOFT GOODS All fashion merchandise and accessories, also linens, piece goods, draperies, etc. See *hard goods*.

SOFTWARE Procedures and materials used to set up computer programs.

SOFT WIG A realistic, soft and washable mannequin wig. The wig often has a degree of curl or wave baked into the man-made fibers, which are used in the wig construction. The resettability of the "hair" will depend upon the original degree of curl. Soft wigs are usually made of Elura or Kanekalon fibers. Also see *hard wig*.

SOFTWOODS The wood of the evergreens or conifer trees such as pine, cypress, spruce, cedar, fir and redwood. These woods are sometimes more difficult to stain or paint because of the graining and surface imperfections. Also see *hardwoods*.

SOLAR HEAT Heat trapped from the sun's rays and utilized in the production of heat and/or heat energy.

SOLDIER ARCH A flattened arch, rather than the traditional semicircular construction, usually constructed of bricks laid on edge and used over lintels of doors or windows.

SOLID MASONRY WALL A solid wall construction with a filling of mortar; no air spaces between the inner and outer walls.

SOLVENT A component with the ability to dissolve or loosen another component. Turpentine is a solvent in an oil-base paint, while water serves the same purpose in a latex-base paint.

SOMBRERO A wide, upturned brim hat, usually made in felt and trimmed with lace or ball fringe. It is part of the traditional Spanish or Mexican man's costume. The sombrero is also executed in straw for the farmer or peon.

SOUNDPROOFING A form of insulation to deaden sound in an area. Used inside walls, above drop ceilings, and under floors. See *acoustical materials*.

SOUTACHE A decorative binding or trimming material—a rounded braid.

SPACE DIVIDER See *divider*.

SPACKLE See *spackling*.

SPACKLING The process of using spackle (a putty-like or plaster substance) to fill small holes or correct imperfections in a surface. Spackle is freely applied to the imperfection and, when it dries, the excess spackle is sanded and the area smoothed out.

SPANDEX A generic term for a man-made elastic fiber which has good stretch and recovery properties and is lighter than rubber. It is important in the manufacture of lingerie, underwear, swimwear and ski wear.

SPANDREL A triangular block or filler between a vertical and a horizontal member in a construction. A reinforcing block that can also be a graphically pleasing addition to the design.

SPANDREL STEPS The triangular-shaped treads in a stairway.

SPANDREL WALL The part of the curtain wall above the top of the window of one story and below the windowsill of the window of the next story.

SPECIAL EVENTS Promotions and store activities produced by the advertising and/or display departments that go beyond the usual merchandise or seasonal promotions: fashion shows, "Import Fairs," Santa's visit to Toyland, and Easter egg hunt for children of the community, a contest or gallery showing of local arts and crafts, etc. See *goodwill*.

SPECIALTY STORE A store that concentrates on a particular type of merchandise. For example, full-figured woman's clothing, children's clothing, tennis, luggage, books, shoes, and jewelry. In more general terms, term refers to a store carrying fashion and accessories only.

SPECIFICATIONS The exact details, measurements, materials, etc., that are stipulated for a given project, job or construction. See *elevation, plan,* and *stress*.

SPECIFIC ILLUMINATION Form-revealing, highlighting and attention-getting lighting used to focus the viewer's attention to a specific object or area. This form of lighting is often accomplished with spotlights and/or concentrated beams of light—sometimes through a colored filter.

SPECTRAL COLORS The colors produced as a beam of white light passes through a prism. The spectral colors are violet, indigo, blue, green, yellow, orange, and red.

SPECTRUM The total range of spectral colors of varying wavelengths. The longest rays create red while violet is produced by the shortest.

SPINDLE A thin, grooved and shaped rod. A thin baluster. A small, twisted column.

SPIRAL COSTUMER A corkscrew or descending waterfall extended out from a central upright post or column; a full round or almost full round merchandise displayer, not a circular or round rack.

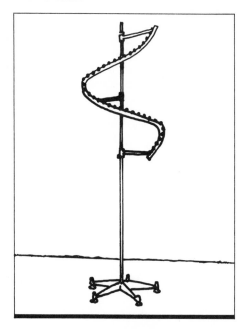

SPIRAL STAIRCASE A series of rising steps, usually triangular or spandrel, that wind around a central vertical shaft. A "winding" staircase. Also see *screw stair*.

SPIT OUT A blemish, bubble or discoloration that may appear on the surface of an electroplated metal; sometimes causes the plated surface to lift or peel off. Usually results from the improper preparation of a surface or the presence of moisture in the air during the electroplating process.

SPLAY An angled or beveled surface. A vertical or horizontal surface that does not continue in a perpendicular or parallel line, but angles out. Splay is a shortened form of "display" since more area is visible when a floor, wall or return is splayed. See *raked window*.

SPLICE *1.* A method of connecting two or more pieces of lumber in such a way that the combined pieces will be as strong and rigid as an equivalent single piece of lumber. The splice that will prove most efficient for compression or where it must sustain weight or exert pressure (the finished splice or the halved splice) may not be the most satisfactory where tension is the problem. In the latter case a square splice would be more effective. *2. (As illustrated)* A joint formed by overlapping, binding or twisting together two or more wires or members. It is a way of extending an electric conducting wire or patching ripped or torn film.

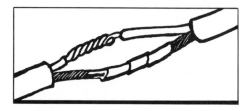

SPLICER A hollow tube with two threaded ends, that serves as a connector or joiner between two pipes or tubes.

SPLINE A thin strip of wood or extender used between two pieces of wood being joined as well as the process of connecting the two pieces. Similar to a mortar and tenon joint.

SPOT CHECK An unannounced or unscheduled "on-the-spot" inventory. A quick, unscientific and not very thorough count of merchandise on the floor or in stock, or of sizes still available. Spot check is done to enable the buyer or retailer to determine how an item is selling and, if item is running low, needs to be reordered.

SPOTLIGHT An electric bulb that throws a sharp, concentrated beam of light with a distinct edge. See PAR *lamp*.

SPRINGER A term used in construction for the jumping off place for an arch.

SPRING-LOADED POSTS Vertical members with retractable spring-like cap and/or foot pieces, which make it

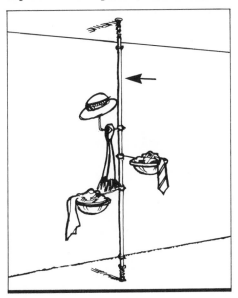

possible to wedge the upright unit between the floor and a surface (such as the ceiling) above. The tension of the spring against the unyielding top and bottom surfaces makes the column or post rigid, secure and capable of bearing or supporting other elements. Also called *vertical tension rods*.

SPRINKLER, SPRINKLER SYSTEM An automatic system to put out fires. The sprinklers are connected to water pipes set into the ceiling, and the water valve set below the ceiling will melt at a low heat point thus releasing the flow of water from the pipes. Because of the low heat point, direct spotlights or other heat-generating items should be kept at a safe distance from the sprinkler caps.

SPUN GLASS See *angel's hair*.

SQUARE *1.* A right-angled instrument, usually of steel or rigid plastic. Used for trueing squares or right angles. *2.* A rectangle with four equal sides: one pair parallel to each other and the other pair perpendicular to the first pair and parallel to each other. To find the approximate *diagonal* of a square: multiply a side by 1.414. To find the *area* of a square: multiply one side × one side. To determine the *perimeter* or measurement of the outer boundary of a square: perimeter + side × 4.

SQUARE NECKLINE A straight, deep neckline with straight upright lines that form the shoulders of the garment.

SQUEEGEE A flat wooden bar with a hard rubber edge or blade. Used in the silk screening process to pull the paint across the screen. See *silk screen*.

STABILIZER See *leveler*.

STAINLESS STEEL A steel alloy with a bright, silvery color; resistant to tarnish, rust and corrosion. It is similar to a "brushed" or "satin" chrome finish.

STAIRWAY DISPLAYER A progression of elevations to show small and related merchandise. It may be a simple arrangement of short risers with treads wide enough to accommodate small accessories such as leather goods, shoes and cosmetics or more complex such as a spiral staircase or a library stepstool. See *build-up* and *risers*. Also called step displayer.

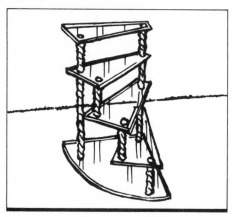

STANCHION A vertical rod or post resting on a heavy or weighted floor base. Often used in series and linked to one another by means of rope or

chain to form a temporary barrier or aisle.

STANDARDIZATION The establishment of specific sizes, procedures, programs, criteria, etc., to which all future projects will be compared. See *prototype*.

STANDARDS *1.* Criteria. The basis of judgment or decision-making. *2.* Vertical U-shaped channels of metal (or metal in wood or plastic frames) applied to walls, columns or any flat, vertical surface. The flattened face of the squared "U" channel is slotted with short, vertical cuts at regular and specific intervals. Brackets in assorted sizes and shapes are made with metal tabs or hook-shaped projections that snap into the standards' slots and lock when tapped. Other accessories, such as shelf supports, are also made to fit into these slots. Slotted standards make it possible to have complete height adjustability within the confines of the standards' length. Standards are available in various lengths, strengths, width and depth of channels, number of slots and, in various distances between the slots, etc. Standards are usually manufactured in steel or aluminum and in finishes such as chromeplated, zinc, brushed brass, bronze, antique copper, assorted enamelled colors or covered with a simulated wood-grain plastic. Most slotted uprights are provided with pre-drilled screw holes which facilitate attachment to wall surfaces— preferably into studs. When applying standards into a part of the wall that is not backed up by a stud, an expansion-type hollow wall anchor is recommended. Fiber or plastic anchors can be used in solid brick or masonry surfaces after the correct size hole is drilled into the wall with a carbide-tipped masonry bit. See *Garcy.*

STAPLE GUN See *stapler.*

STAPLER A tool—usually hand-held—for fastening papers, fabrics, etc., by means of clinching a wire staple through the various thicknesses of materials. Some staplers work like hand pliers and can be used to make quick (temporary) hems or seams, while others are particularly suited for applying papers and fabric panels to walls. Heavier models—often power-driven—can actually be used in light construction work or packing.

STAR RACK A variation of the four-arm or quad rack with arms overlapping at the inner junction. Similar to a pinwheel in configuration.

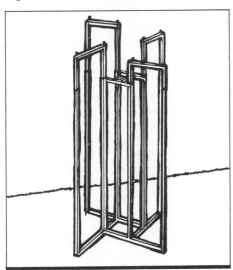

STATUARY BRONZE An antiqued, brushed, golden-brown metallic finish. An attempt to reproduce the color of statuary cast in bronze and rubbed for highlights. See *bronze.*

STEAMBOAT GOTHIC See *bargeboard.*

STEEL ENGRAVING A technique in graphics reproduction in which a very thin film of steel is electrolytically deposited onto a copper plate. It is possible to make many clear reproductions without affecting the fine lines on the plate. Prior to the use of steel, the softer copper plate wore out more readily.

STEEL SQUARE A carpenter's square, made of steel. Used to indicate and correct right angles.

STEEL WOOL A mass of finely intermeshed and intermingled metal fibers, available in a variety of grades (fine to coarse). Used for fine finishing or polishing wood or metal surfaces.

STEM-SUSPENDED FIXTURES A term for lighting fixtures that hang down from the ceiling by rigid metal tubes of desired lengths. Electric wires are enclosed within these tubes. See *droplight.*

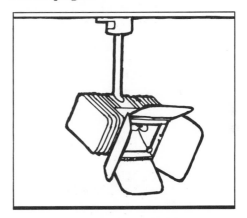

STENCIL Cardboard, metal, plastic, fabric or a specially prepared tough, oil-impregnated paper that is prepared in such a manner as to provide a cutout impression area as well as a surrounding masking area. Used to transfer design onto another surface.

The design is drawn onto and then cut out; the uncut area is the mask which will protect the surface around the open design area. See *silk screen* and *stenciling*.

STENCILING A method for transferring an allover or special motif or pattern cut onto a stencil onto a flat surface. The cutout area of the stencil is treated with colored paints or dyes. Color may be sponged on, dry brushed, squeegeed or sprayed, but care must be taken to avoid getting color under the edges of the masked area. If properly prepared and treated, the same stencil may be used many times.

STEP ARRANGEMENT Merchandise shown in a step-up arrangement; each item raised above the previous one.

STEP DISPLAYER See *stairway displayer*.

STEREOBATE The foundation or basement of a building. The continuous platform or pedestal under a wall.

STEREO PAINTINGS See *holographs*.

STETSON HAT Originally produced as a quality hat by John Stetson of Philadelphia in the 1870s. Trade name for a man's hat manufacturer. A high crown, brimmed hat; a ten-gallon hat; the American cowboy hat.

STICK See *roll (of wallpaper)*.

STILE The vertical strips between panels of wood or glass; the vertical separating bars. The horizontal bars are called "rails."

STILL LIFE A painting or graphic representation of inanimate objects such as flowers, fruit and books, or a decorative arrangement of accessories.

STILLSON WRENCH A large, hand-held vise with a pair of clamp-like jaws that can be brought together and secured or set by means of a knurled ratchet device located above the holding handle.

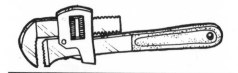

STIPPLING A painting technique which creates a textural and decorative finish. A stiff, fairly dry brush or semi-dry sponge is applied to the surface and *quickly* picked up without any attempt at blending or melding the color. The resulting effect can be similar to a flat, stucco-like finish.

STOCK A starched neck cloth originally wrapped twice around the neck and buckled in the back. Eventually gave way to the cravat, but it is still part of the formal riding attire of both men and women.

STOCKING FORMS Flesh-colored, three-dimensional plastic leg shapes, usually with hollow tops; available in assorted lengths depending upon the type of merchandise to be displayed, such as thigh-high, knee-high, or calf high. The forms are often shown with the instep arched and the "weight" on the ball of the foot. Some stocking forms are two-dimensional with a twist, which are presented with the thigh end as the base of the form.

STOLE A long straight scarf made of fabric or fur and often with decorative bands or tassles at the ends. See *boa*.

STORE DIVISION Major groups of a store such as merchandising, controller, operating, personnel, sales promotion and often in larger stores, branch-store division.

STORE'S OWN BRAND The store's name and label appears on the product rather than the name and label of the manufacturer.

STOVE BOLT A connecting piece of hardware with a threaded shaft and a head that is slotted like a screw.

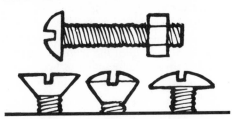

STRAIGHT STAIR An uninterrupted flight of stairs.

STRAIGHT STORE FRONT The store entrance and its display windows are aligned and parallel to the street. See illustration of *bank (of windows)*.

STREET ART The whole range of art in the open: outdoor sculpture; graffiti on walls, trains and sidewalks; giant murals on the sides of buildings; painted signboards; "happenings" or "street theater." In many cases street art makes political statements. See *street theater*.

STREET THEATER Display windows commenting on current social or political controversial issues; often shocking, always attention-getting. Especially popular in the larger urban areas during the 1970s. See *street art*.

STRESS The reaction of a material or structure to the weight load applied to it or on it. Certain building materials will carry "X" amount of weight per square foot and, in determining the materials to specify, the designer or engineer must know how much of a load the materials will be expected to carry.

STRETCHER *1. (As illustrated)* The connecting bar or brace between two uprights. Also between chair or table legs. It can be decorative as well as functional. *2.* The long, straight flat edges of a brick—the long faces.

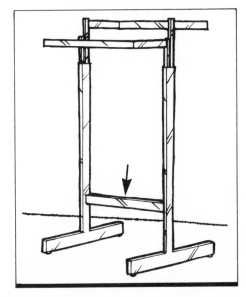

STRIP CENTER A small group of stores clustered together, often along a road or highway; a group of independent enterprises joined together for a common good.

STRIP LIGHTING Long lines of exposed fluorescent fixtures on a ceiling.

STRIPLIGHTS A broad term that includes borderlights, footlights, cyclorama border or footlights, and backing striplights. A striplight usually consists of a row of individual reflectors, each containing one lamp and a round glass color-medium that covers the entire top rim of the reflector. Striplights are usually wired in three or four circuits for the primary colors (red, green and blue) and possibly one for white. The color media or roundels are interchangeable, as are the spot-lamps for flood lamps and visa versa.

STROBE LIGHT A special-effects light that flickers or flashes on and off at a set rate (30 to 1500 flashes per minute); has no filament to burn out. Economical in the use of electric current. It creates stop-motion effects, similar to old-time movies, and it appears to slow down fast movements.

STRUT A horizontal separating and supporting construction member set between vertical supports; similar to an oversized stretcher.

STUB OUT The exposed and capped pipe ends or traps which are brought out from the wall or up from the floor, but to which plumbing or other water or waste fixtures have yet to be attached.

STUCCO A rough, stippled textured finish for interior or exterior walls. A compound of plaster or cement is troweled onto the walls and then sponged, combed or patterned. It can be tinted. See *composition* and *gesso*.

STUD *1.* A heavy, sturdy wooden post, usually 2″ × 4″, used in the construction of walls and partitions. *2.* A large decorative nailhead, often dome-shaped, made of copper, brass or other metallic or enamel finish.

STUFFER The coarse, firm fiber, similar to jute, used for the carpet construction. The weft and woof fibers are woven into it.

STYLE The obvious elements of a design. The specific characteristics, motifs and materials that make up the look and special qualities of a particular period in time or trend.

STYRENE See *polystyrene.*

STYROFOAM A lightweight, porous material available in sheet or log form. It can be carved, shaped, shredded, painted with water soluble, paints or dyes and appliquéd. See *polystyrene.*

SUB-TEEN SIZES A retailing term for clothes designed for the junior high school girl (ages 9 to 13). The figure development at this age is: slight bust and hip development, more defined waistline, longer waisted bodices, but shorter than the young junior.

SUEDE A French word for "swedish" where this velvety finish for leather originated. Originally a finish on kid-skin, but the same soft, napped finish is available on baby lamb and calf-skin. It also may be simulated with natural and man-made fibers.

SUGGESTED RETAIL PRICE A retail price recommended by the manufacturer and often printed on the labels or boxes as the one suggested for use by the store.

SUMP A collection basin or an area to drain into.

SUNBURST PLEATS Stitched or pressed-in folds, narrower at the beltline and wider at the hemline.

SUNFAST A term applied to dyed fabric treated to resist fading caused by exposure to the sunlight.

SUPERGRAPHICS Environmental designs of huge scale often executed with a bright, rainbow palette. Generally simple, bold repetitive lines and forms. Used on walls, ceilings, columns, doors, etc., to "break" the dullness of box-like interiors, accentuate areas, create movement or flow between rooms or spaces, camouflage dated architectural details or decorate a wall without using wallpapers or a collection of graphics or wall arrangements. See *emblematic art.*

SUPERIMPOSED ORDER A structure in which each succeeding level has a different classic architectural order; Doric, followed by Ionic, Corinthian, Composite.

SUPERSTRUCTURE An extension fixturing unit set on top of a gondola, shelf unit, promotional table, rack, etc., to provide additional space for merchandise, display or both. See *top deck.*

SUPPORT ROD See *butt rod* and *foot spike.*

SURAH A silk fabric with a fine twill weave.

SURFACED LUMBER Lumber that is dressed or smoothed down by being run through a planer machine before being offered for sale. It may be smoother on one side only (S1S), finished on both sides (S2S), one edge only (S1E), both edges (S2E), or a combination of edges and sides (S1S1E or S1S2E, etc.). The most finished piece

of lumber would be finished on all four sides (S4S).

SURREALISM A 20th-century school of art that is a continuation of the art of Hieronymus Bosch, Goya, Odilon Redon, etc., as well as Nihilism, Dadaism and Cubism of the early 20th century. The art of the mind—beyond realism.

SUSPENDED CEILING See *hung ceiling.*

SWAG A suspended drape of fabric, foliage, etc., which is caught up and/or gathered at the elevated ends and bellies out and hangs lower in the middle.

SWASH LETTERS Ornamented and embellished letters. Often italic letters with flourishes added in to fill up the gap of the inclined stroke of the letter. The swashes extend beyond the body on which the main part of the character is found. Any unusual or odd letter added to a font for ornamental purposes.

SWEATER DRESS A knitted or crocheted garment; styled like a sweater.

SWEETHEART NECKLINE A neckline consisting of two arcs over the breasts that swoop back to the neck and leave the chest revealed but the shoulders covered.

SWITCHBOARD A portable or fixed panel with switches, dimmers, etc., used to control all the lights in a window or group of windows. By means of a switchboard, it is possible to turn specific lights on and off without having to climb or reach up to them.

SWIVEL SOCKET A socket with a 360-degree swivel joint between the screw in the socket end and the receptacle that receives the lamp or bulb. It is possible to rotate and direct the lamp or bulb into any direction—up or down. The swivel socket sometimes comes with an extension pipe before the swivel device.

SYCAMORE A whitish or light-brown, strong, tough, and heavy wood; stains well.

SYMMETRICAL BALANCE A regular arrangement of equal parts on either side of an imaginary axis thus creating equal halves or mirror images. A perfect and exact balancing of objects, colors, lines, etc.

SYNDICATE BUYING OFFICE See *buying group, buying office.*

SYNTHETIC FIBERS Materials made from chemical sources rather than natural elements. Also called man-made fibers.

SYSTEM A simple method of joining fixtures, merchandisers, dividing walls, screens, platforms, etc., of assorted lengths and dimensions to each other by means of molded connectors. The concept calls for easy assembly, few tools and the ability to disassemble and rearrange the parts when desired. See *Abstracta, Anchor-Lok, Apton, Cubicon, Klem, Opto,* and *Rocker-loc Systems.*

T

TABARD A sleeveless or short-sleeved garment that is open at the sides. Usually decorative and, sometimes, embroidered.

TABI A white, cotton sock with a separate area for the big toe. Worn indoors or outdoors by Japanese.

TABLEAUX The arrangement or grouping of mannequins and props into life-like scenes. A three-dimensional representation of a scene, an incident or an event.

TABLE GOODS Merchandise that sells off of aisle or dump tables.

TABLE SAW A one-horsepower, electric power saw with a 10″ blade. It has a tilting arbor, miter gauge and rip fence, and is heavy enough to do precision quality work. It both rips and miters the wood.

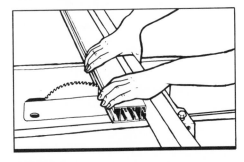

TAFFETA A crisp, plain weave fabric with equal warp and weft threads. Smooth and lustrous. Named for the Persian fabric "taftah."

TAILLEUR French for tailored suit.

TANK TOP A sleeveless jersey with a rounded neckline.

TAPA CLOTH A fiber cloth produced in the South Seas and often decorated in bold, bright allover patterns printed in vegetable and animal dyes. Used as decorative pieces.

TAPERED SAW A saw blade that is thicker at the base where the cutting teeth are located than above at the body of the blade.

TAPESTRY From the French "to line." A pictorial design woven during the manufacturing of the fabric. Originally used to line or cover drafty walls. Used in home furnishings and as decorative pieces.

TAPESTRY CARPET An uncut pile fabric woven on a velvet loom.

TAPPED HOLE A predrilled opening or one prepared for drilling.

TARGET MARKET The particular market based on age group, financial or social strata, taste level, etc., that the manufacturer or retailer hopes to appeal to and to attract.

TARLATAN An open-mesh fabric heavily sized and dyed in solid colors. Used for theatrical costumes.

TARNISH PROOF The ability of a material to resist discoloration or oxidation. The term usually refers to a material that has been sealed and/or coated with a clear plastic finish to keep the actual surface bright and shiny.

TARTAN A woven wool plaid fabric with the pattern and colors of a particular Scottish Highland family or clan.

TASK LIGHTING An expression used to describe specialized lighting for specialized purposes; brighter or more direct light at a specific area where a special "task" is being performed or where a specific object is being displayed. Non-uniform lighting.

TATAMI A woven matting of natural straw fibers and usually uneven. Used by Japanese for floor mats, wall coverings, etc.

TATTERSALL A check fabric of narrow, perpendicular crossing lines on a neutral-colored background. Originally a woven woolen fabric used for sporty vests. Named after a London sales room which dealt in racehorses and thoroughbreds.

TAXPAYER A term used in store planning for a commercial or semi-commercial building producing enough income to cover the taxes on the structure and the actual building investment, but not enough income to provide adequate returns on the value of the land, which has been used for the structure.

TEAK A light- to deep-brown wood with blackish streaks. Desirable for its attractive mottled or rippled figured surface as well as for its resistance to moisture, heat and insect attack.

TEASER The upper border or valance of a window. The horizontal, adjustable mask set closest to the window. Usually conceals lights and lighting equipment. It is adjustable and can be lowered to decrease the height of the window. See *mask* and *tormentor*.

TEDDY A women's one-piece undergarment which combines the features of a chemise and panties.

TEE-DISPLAYER, TEE-RACK In plan view; a T-shaped unit in which one member is perpendicular to the other; both members are joined in their centers. The flat surfaced member is usually the supporting element and the joining member is the hang rod, which is supported by a single leg at the end.

TEE-STAND A freestanding floor unit with a horizontal bar or rod on top, which will hold and display a very limited number of garments. Tee-stands are also designed with one straight arm and one waterfull, or with two waterfalls (see *slant top stand*), and depending upon the construction of the vertical support, the arms or rods may be individually adjustable, or adjustable as a unit. Since the tee-stand is a highlighting unit on the selling floor, it is available in

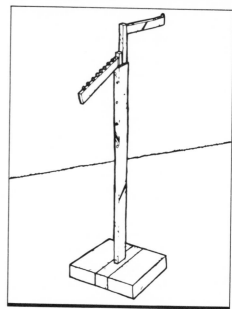

many materials, finishes, and with decorative bases, details, finials, etc.

TELESPAR Trademark for telescoping square tubing. Also available perforated for adjustable shelving units. Used in fixturing and store planning.

TEMPERA A quick-drying, flat water-based paint. Also called poster paint. Similar to gouache. Originally tempera was applied to a panel coated with gesso. The colored pigment was combined with egg yokes and thinned with water. See *gesso* and *gouache*.

TEMPERED GLASS A safety glass which shatters into relatively harmless fragments when it breaks.

TEMPLET A pattern for a construction or design made of a heavyweight paper, board, wood, etc., in the exact shape and size of the design to be reproduced. Also spelled template.

TEN-GALLON HAT See *Stetson hat.*

TENON A projection from one piece of material that is shaped to fit into a groove or depression of another piece (mortise) to make a joint. See *mortise and tenon joint.*

TENSION POLE See *spring-loaded posts.*

TENT SILHOUETTE A simple, flaring garment that starts at the neckline and sweeps out to the hemline.

TERM, TERMINUS A pedestal or base that tapers as it goes down to the floor. An inverted truncated obelisk.

TERRACE *1.* A raised or above-the-level piece of land of the surrounding ground; a flat, hard-surfaced area surrounded by a balustrade or low retaining wall. The terrace is often flanked or adjacent to a structure or building. *2.* A continuous row of connected houses.

TERRA COTTA Baked earth. A reddish-brown clay shaped and molded into forms, figures and decorative items and then baked to harden. The clay may be painted or glazed, or left in its natural matte finish.

TERRAZZO A floor-surfacing material, like concrete, which is made up of small pieces of crushed marble and cement. A hard, durable and decorative material that can also be used on walls.

TERRY CLOTH A loopy and nubby fabric made of cotton or blends of cotton and other fibers. Highly absorbent. Used for toweling as well as sportswear for men, women and children. Also called Turkish toweling.

TEVIRON See *wigs.*

TEXTILITE See *melamine formaldehydes.*

TEXTURE The surface pattern or feel of a paper, fabric, wall, etc. See *combing, eggshell finish* and *stucco.*

THAI SILK Handwoven silks of Thailand. Most Thai silks are in rich, full colors, often slubbed.

THATCH ROOF A roof covering of reed or straw, usually associated with Elizabethan and half-timber houses—or provincial farm houses.

THEATRICAL GAUZE A lightweight cotton or linen fabric in a plain, open weave. The semisheer fabric is often sized for body and available in a variety of widths—including extra wide widths for theatrical use (borders and overhead cutouts). Used in window displays and for decorative semitransparent panels.

THERMOFORMING A process for forming a sheet of plastic into a three-dimensional shape. The sheet is clamped into a frame, heated to make it soft and fluid, then pressure formed (see *vacuum forming*) to conform with the shape of the mold or die below the frame. Used in point-of-purchase displays and decoratives. See *thermoplastic*.

THERMOPANE INSULATING GLASS Trademark of LOF Glass, a division of Libby-Owens-Ford Company, for a factory-fabricated unit composed of two or more pieces of glass separated by a sealed space containing dry air. Used for insulation. See *insulation*.

THERMOPLASTICS Plastic or resin compounds which in their final state can be softened and reshaped over and over again by increasing the temperature around them. The plastic material sets or rehardens when cooled. See *bakelite* and *thermoforming*.

THERMOSETTING PLASTICS Resin or plastic compounds that are insoluble and infusible in their final state. Most thermosetting resins are in a liquid state at some point in the process and are cured, hardened or set by heat, catalysts or other chemical means. Once cured, this group of resins and plastics cannot be reshaped, reliquified or reformed. Also called thermosets.

THERMOSTAT An electric switch activated by changes in temperature.

THIRTEENTH MONTH A retailing term for the five selling days between Christmas and New Year's.

THOMPSON PROCESS See *welding*.

THREADED A term used to describe the fine, spiraling, corkscrew groove around a tube or rod. It can be rotated into a socket with a similar ridging or grooving, for example a lightbulb into an electric socket. See *nipple*.

THREE-PART RACK A circular rack made up of three equal arcs, often each may be adjustable in height; a single unit with three adjustable sections or three separate arcs. It is possible to have all the spatial advantages of a circular rack and the adaptability and display potential of a merchandiser to show coordinated garments on one fixture. Also see *round rack*.

THREE-QUARTER FORM A three-dimensional body form with head, arms and parted legs that end at the knees or just below the knees. Often used on ledges or where there is insufficient height to accommodate a full, standing mannequin. Also called three-quarter mannequin.

THREE-QUARTER MANNEQUIN See *three-quarter form.*

THREE-SHEET POSTER An outdoor advertisement 41″ × 82″ high. See *billboard.*

THUMBNAIL A quick, rough, idea sketch, usually one of many, undetailed and unspecified; a layout of line, form, mass and possibly color. See *croquis* and *rough.*

THUMBSCREW BRACKET A bracket designed to fit into a slotted standard and equipped with a knurled screw at the hook-in end. By turning the screw, the bracket is held more securely into the slots of the standard. See *knurled screw* and *standards.*

TICKING A broad term for a sturdy, tightly woven fabric used to cover pillows and mattresses. Decorative and strong enough for other uses. The striped pattern associated with ticking is available as a wallpaper ground.

TIERS Layers or rows set above or behind each other at different heights, such as the ascending rows in a mezzanine or balcony.

TIGHTS Skin-fitting garments covering the hips and legs. Made of clinging, stretch-knit fabrics. Used alone by dancers, acrobats, skaters and gymnasts, or worn under abbreviated skirts or shorts. See *leotards.*

TIMBER TOPPER Trademark for tension spring mechanisms made to fit on the top and bottom of 2″ × 3″ pieces of lumber. The lumber is then wedged into an upright (or horizontal) position between the floor and ceiling (or between two walls) and held rigid by the tension of the springs at either end. See *spring-loaded posts.*

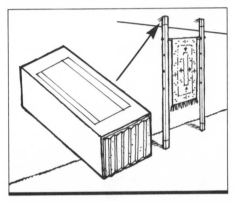

TINT A pastel or lighter version of a color or hue. A color with white added to soften the look.

TINTYPE An early form of photographs with a limited contrast range; whites were usually more gray than white.

TISSUE PAPER A lightweight, semi-transparent paper generally associated with wrapping and stuffing. Available in a multitude of colors. Its stiff, glazed, crinkled crispness has a decorative value.

TISSUES A broad term for thin and semi-sheer fabrics.

TIVOLI LIGHTS Small, clear decorative globular lamps of low wattage, with small or candelabra screw bases. Generally used in clusters, in groups or in continuous rows for decorative graphic designs in light rather than for actual illumination of areas or merchandise. Named for the flamboyant light outlines used in the amusement park, Tivoli, in Copenhagen.

T-LAMP See *showcase lamp.*

TODDLER SIZES A retailing term for sizes 1T, 2T, 3T and 4T. For children that walk, but are usually not over three years of age. These children generally are chubby with short waistlines and bulging "tummies."

TOE CAP Also called footpiece. A protective, sometimes decorative, device attached to the bottom end of a vertical supporting element or leg in fixturing or furniture design. In structural systems using hollow tubes, the toe cap may be the plug at the end of the tube. The footpiece also serves to protect the floor surface under the leg from being marred or scratched. Also see *top cap.*

TOGGLE A rod-shaped fastener, usually wood, attached by a loop. Fastened by a similar loop which catches around the toggle.

TOGGLE RAIL A horizontal cross member on the frame of a scenic "flat." Used to strengthen and to hold square the shape of the outside framing. Used in scenic design. See *flat*

and *rail.* Also see illustration under *diagonal brace.*

TOILE, TOILE DE JOUY Handblocked, screened or printed designs on a natural or white sturdy cotton, linen or silk base. The designs are usually "provincial" in subject matter and are based on the "indienne" designs produced in Jouy, near Versailles, in the 18th and 19th centuries. The patterns are generally printed in one color on the neutral ground. Originally a linen- or canvas-like fabric used by artists as a surface for paintings.

TÔLE From the French for "sheet iron." Objects made from sheet metal or tin, such as lamp shades, trays, boxes and small decoratives, and then painted or enamelled and ornamented.

TOLERANCE The permissable allowance for variation from a specified measurement, weight, etc. The slight difference from the proscribed.

TONE The shade or degree of light or dark of a color or hue.

TONGUE & GROOVE JOINT A type of wood joinery in which the long, narrow projecting edge of one piece of wood fits into the grooved edge of another piece of wood. A rectangular extension fitting into a recessed rectangular opening.

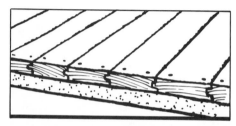

TONNEAU SILHOUETTE See *pegged skirt.*

TOP CAP The finishing plug or cover used to seal the exposed end of an open tube or rod. Used especially in modular systems on precut hollow tubes. Also see *toe cap*.

TOP COLOR In printing, the color placed on top of the ground or base color.

TOP DECK A superstructure on top of a rack or gondola to store additional merchandise, or to display one of the stored garments. See *superstructure*.

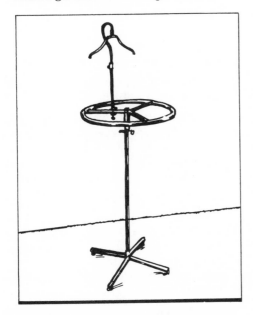

TOPIARY ART The clipping, cutting and shaping of trees and shrubs into decorative and fanciful forms, sometimes into animal and bird forms.

TOP STOCK Merchandise that is stored or displayed on top of a counter or showcase. An open display rather than a closed display. Also see *closed display*.

TOQUE A soft, brimless fabric hat. Fitted close to head.

TORMENTOR The vertical, adjustable masks of a window frame, valance or proscenium. Usually set close to the glass line and conceals the lighting equipment. It is adjustable and can be brought in to decrease the width of the window. Also see *mask* and *teaser*.

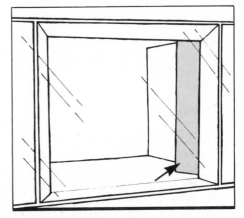

TORSO, TORSO FORM A full round, headless and armless body form that ends just above the knees. The average height is about 38″ for female

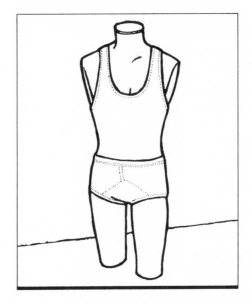

forms and 43″ for male forms. The form differs from the usual dress form in that the body line is more animated and the legs are parted and defined. Used to show bathing suits, lingerie and sportswear.

TOWER A tall, freestanding, merchandising unit on the selling floor which may be equipped with shelves or hang rails. It is open and full round with access to merchandise from all sides. Sometimes called an étagère. See *étagère*.

TOYOKALON See *wigs*.

TRACERY The arcs, lines and sweeps that appeared in Gothic architecture. The "cut-out" decorative designs in stone of Gothic windows separating the panels of colored glass.

TRACING CLOTH A translucent, semi-transparent cloth. Used to duplicate or trace artwork or designs.

TRACING PAPER A crisp, stiff, semi-transparent paper. Used to trace or copy by drawing over an existing design.

TRACK LIGHTING The arrangement of assorted spot- or floodlights, in decorative housings, on a channel or track, attached to a ceiling, wall or other surface with one end plugged into a source of electrical current. Length of channel may measure 4′, 6′, 8′, etc. Fixtures can be moved anywhere along the track, aimed at any position along the track and need not be turned on at the same time. Used for selective or task lighting. Also called overhead track. Track lighting may

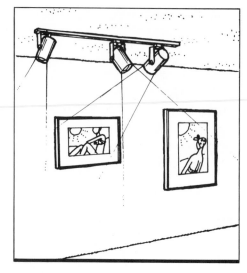

be either the primary or secondary type of store lighting.

TRADE ASSOCIATION Organizations involved in a specific market, or a particular industry. The organization may consist of manufacturers only (such as N.A.D.I.) or manufacturers plus customers (such as P.O.P.A.I.).

TRADE DISCOUNT Special price reductions or discounts for persons or companies who will resell the product. A complimentary discount to a person in the trade.

TRADEMARK According to the U.S. Trademark Association (U.S.T.A.) ". . . a word or design or a device or a combination of these used to designate the product of a particular company, organization or trade association . . . used to identify a single product or a line of products made by one manufacturer or sold by one company. It may also designate the services performed by a company of an organization . . . may be applied to products or services offered by members of a single trade association. *. . . never the generic term for the product . . .* used on goods, packaging, business documents, advertising, promotion and display."

TRADE SHOW An exhibition or joint showing of products or innovations by a trade association for a particular field or market. For example, a showing of display products by the N.A.D.I. membership for visual merchandisers and store planners.

TRADE TERMS The special prices, discounts, arrangements for sales and payments, etc., allowed by manufacturers or vendors to persons or companies in specific trades or fields.

TRADING DOWN Lowering image, ambience and target market of a store by presenting and stocking cheaper merchandise in an effort to attract lower-income level customers.

TRADING UP Raising the image, ambience and target market of a store by presenting and stocking upgraded and better merchandise. Bringing in better goods to make a better store.

TRAFFIC Amount of people who frequent an establishment.

TRAFFIC FLOW, TRAFFIC PATTERNS The movement of persons in a store or department; the directional flow. The customer's route up and down aisles, escalators, etc.; the pattern of predicted movement.

TRANSFORMER An electrical device which, by electromagnetic induction, transforms electrical energy in such a way that the energy remains unchanged while the voltage and current changes.

TRANSLUCENT A material such as glass, plastic or vinyl which permits the passage of light without an actual view. A semi-transparent quality similar to a window covered with a gauze curtain or tissue paper.

TRANSOM A cross piece that separates a door from a window directly above it, or the window placed above the door. A fanlight. See *fanlight.*

TRANSPARENCIES Positive images produced on transparent film—in black and white or in full color.

TRAPEZE SILHOUETTE Similar to the A-line and the tent silhouette created by Yves St. Laurent in the late 1950s. See *A-line silhouette* and *tent silhouette.*

TRAPS Openings in the floor of a stage or a window.

TRAPUNTO A design or motif is outlined in stitches and puffed with stuffing from behind.

TRAVERTINE A light beige onyx-type stone with irregular depressions and veining. Used as a facing material for interior and exterior walls. The color of the stone can be as deep as rust.

TRAY A flat, dish-like container with a short rim or lip. Used to hold merchandise.

TREAD The flat, horizontal part of the stairway; the step between the two risers.

TREADMILL A seemingly endless horizontal belt that moves across an area. It consists of narrow wooden slats, like a tambour, or a firm plastic material stretched between two rotating drums. The horizontal surface goes from one drum across to the other, arcs around the drum and then continues below the visible surface of the treadmill to the other drum, arcs up and once again becomes the visible, moving surface.

TRELLIS A criss-cross design made of wood, metal or plastic slats. A fretwork design. See *lattice*.

TRENCH COAT Originally the coat worn by the British officers in World War I. A full-length double-breasted coat trimmed with epaulets, gun flaps, and belted.

TREND A prevailing direction or course in which fashion styles or businesses are heading. A general tendency—a popular movement.

TRENDY A forward, high-fashion, attitude in merchandising. The presentation of the very newest in fashion concepts. See *attitude shop* and *avant garde*.

TRESTLE A supporting frame, often in the shape of an inverted "T," on a table or cabinet. Usually used in pairs.

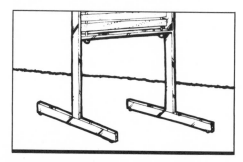

TRIAL PROOF See *artist's proof*.

TRIANGLE A closed plane figure consisting of three sides and three angles. *Right Triangle:* A triangle with two perpendicular sides or legs, at right angles (90°) to each other and one long side or hypoteneuse connecting them.

30-, 60-, 90- degree triangle. In a right triangle: $\text{leg}^2 + \text{leg}^2 = \text{hypoteneuse}$. Area of a right triangle: $\frac{1}{2} \times \text{leg} \times \text{leg}$. *Equilateral Triangle:* A triangle with three sides equal in length and three 60 degree angles. *Isosceles Triangle:* A triangle with two equal sides. *Obtuse Triangle:* A triangle with one angle greater than 90 degrees, but less than 180 degrees. *Acute Triangle:* A triangle with three angles each less than 90 degrees. *Area of a Triangle:* $\frac{1}{2} \times$ base (the bottom or width of a figure) $\times$ height [a line drawn from the top of the figure meeting the base at a right angle (90 degrees)].

TRICOT See *jersey*.

TRIM *1.* A broad term for woodwork frames around windows and doors, dadoes, coves and cornices, picture moldings, panel frames, etc. *2.* A molding strip or other decorative device used to cover joints and conceal imperfections in butting and joining. *3.* The arrangement of merchandise and props into a pleasing and selling composition. *4.* A holiday or promotional decorating scheme or theme, which is followed through in windows and the interior. *5.* The actual dressing of a mannequin or display area.

TRIM MARK The marks or lines used to indicate the end of a design or pattern, and where the excess can be cut off, removed or masked. The marks on a roll of printed or screened wallpaper which indicates the place to cut—to remove the selvage.

T-ROD An inverted T-shaped metal device serving as an easel base for the mannequin. The upright end secures into the butt fitting of the mannequin while the flat, horizontal bar rests on the ground.

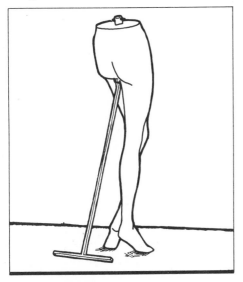

TROMPE L'OEIL The French term for "deceive the eye." A graphic technique for rendering objects with such skill as to look dimensional rather than painted or drawn on a flat surface. In Italian, this art form is called "quadrature."

TRUNK FORM A male body form that extends from above the waistline (the diaphragm) down to the knees or

slightly below. It is ideally suited for showing shorts, swim trunks, briefs and assorted underpants. Usually designed to wear a size 30. Longer forms will show more leg, while the shorter forms will be cut in mid-thigh.

TRUSS An arrangement of structural members to form a support for a wide span without the use of intermediate supports or members.

T-SQUARE A drafting or mechanical drawing aid by which parallel lines are drawn at right angles to the edge of a drawing board or table.

TUBULAR INCANDESCENT LAMPS "T" lamps. See *showcase lamps.*

TULLE A very fine net or gauze made of cotton, silk or man-made fibers. Used for millinery trim, bridal veils, and gowns.

TUNGSTEN FILAMENT LAMP An incandescent lightbulb with a tungsten wire filament. The tungsten wire has a high melting point and a low rate of evaporation. The bulb itself is filled with a mixture of argon and nitrogen.

TUNGSTEN HALOGEN LAMP An incandescent lightbulb which contains halogen gas in addition to the tungsten wire filament. The gas recycles the tungsten (which would ordinarily collect on the bulb wall) back onto the filament. It supplies an almost constant light output throughout the life of the bulb. It emits a slightly whiter light than the usual incandescent lamp.

TUNGSTEN IODINE LAMP See *tungsten halogen lamp.*

TUNIC Originally, the below-the-hip length garment worn by the ancient Greeks and Romans. *1.* A hip- or knee-length overgarment generally worn over a sheath or slim line skirt. *2.* A military jacket.

TURBAN An Oriental headdress of a long scarf of silk, linen or fine cotton, artfully wrapped and draped around the head—covering all the hair. Worn by Mohammedan men. Any headdress or hat that is draped and shaped to simulate the Oriental turban, or a variation thereof.

TURKISH TOWELING See *terry cloth.*

TURNBUCKLE A type of coupling or joining device having internal screw threads or nuts with opposite screws at the ends. By turning the internal screws, it is possible to connect two metal rods and regulate the length and tension of these rods.

TURNING A shaped dowel with nodules, bumps and bulges. A spindle.

TURNIP DOME A dome or cupola that often appears on churches in Slavic and Near Eastern countries. A bulbous shape—an inverted turnip—that overlaps the cylindrical structure below it.

TURNKEY LEASE A lease for a finished store or building in which all walls, partitions, floors, ceilings, elec-

trical installations, bathroom and water facilities, and general decoration have been completed. Usually ready for the merchant to move in with his own merchandise and any specific or special fixtures his operation may require. See *shell & allowance lease.*

TURNOVER *1.* The number of times merchandise is sold and replenished within a given period of time. *2.* The ratio of net sales per year divided by the average inventory—at retail.

TURNSTILE A one-way rotating device consisting of horizontal, revolving arms pivoted on top of a post. A method of controlling traffic in and out of an area.

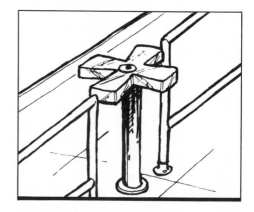

TURNTABLE A mechanically rotated horizontal plane or disk, sometimes set into a floor or platform, flush with the surrounding surfaces.

TURPENTINE A reducing or thinning and/or drying agent for oil-base paints and certain types of inks. A cleaning agent.

TURTLENECK A high and close-fitting, usually knitted, collar.

TUSCAN ORDER A classic order of architecture used by the early Romans, and the later Italian architects. Similar to the Doric, but of greater simplicity.

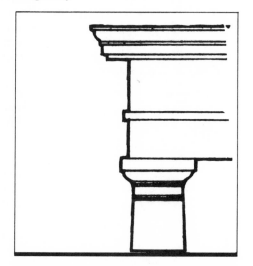

TUSCHE A special transfer ink composed of shellac, lampblack, wax, soap and/or tallow. Used in lithography, painting and drawing.

TUSSAH, TUSSEH, TUSSER, TUSSORE See *pongee, shantung* and *tissue.*

TUTU A filmy, many layered, bouffant skirt associated with classic ballet costumes.

TUXEDO See *dinner jacket.*

TUXEDO COLLAR Similar to a "shawl collar." A long, straight fold that goes around the neck and tapers down towards the waistline of the jacket or coat.

T-WALL A wall with a short, end cap used to divide or separate two areas on the selling floor. The short or "T" end, which is often parallel to the perimeter wall and approximately 5 feet wide, provides space for featured displays or for a special display fixture.

The divider wall generally carries hang rods, bins, or shelves for both areas.

TWEED A rough-surfaced, homespun material that is often woven in a check, plaid or herringbone pattern. See *Harris Tweed.*

TWILL *1.* A basic weave with a diagonal line in the surface finish. Herringbone is a variation of the twill weave. *2.* A type of fabric that is woven in this means.

TWINKLE LIGHTS Tiny, sparkling lights, of very low wattage, that are available in sets of 20, 36 or 40 lights to a string. Used to simulate flickering stars behind a gauze, silk or translucent panel and as Christmas tree decorations.

TWIST CARPET A firm and fairly wear resistant floor covering made of uncut, twisted yarns. The yarns or fibers may be of wool, nylon, acrilan, Herculon, etc.

TYPEFACE The style of letters, or characters in a particular appearance: size, thickness of stroke, with or without serif, degree of blackness, etc. Cast in metal in relief, mounted on wooden or metal blocks. Used in printing.

TWIG STORE A mini-branch store that often carries a partial or limited group of the total merchandise sold in the parent store; a women's fashion shop, a housewares shop, a furniture shop, an auto accessory shop. See *branch store.*

U

ULSTER A long, loose-fitting, heavy outercoat. Originally worn by men and women in northern Ireland, in Ulster. Made of a wool fabric called Ulster Frieze. Usually double-breasted and belted either all around or in the back only. Introduced into the United States in the early 20th century.

ULTRAVIOLET LIGHT See *black light.*

UMBRELLA COVER A woven, palm thatching, usually 7 to 9 feet in diameter. Used in decoratives, for example, it may be dropped over a beach or sun umbrella to create a tropical setting.

UMBRELLA SET-UP An architectural design firm that not only has architects and engineers on staff, but may also include landscape artists, interior designers and furniture specifiers, and store-fixturing specialists in their group. A design firm that can satisfy all the construction and furnishing needs for a client—inside and outside of the structure.

UNDERBRACING The braces and stretchers used to support a fixturing unit or a superstructure from the bottom such as a mezzanine.

UNDERCOAT The first or bottom coat; the preparation or priming on a wall, panel, etc., in readiness for a finished color or layer of paint. See *prime coat* and *size coat.*

UNDERFRAME The horizontal frame or panel of a table, case, cabinet, etc., which is directly supported by the legs or base of the unit.

UNDERPINNING Additional supports added to the foundation of a structure to reinforce the structure, especially during renovations when there may be drastic changes in the structure as shifting or weaknesses in the construction may appear.

UNICUBE SYSTEM Trademark for a group of structural, modular-type systems which combine round metal tubes by means of assorted joints or connectors. Some joinings are accomplished with finger-like connections that fit inside the round tubes to form "L," "T," "Y," "X," etc., arrangements. Another Unicube system is based on two identical, mating, die-cast segments which clamp down on the horizontal tubes as the internally threaded vertical tubes are tightened. Only the one universal connector is required. These systems are provided

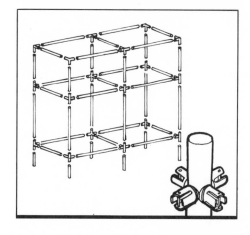

with various accessories and are available in a standard chrome finish, in brass and can be custom finished on special order.

UNION SHOP An agreement between management and a specified union which requires all workers to become members of that union after a probationary or testing period.

UNISEX Merchandise, materials and services that are applicable to both sexes. A "unisex" shop would sell clothes and/or appliances that could be used by both men and women. An active sportswear shop that sells tennis and jogging equipment could be a "unisex" shop.

UNIVERSAL JOINT A joint or connector which allows one or both members joined at this point free movement in any direction and at any angle.

UNPRESSED PLEATS Soft, unstitched or pressed down folds in the fabric that are allowed to gently fall or flare.

UPLIGHTS Store lighting fixtures that wash or light up the ceiling rather than the area below. See *ceiling washer*.

UPPER CASE The capital letters in a font of type.

UPSON BOARD See *fiberboard*.

UPSTAGE The back of a display window. The area farthest away from the glass line or the viewer.

U-RACK See *C-rack*.

URN A large vase or decorative container of pottery, wood or metal. An ornamental finial.

V

VACUUM FORMING The thermo-forming process in which a thermo-plastic material is shaped and formed by means of applying differential pressure to make the sheet conform to the shape of the die or mold positioned below the frame, which holds the sheet of plastic. Used in point of purchase displays and decoratives.

VALANCE A horizontal band, such as an interior curtain wall, which finishes off the area above the wall fixtures, the hang rods, bins or shelves. Also serves to hide any lighting that may be used to illuminate the merchandise in or on the wall units. Also called lambrequin. See *cornice, curtain wall,* and *lambrequin.*

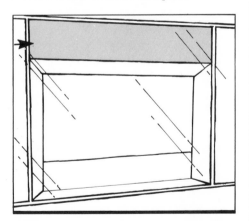

VALET A costumer for men's clothing displays which in addition to a contoured hanger on top of a vertical rod or frame may include attachments for the display of a shirt and tie, a pants clip, a shoe carrier, etc. A highlighting device. Usually decorative as well as functional. See *costumer.*

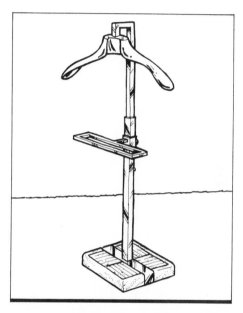

VALUE The light to dark variation of a color. A color or hue can be raised (lightened) by adding white or lowered (darkened) by adding black. See *shade, tint,* and *tone.*

VAN DYKE PRINT See *velox print.*

VANISHING POINT The point (or points) on the horizon (or eye level) to which all parallel, horizontal lines on one plane, or on parallel planes, appear to converge and meet. Also see *eye level, horizon* and *perspective.* (See illustration under *perspective.*)

VARIETY STORES Retail stores that sell a wide variety of inexpensive

211

items, such as a "five and ten cents store."

VARIETY WINDOW See *assortment window.*

VARNISH A liquid medium used to create a shiny, transparent, water-resistant finish. A sealant. A finish to brighten and preserve colors.

V.A.T. See *vinyl asbestos tiles.*

VAT DYES A type of dye in which cotton, linen, rayon and other vegetable fibers are made colorfast and will resist fading. The dye is applied to the fiber rather than to the fabric.

VAULT *1.* A semi-circular or barrel-shaped ceiling. *2.* An underground room or area. *3.* A large walk-in safe for storing precious materials or merchandise—a fur vault.

VEHICLE The liquid material in which the pigment or dye is mixed; responsible for the spread and coverage of that medium. See *casein paint* and *medium.*

VELCRO A non-metallic fastener consisting of two strips of specially treated fabric, each with thousands of tiny "grippers." Strips adhere to each other and to "open" one just pulls the strips apart. Trademark of Velcro Corporation.

VELLUM *1.* A natural or light-beige-colored paper with a texture and look of fine parchment, originally obtained from calf-skin. *2.* A heavyweight tracing paper.

VELON Extruded plastic filaments. Used to make plastic upholstery and wall coverings as well as webbing materials. Trademark of Firestone Plastics Co.

VELOUR French for velvet fabric. A smooth, lustrous, short pile knit or woven fabric.

VELOX A glossy photographic print produced from an original photo or piece of artwork which breaks up gray gradations into black and white dots and will reproduce as tones. These velox prints can be retouched and combined with line art and type proofs. Also called Van Dyke print.

VELVET A plushy, pile fabric. Velvet can be manufactured from a variety of fibers such as silk, rayon, cotton, or blends, which will affect the feel, luster and wearability of the finished fabric.

VELVET CARPET A cut pile floor covering which can be tightly woven with a short pile or loosely woven with a more open weave with a longer or "shag" pile.

VENDOR The seller. It can apply to the retailer selling to the consumer or the manufacturer (or his representative) selling to the retailer. The term is usually applied to the latter situation.

VENDOR MONEY A contribution in money or materials by a manufacturer to a retail store to help cover the cost of promoting the manufacturer's product. It may be in the form of a television commercial, by the manufacturer, which gives the store's name as where the product is available, or it may be a partial or full payment for a store's ad in a newspaper. It can also be in the form of fixtures or props supplied to the store at a minimal cost, or at no cost at all. See *cooperative advertising, cooperative display.*

VENEER A better or more decorative material to face or cover a body of coarser material. Thin slices of wood (1/16″ to 1/32″ in thickness) which are cut through the vertical section of a log or flitch. Used in cabinetry, store planning and interior design.

VENETIAN BLINDS Window coverings consisting of a multitude of horizontal slats made of wood, metal, plastic, etc., joined together by vertical tapes and cords, which end in pulleys to control raising, lowering and slanting of the blinds or the individual slats. Used to filter sunlight. See *vertical blinds*.

VENT A passageway for air, or a duct through which air moves. Usually a louvered opening into a hollow tube or tunnel through which air is drawn or passed.

VERANDA A wide, sun-shaded porch or patio attached to a house or building. It is often associated with the late 19th- and early 20th-century one family residences, especially on the Shingle style or Steamboat-Gothic houses.

VERDIGRIS The blue-green coating or patina that forms on metals such as copper, brass and bronze when the metals have been exposed to the elements for a period of time. Also, a decorative finish of gray-blue-green color on wrought iron furniture and fixtures.

VEREL Trademark of the Eastman Kodak Company for a modacrylic fiber. Used for fire-resistant fabrics and carpeting.

VERTICAL BLINDS A continuous vertical pattern of strip blinds made of lightweight metal strips, fabric or wood slats. Used to cover windows, as dividers or screens in open back windows, or interior separators. They can be colored and pattern-coordinated to the interiors. The fabric or vinyl strips are removable and interchangeable. Also called *Boston blinds*.

VERTICAL TENSION RODS See *spring-loaded posts*.

VEST A sleeveless garment ending just below the waistline and often with a V-neckline. Traditionally worn under a jacket in a man's "three-piece suit."

VICRTEX A wall covering and upholstery fabric of electronically fused vinyl sheeting. Available in a wide range of colors, textures and patterns. Trademark of L.E. Carpenter & Co.

VICTORIAN LETTERING One of the many variations of the "Gay '90s" style of type—ornate and curleycued, sometimes partially shaded. Reminiscent of the circus "Barnum," old-fashioned and Early Americana styles of lettering.

VIDENE See *polyester*.

VIGNETTE *1.* A design or ornament with washed-out or faded edges; not confined or restricted by a border or frame. *2.* A design of meandering and intertwining vines and leaves. From the French word for "small vines." *3.* See *vignette setting*.

VIGNETTE SETTING A display that is semi-realistic and suggests rather than shows a complete room or place. It is the essence of the area that is presented and some of the details are omitted in favor of a few basics which create the effect. A crystal chandelier, a table covered with a long white cloth, two elegant gold chairs, a wine cooler and a few potted palms and the setting could be an elegant restaurant —a hotel room—a romantic tryst for two. A suggestion or fragment of a total entity.

VINYL Fabrics of fused or coated vinyl plastics. Drapable, pliable and resistant to peeling. Used for upholstery or wall coverings. See *Naugehyde* and *Vicrtex*.

VINYL ASBESTOS TILES A flooring material similar to asbestos tile but more resilient and with more "give" underfoot. It is resistant to oil, grease and some acid stains, easy to maintain, wears well and will not crack or chip as readily as asbestos tile. Available in a wide range of colors, patterns and textures depending upon the manufacturer.

VINYL TILE A tile, similar in feel to a rubber tile but resistant to oil, grease, moisture and mildew. Available in a range of colors, textures and patterns; can be made in white and very pale pastels or high, bright fashion colors. Because it is "soft" and resilient, vinyl tiles will scuff and scratch and can be dented.

VISE A mechanism with two parallel, ridged jaws and a radial screw closing device that brings the jaws together. The element that is to be held rigid is set between the two jaws and the vise is tightened till the jaws are close enough to hold the element firmly and securely. The vise is usually attached to the work bench to secure the work at hand while drilling, sawing, sanding, etc.

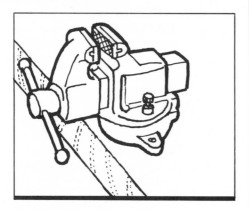

VITREOUS ENAMEL A shiny, porcelain finish fused onto a metal base.

Popular for wall cladding, exterior signs, or any surface which must withstand the affects of weathering.

VITRINE A glass enclosed cabinet or showcase. Used as a storage and/or display unit. A see-through cabinet with glass partitions that display and protect the objects contained within. Often a period design with glass shelves, glass front, and sides; ornate legs, apron and cap. A "china closet." Also called cabinet vitrine.

VIYELLA Trademark for an English fabric made of wool combined with cotton in a twill weave.

"V" NECKLINE A neckline that cuts down to a sharp point at the chest or bustline. A plunging "V" descends past the cleavage.

VOILE A lightweight, sheer fabric that can be woven from cotton, wool, silk, man-made fibers or blends.

VOLT A unit of "electromotive force" (e.m.f.). When one e.m.f. is applied to a conductor with a resistance of one ohm, a current of one ampere will be produced.

VOLUME The gross earnings based on the retail value of the total merchandise sold in a year.

VOLUME OF GEOMETRIC FORMS
Volume of Rectangular Solid = length × width × height.
Volume of a Cube = edge × edge × edge.
Volume of a Cylinder = Π (3.14) × radius × radius × height.
Volume of a Sphere = 4/3 × Π × radius × radius × radius.

VOUSSOIR See *arch brick.*

W

WAINSCOT *1.* Wood panelling used to line interior walls, often made up of panels set into frames. *2.* A superior grade of close-grained oak.

WAISTCOAT See *vest.*

WALLBOARD TUBES Hollow cardboard tubes of assorted diameters in lengths up to 10 feet. The heavy, multi-layered cardboard walls of the tubes keep them rigid.

WALL FURNITURE Architectural furniture, cabinets, cupboards, hanging or shelving devices which are built as stationary units and thus an integral part of the interior architecture of an area or room. Permanent fixture installation.

WALLPAPER Printed, screened, embossed or textured paper which is used to line or decorate interior walls. Usually sold by the roll, but printed and packaged as "doubles" or "triples." An average roll of paper will cover about 36 square-feet of surface, depending upon the scale of the design, the "repeat" and the "match." See *domino paper, flocked paper* and *roll (of wallpaper).*

WALL POLE A vertical rod or tube kept rigid and upright by means of horizontal attachments which secure into a wall, column or partition. See *outriggers.*

WALL THICKNESS The actual measurement or gauge of the solid part of a hollow tube or rod.

WALL UNITS, WALL SYSTEMS Any device or system that is bolted, screwed or fastened into a vertical supporting surface and does not depend upon legs or a base for support. A wall-hung unit or system. See *garcy* and *standards.*

WALL WASHING Bathing the walls with light, usually from an overhead source. It creates the illusion of a brighter floor or sales area.

WALNUT A light brown wood with a wide range of grains, depending upon how it is cut or sliced.

WALNUT (OILED) Walnut wood or veneer treated with a linseed oil finish rather than varnish or shellac. The wood takes on a low satin finish and the grain is accentuated. This oiled finish is usually more resistant to heat, alcohol and stains. Used in woodworking and furniture design.

WAREHOUSE A storage area for merchandise, sometimes remote from the store. It may be part of a merchandising set-up and the selling space may be in the warehouse (discount operation). Usually it is especially built to make the transport of merchandise simple and fast, made to withstand heavy floor loads, fireproof, and secure from pilferage and the elements.

WARM COLORS Yellow, orange, red-orange, red, and red-violet. The colors that psychologically and emotionally suggest warmth and heat. Also see *cool colors.*

WARM DELUXE MERCURY LAMP A color corrected and improved mercury lamp with a warm, pleasant color similar to that of the incandescent lamp. See *mercury vapor lamp.*

WARP *1.* To twist or turn out of shape. The arc or "bend out" of a flat plane. *2.* The lengthwise threads in a weave.

WASH *1.* The indirect or soft lighting of an area. *2.* A light coating with paint or dye.

WASH DRAWING A drawing in which tones and shades are built up by successive layers of superimposed monochromatic washes. These renderings are usually built up in gray or sepia washes and sometimes ink is added to outline or "snap-up" the drawing. In illustrations and advertisements, the drawings may be combined with crayon, spatter or may be airbrushed for halftones. See *line drawing.*

WASHER A small, flat, perforated disk of metal, leather, rubber or plastic, in assorted sizes and thicknesses. It is generally placed under a nut or screw, or at an axle bearing or joint to act as a cushion and to relieve friction; also may be used as a "build-up" where two surfaces do not make a close fit.

WASP WAIST The narrow, cinched-in waistline which accentuates the bust

and hips. The "hourglass silhouette" of the turn of the century.

WATER-BASE PAINTS Paints which are thinned or made more soluble by the addition of water such as Casein or Latex paints.

WATERCOLOR A painting technique in which the pigment is compressed and contained in water-soluble gums. A light, transparent stain is produced when the watercolor paint is moistened with water. Tones and gradations are accomplished by the addition of washes over the original layer. See *wash drawing.*

WATERFALL An arm that is fixed perpendicular to a wall, column, fixture or any supporting upright surface, and is used to present a face out selection of merchandise in a stepped down, back to front alignment. Usually, the waterfall arm makes it possible to remove one or more garments from the ordered arrangement and to restock the arm easily. Most waterfalls are equipped with hooks, notches, knobs or stepping devices to make for an orderly effect. In specific designs, the waterfall may make a right-angled turn before the descending presentation to accommodate spatial requirements, but not loose the front on or face-out viewing of the merchandise.

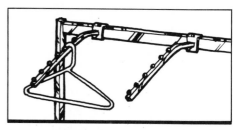

WATER TABLE A ledge constructed near the base of a foundation of a building, raised or angled to divert the rain water and melting snow away from the foundation. An asset in keeping foundations dry.

WATT A unit of electric power, approximately 748 watts to equal one horsepower. Watts = volts × amperes.

W.A.V.M. Western Association of Visual Merchandising.

WEATHER BOARDING An exterior wall surfacing treatment of horizontal wood boards overlapping one another—like closed Venetian blinds. The same technique can be used for decorative effects on interior walls. See *clapboard.*

WEATHERING *1.* The sloping surface on a buttress, cornice, roof, etc., to help shed or throw off the rain and snow. *2.* The aging such as cracks, splits, bleaching, fading and patinas, of exterior building materials due to the effects of rain, snow, cold, heat, sun, etc.

WEAVE The interlacing of warp (lengthwise) threads with filling (horizontal) threads to produce a fabric. Assorted patterns and textures can be produced depending upon the yarns used, the type of loom used, and the pattern of filling threads crossing the warp threads.

WEB OFFSET An important development in lithographic reproduction which makes for greater speed in printing (over 1000 feet of printing per minute). The web offset press can produce single or multicolor work for small or medium runs of newspapers, books, decorative papers, business forms and catalogues. See *offset lithography.*

WEDGE SHOES A platform shoe where the heel is made continuous with the sole and is available in a variety of heights.

WEDGIES See *wedge shoes.*

WELDING The act of joining two pieces of metal; sometimes by hammering and applying pressure or by applying heat along the area of contact with the use of solder. In most welding processes, the metals are melted at the points that are to be joined and an additional molten metal (the solder) is added as the filler and joiner. The Argon Arc method of welding is used on stainless steel, aluminum, magnesium, and titanium. The use of argon prevents the slag from forming at the welding junction and speeds up the welding process. Other welding techniques are: electric arc, oxyhydrogen, oxyacetylene and the Thompson processes, in which the pieces that are to be joined are "melted" by the resistance to an electric current passing through them.

WELDWOOD FLEXWOOD Trademark for a wide selection of wood veneers available bonded onto a strong cloth backing. Used as wall coverings. It is possible to go around curves and conform to angles with this type of veneering.

WELTING An edging produced by covering cord with bias strips of fabric. Used as a reinforcing edging on upholstery or slipcovers. It can be decorative as well as functional.

WESKIT A waistcoat or vest.

WESTINGS The single, braided strand of mannequin wig "hair" made of man-made fibers. These westings are sewn or hand-tied into the wig cap, baked, shaped and set.

WHITE SALE A retailing term for sales promotions or for merchandising sheets, pillowcases, household linens and related items. What was once a "white" promotion is now multi-colored, patterned and signed by top designers.

WHITE SPACE A printing, graphics or design term for the area which is not occupied by the copy or the artwork.

WHOLESALE The purchasing of goods or merchandise in quantity from a manufacturer or importer, at a reduced price. See *retail price.*

WICKER Small, flexible and pliable reeds that can be woven and shaped into furniture and decorative devices. See *rattan.*

WIG FOUNDATION The "skull cap" or "bathing cap," to which the "hair" fibers of a mannequin's wig are attached. This foundation fits on the head of the mannequin, sets the wig correctly, and keeps it in place.

WIGGLE NAILS See *corrugated fasteners.*

WIGS The detachable hair pieces or head coverings for some mannequins. Usually made of man-made fibers that appear to be "life-like," but they can also be decorative "hair-dos" of twine, yarn, papier-mâché, tissue, spun glass, raffia, etc. Man-made fibers produce soft, natural-looking wigs, which are washable, heat-resistant and can be reset with hot rollers. Man-made fibers for wig production are produced under trademarks such as Cordalon, Cy-belle, Elura, Eurolyn, Kanehalon, Teviron and Toyahalon.

WILTON A multicolored and/or patterned, cut-pile floor covering produced on a Wilton loom.

WIND A woodworking term for the longitudinal twist in a board or piece of lumber.

WINDBREAKER Trademark for a short, nylon jacket with zippered front opening and elastic cuffs and waistband.

WINDER The tapered or pie-shaped step used in spiral or screw staircases. Eliminates the need for a landing platform as the staircase changes direction.

WINDING STAIRCASE See *screw stair* and *spiral staircase.*

WINDOW LEFT, WINDOW RIGHT See *left window* and *right window.*

WINDOW SCHEDULE A timetable for the advance planning on the in-and-out of window displays. Information includes which window will be put in, when, with what type of merchandise, for how long the display will remain, and when it will be removed as well as what is planned to replace it.

WING A flat, flap or single panel, usually framed, used as part of a display window's decor or as a mask, valance or part of a proscenium. Sometimes the wing is used to add depth to the window setting or to separate one window grouping from the next grouping. See *tormentor* and *valance.*

WINGED NUT See *butterfly nut.*

WING PIN A T-shaped pin used in pinning and draping garments and fabrics as well as attaching or joining papers. The "T" head makes the pin easier to grasp, push or pull out.

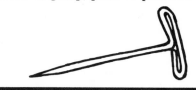

WIRE NAIL A metal fastener, circular in cross section and not tapered at the end. Available in assorted sizes and shapes, with or without heads. Generally used for indoor projects.

WOMEN'S SIZES A retailing term for dress or suit sizes 34 to 46. For the fuller, heavier woman with fuller and lower breasts, larger diaphragm and abdomen, and with the hips smaller in proportion to the rest of the body.

WOMEN'S STOUT SIZES A retailing term for dress or suit sizes 48 to 52. Heavier than Women's Sizes.

WOODCUT A printing technique; a graphic end result of the technique. The design is carved into and below the surface of a block of wood (or linoleum). When the plate or block is inked, the plane surface will print onto the paper or fabric which is pressed against it—the gouged out areas will not print. This technique was used on the earliest wallpapers.

WOOD ENGRAVING See *woodcut.*

WOODEN JOINTED ARM An articulated wooden or plastic manne-

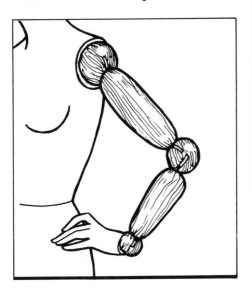

quin arm, which fits into the standard mannequin shoulder fitting and is designed to accept a realistic hand. Under a shirt, jacket or coat, the jointed arm can be positioned into a variety of realistic poses and only the flesh-colored hand is visible. A pocket or paddle hand can also be used with this re-positionable arm. See *pocket hand.*

WOOL The natural fiber produced from the fleece of sheep as well as similar fibers of goats.

WORKED LUMBER Lumber which has been shaped into moldings of assorted shapes, profiles and sizes.

WORKING DRAWING A detailed, scaled and clearly defined drawing with all the specifics and points of clarification included. A drawing or layout ready for reproduction. See *comprehensive.* Opposite of rough or croquis.

WORKING PROOF A trial print or strike-off of a design with the corrections, changes and additions included.

WORMY CHESTNUT A pitted, scarred and irregularly textured, light brown wood which simulates a "blighted" wood. Decorative and "Provincial," but not too sturdy for construction work.

WORSTED A woolen fabric produced from sturdy, compact yarns which have been combed as well as carded. Worsted fabrics are sturdier and wear better than woolen fabrics.

WOVEN BAMBOO Blinds or panels made from the outer skin of bamboo, generally prepared in 3' × 6' modules. Used to create a tropic look.

WRAP, WRAPAROUND Garment that closes by overlapping one side of the garment over the other and securing with a belt, tie, sash, etc.

WRAP DESK, WRAP COUNTER A table surface that is high enough, wide enough and long enough to accommodate the wrapping and packaging of merchandise. Ideally, there should be storage space behind, above or underneath the wrap surface for tissue, bags, boxes, ribbons, ties, etc. Sometimes the wrap desk will also accommodate a cash register or drawer and serve as a cash desk as well.

WRAPPER A loose robe or dressing gown. An informal house dress.

WROUGHT IRON Iron which has been worked, bent, twisted and formed. Iron contains a low percentage of carbon and is malleable (can be drawn out and extended by beating, or under pressure). The material lends itself to decorative units such as scrollwork, ornate brackets, twisted stands, furniture and fixtures. Often finished in matte black or painted a color. See *verdigris*.

X

X-RACK Two vertical X-shaped sides joined together by connecting hang rods through the upper and lower arms as well as through the midpoints of the "X" for additional rigidity. A double-sided hang rack which is sometimes made with adjustable hang rods.

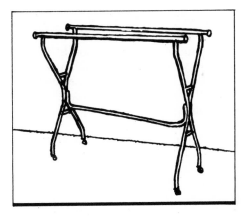

Y

YANKEE SCREWDRIVER See *ratchet screwdriver.*

Y-MERCHANDISER, Y-FIXTURE
Many types of fixturings racks based on three fins or merchandising surfaces, equidistant and radiating out from a central core or upright. A "Y" in plan view. Three arms or hang rods splayed out from a central point.

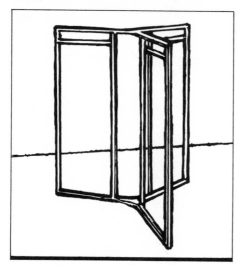

YOUNG JUNIOR (TEEN) SIZES A retailing term for sizes 3, 5, 7, 9, 11, and 13. The age group for girls from 13 to 16 years old. The waistlines are defined, hips are developed and the busts are high and rounded. The department that caters to this size group is often called "Young Junior," "Miss Junior," Junior Deb," etc.

YOUTH MARKET The market for those under twenty-five with an interest in trendy, different and new ideas.

YUCCA POLES The long, thin natural wood trunks of the yucca plant which grows in the southwestern part of the United States. Similar in appearance to a bamboo pole. Used as display standard.

Z

Z-CLIP A shelf bracket resembling the letter "Z" with two right angles and an additional lip at one of the horizontal ends. The lip hooks over a square tube or member with the remaining bracket extending out at a right angle to the vertical plane of the tube. Used to receive and support a shelf or horizontal member.

ZIP-A-TONE See *dry transfer*.

ZONE & CLUSTER PLAN The sales floor is subdivided into large areas or zones of associated merchandise groups, separated by partitions or divider fixtures. Each zone houses coordinated or related merchandise which is stocked and displayed on clusters of movable, flexible and adaptable fixtures. The cluster or grouping of fixtures serves to delineate the individual departments in the particular zone.

ZONING The legal restraints or controls on what may or may not be built, and where and by whom. The limits set on heights, widths, depths, uses, the number of people a structure can safely accommodate, the products, trades or types of businesses that can be conducted in a particular structure or area, etc. See *code*.

ZORI The Japanese shoe made of felt, straw or wood, similar to a sandal.

Z-RACK In plan view this merchandiser is similar to a three-part screen with two parallel elements connected by a single perpendicular plane. In actual floor appearance, the parallel vertical elements may be panels, legs, or structural elements of wood, metal or plastic, and the connecting rod between the two is the hang rail. Depending upon the construction, intended use and the decorative elements involved, the hang rail may or may not be adjustable. The basic "Z" construction also lends itself to other uses such as outposts, free-standing displayers with mannequin platforms, and dividers.

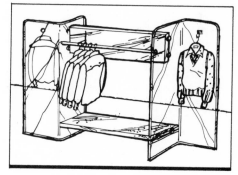

Appendix

THE HISTORICAL FRENCH PERIODS

PERIOD	INTERIOR ARCHITECTURE	FURNITURE	DECORATIVE MOTIFS	FABRICS, COLORS & WOODS	ARTISTS & ARTISANS
The Baroque Period/ Louis XIV (1643–1700)	Height of French Renaissance	Massive thrones	Classical architectural orders	Heavy tapestries, velvets and damasks	Le Brun
	Grand, dramatic and sweeping halls	High, cane-back chairs	Historical and allegorical scenes	Large scaled patterns	Bernini
	Symmetry and balance	Square backs and seats with heavy, square or tapered legs enriched with carving	Sun with spreading rays	Deep rich colors	J. Berain
	Marble, mirror and multipaned glass windows	Squat C-scroll legs (introduced at end of period)	Apollo	Oak	Lefevre
	Period of Versailles, the Louvre, St. Germain and Fontainebleau palaces with enormous rooms and furniture	Marble-topped tables and commodes	"Le Roi Soleil"	Walnut	P. Caffieri
	Compass curves relieve straight lines of woodworked walls (boiseries)	Bureau plats	Lions, rams, stags	Ebony	Coysevox
	Gobelins artwork and rugs	Monumental beds with massive draperies and testers	Weapons and symbols of war	Dark-finished wood	Moliere
		Heavily carved stretchers between legs and ornate chests	Chinoiserie	Marquetry and inlay	Racine
			Entwined "L's"	Carving and gilding	Corneille
			Boulle work (an inlay of pewter, brass and tortoise shell)		Lulli
Transitional/ Regence (1700–1730)	Softening and lightening up of Baroque Period	Bombe commode becomes more curvilinear	Foliage and ribbon ornaments	Similar to Baroque period, but softer, more muted and gentler	A. Watteau
	More curves	Squat cabriole legs replace squared and tapered legs	Ormolu and bronze d'ore trim on furniture	Mahogany	C. Gillot
	Lower ceilings	More curves in chair backs and seats (a forerunner of the Rococo period)	Chutes and sabots	Rosewood veneers	C. Audran
	Smaller scale to interiors and furnishings			Walnut	Oppenord
				Oak	H. Mansart
					Chas. Cressant

PERIOD	INTERIOR ARCHITECTURE	FURNITURE	DECORATIVE MOTIFS	FABRICS, COLORS & WOODS	ARTISTS & ARTISANS
Rococo/ Louis XV (1730–1760)	Soft, feminine, frivolous attitude	Ornate and flamboyant carving	Rocks and cockle shells	Moiré	F. Boucher
	Asymmetrical and curvilinear	Lacquerwork	Chinoiserie	Striped taffetas	Meissonier
	Style of Mme du Barry and Mme Pompadour	Elongated, S-curved cabriole legs	Bean and lozenge shapes	Small allover patterns	Rousseau
		Light chairs with cartouche-shaped backs	Cartouches and oval frames	Toile de Juoy	Voltaire
	Age of the Boudoir and the Salon	Canapes (love seats)	Garlands of fruit and flowers	Needlepoint	
	Rich, ornate and gilded boiserie	Poudreuse (powder tables)	Doves	Light, soft pastels—rose pink, chalky blue, muted celadon green, lilac, lemon, gray	
	Scale is charming and comfortable	Chiffonieres (multidrawer commodes)	Cupids		
	Parquet floors		Musical instruments	Mahogany	
	Soft Aubusson and Savonniere rugs	Kidney- and crescent-shaped tables and desks	Gardening supplies	Fruitwoods	
	Chinese porcelains		Monkeys at play (singerie)	Satinwood	
	Mirrors and painted scenes in curved and gilded frames	Chaise lounge	Exotic scenes, settings and people	Marquetry in a wide selection of colored woods	
		Twin beds are introduced		Lacquered and painted woods	
		Bolster roll is popularized			
		Lighter drapery treatment on beds			
		Serpentine front servers and commodes			
		Human-size, movable and comfortable			

PERIOD	INTERIOR ARCHITECTURE	FURNITURE	DECORATIVE MOTIFS	FABRICS, COLORS & WOODS	ARTISTS & ARTISANS
Neo-Classic/ Louis XVI (1760–1789)	Petit Trianon (designed by Gabriel) Return to reason, symmetry and simplicity with emphasis on Pompeiian painting and decoration Simple, straight-lined boiseries with key corners and rosette fillers Grisaille paintings over doors and mantles Stucco arabesques and bas relief classic figures and garlands painted in contrast to background such as Wedgewood plaques Wedgewood plaques Wall panels are filled with fabric, wallpaper or Pompeiian-painted designs. Oak parquet floors Aubusson, Savonniere or Oriental rugs	Straight and fluted legs similar to miniature Ionic columns Oval and straight back small chairs Bergeres, fauteuils and straw-seated chairs Many styles of small beds Lit à polonaise, lit d'ange also Imperial, Turkish and Chinese styles Rectangular case furniture enriched with metal moldings surrounding broken or segmented panels Macaroon or rosette motifs appear in the cut-off or cut-out corners of the panels and in a square above the column-like legs on chairs and tables	Pompeii revisited Greek and Roman classic motifs: columns, volutes, masques, cadeusus, acanthus leaf, garlands, animal heads, bows and arrows, pomegranates Marie Antoinette roses Ribbons and lover's knots shaped into chair backs and frames Cupids Doves Montgolfier's balloon		Fragonard Houdon Clodion H. Robert Boucher Reisiner Roentgen Rousseau Huet Fay

PERIOD	INTERIOR ARCHITECTURE	FURNITURE	DECORATIVE MOTIFS	FABRICS, COLORS & WOODS	ARTISTS & ARTISANS
Directoire/ The French Revolution (1789–1800)	Classic look of Louis XVI continues only devoid of the delicate, the pretty and the romantic Simple, stark, more virile version with red, white and blue as the major color scheme	The simplified version of Louis XVI Salute to Napoleon's successful campaigns Bent- and wrought-iron and bronze furniture Campaign and portable furniture Camp beds Collapsible tables, chairs and stools Tripod tables	Symbols of liberty: spears, oak boughs, clasped hands, Liberty caps, triumphal arches, cockades, drums, pikes Stars and symbols of war and victory	Toiles with scenes of Revolution and victory dark, vibrant reds and blues with a field of white	

PERIOD	INTERIOR ARCHITECTURE	FURNITURE	DECORATIVE MOTIFS	FABRICS, COLORS & WOODS	ARTISTS & ARTISANS
Empire/ Napoleonic (1800–1830)	Armed camp tent	Beginning of mass-produced furniture and accessories	"N"	Leather	
	Antique Roman hall		Bee	Velvet	
	Symmetrical	New style created by Percier et Fontaine for Napoleon	Victory wreaths	Damask	
	Heroic		Fasces	Rich, deep colors such as wine, purple, royal blue, emerald green	
	Virile	Return of the klismos and Greek, Roman and Egyptian styles and motifs	Rosettes		
	Severely decorated and ornamented with the emphasis on the vertical: columns, pilasters, niches, arches		Anthemions	Woods include ebony, rosewood, mahogany enhanced with bronze moldings and appliqués	
			Antefixes		
		Massive bookcases and cabinets	Classic Egyptian and Roman motifs		
	Empire draperies cover walls or draped over ceilings to create tents	Round tables			
		Throne-like chairs			
	Marble floors	Arms of sofas and chairs resemble swan's necks and heads, lion's head with paw below, winged sphinx, gargoyle			
	Raised platforms (for beds and thrones)				
	Walls painted in soft gray, gray-blue, gray-green and highlighted with white and gold	Heavy beds with both ends even and equipped with bolsters			
		Boat bed			
		Case goods with large veneered areas, metal moldings, bronze appliqués			

THE HISTORICAL ENGLISH PERIODS

PERIOD	INTERIOR ARCHITECTURE	FURNITURE	DECORATIVE MOTIFS	FABRICS, COLORS & WOODS	ARTISTS & ARTISANS
Tudor/ Age of Oak (1500–1558)	Period of Henry VIII—Transitional—Gothic to Renaissance	Mixture of Gothic and Italian Renaissance forms	Linenfold and diamond designs	Vigorous and somber, masculine-oriented damasks	
	Perpendicular Gothic blended with Norman castellated motifs	Serviceable rather than comfortable pieces	Arcaded panels	Tooled leather	
		Chests	Arabesques	Heavy velvets	
	Spacious and dignified	Cupboards	Italian Renaissance forms	Deep, dark colors	
		Wardrobes	Caryatids	Oak	
	Tudor arches frame doors, windows and fireplace openings	Dressers	Therms		
		Settles	Crudely carved classic columns		
	Bay and oriel windows filled with small diamond-shaped pieces of glass	Stiff and square chairs			
		Stools			
		Massive and heavily draped tester beds			
	Half-timber houses with rough plaster walls banded and broken with visible wooden beams and posts				
	More elegant homes have wood-panelled walls; wainscoting in small oak panels, sometimes carved with linenfold or diamond designs				
	Floors are covered with slate, stone, rush or wood planking				

PERIOD	INTERIOR ARCHITECTURE	FURNITURE	DECORATIVE MOTIFS	FABRICS, COLORS & WOODS	ARTISTS & ARTISANS
Elizabethan/ Age of Oak (1558–1603)	Strong influence of Spanish and Italian Renaissance designs	Wainscot chairs with heavy triangular seats and short, thick, turned legs	Bulbous forms	Palampores (Indian-painted cotton)	Wm. Shakespeare
	Architectural orders of the Renaissance pilasters, columns, entablatures	Trestle and Rectory tables with massive-turned legs	Melon turnings with gadroon edgings and acanthus leaves	Crewel embroidery	Christopher Marlow
	In smaller rooms—often wood paneling from the baseboard to the ceiling where paneling is topped with a classic-carved cornice molding	Drop-leaf or gate-legged tables	Crudely sculpted Ionic and Doric columns	Silks	Sir Francis Bacon
		Heavy, four-poster beds with wide wooded tester tops	Strapwork and arabesques	Velvets	
	In state rooms—often a 3′ oak dado or pedestal topped with wood molding and an enriched entablature	Tridarn, Welsh dresser and buffet and credence from France appear in dining halls	Geometric interlacings	Mortlake tapestries	
			Split spindle decor on chests	Deep reds, browns, yellows (ochres) and greens	
	In some large areas exposed carved beams either in triangular wood truss forms or a hammerbeam truss construction	Hutches, settles, box settles, chests and coffers of various sizes and with degrees of sculptured enrichment	Grotesques rising up from scrolls and leaves are used as caryatids and fireplace mantel supports	Oak	
	Plasterwork ceilings introduced at end of this Period, sometimes simulating wood beam with applied moldings	Furniture decorated with "trompe l'oeil" ("nonsuch" furniture)	Small mirrors and "nonsuch" marquetry		
		Wrought iron, brass, pewter and silver lanterns (chandeliers)	Romayne work (carved medallions or heads) used as knobs on furniture or to add relief to panels		

(continued)

PERIOD	INTERIOR ARCHITECTURE	FURNITURE	DECORATIVE MOTIFS	FABRICS, COLORS & WOODS	ARTISTS & ARTISANS
Elizabethan/ Age of Oak (1558–1603) (continued)	Some ceilings have a geometric allover pattern of Tudor roses, scrolls, cartouches or elaborate interlacing designs called Pargework Fireplaces become even more dominant as are stairways, which are often enhanced with carved balustrades and newelposts Main level floors are covered with slate, flagstone or rush Upper level floors are covered with random width oak planks	Oriental ornaments and porcelains			

PERIOD	INTERIOR ARCHITECTURE	FURNITURE	DECORATIVE MOTIFS	FABRICS, COLORS & WOODS	ARTISTS & ARTISANS
Jacobean/ The English Palladian Period of Inigo Jones (1603–1649)	Similar to Elizabethan interior but with a greater refinement in the use of Italian Renaissance motifs	Larger panels on case furniture with molding strips outlining diamond, hexagonal or double-rectangular shapes	Similar to Elizabethan Period with more sophisticated use and reproduction of Palladian Renaissance motifs	Similar to Elizabethan Period	Inigo Jones John Milton John Donne Robert Herrick
	Style and talent of Inigo Jones dominates	Supports resemble dwarf columns with fluted or spiraling shafts			
	Panels are enlarged	Twisted rope turnings			
	More geometric forms	Upholstered seats are added to the wainscot or wood-paneled back chairs			
	Broken corners on rectangles	In smaller rooms—Yorkshire and Derbyshire chairs			
	Hexagon				
	Arches are introduced as a softening element in the tradition of the Italian designer, Palladio	Heroic four-poster beds with architectural capital supports wooden testers, which resemble classic entablatures			
	Rich plasterwork ceilings	Long velvet draperies envelop beds			
		Small tables for service of tea, coffee or chocolate			

PERIOD	INTERIOR ARCHITECTURE	FURNITURE	DECORATIVE MOTIFS	FABRICS, COLORS & WOODS	ARTISTS & ARTISANS
Restoration/ Stuart or Carolean (1660–1689)	Influx of French and Flemish taste Charles II imitates French court of Louis XIV Under James 11, 400 French Huguenot craftsmen enter in English interior design Great Fire of 1666 in London creates new opportunities for new and different architecture and decoration Wood-paneled interiors are still popular in oak and walnut often with projecting surfaces Grinling Gibbons-type relief sculpture appears as "trophies" on panels, over mantels, around frames on walls, windows and doors Molding strips are often gilded	Comfortable Spiral turnings are favored for legs and trimmings Flemish "S" and "C" scrolls used for supports, arm stumps, stretchers, aprons and crestlings Chairs often have slanted backs with cane inserts and seats to match Loose pillow seats are added Wing chair is introduced Elaborate backless benches and stools Bookcases, gaming tables and small tables are trimmed with marquetry or Japanese lacquerwork Daybeds (similar to chaise lounge) become popular	All Gothic influence is gone Height of Renaissance designs Grinling Gibbons, the master sculptor, carves trophy panels filled with hunted animals, weapons, musical instruments, ribbons and swags of entwined fruits and leaves Restored Crown appears on furniture often flanked with cherubs Romayne work is abundant In many ways, similar to the decorative devices of Louis XIV of France	Elaborate upholstery fabrics Plain, tooled and gilded leather Heavy fringe and tassels plus prominent nailheads or studs used to finish upholstered pieces Strong and brilliant colors Walnut is favored wood Woods are highly polished or painted to simulate marble (faux marble) Cheaper woods are painted to resemble walnut or olive wood Velvet or tapestries are sometimes used to cover the plaster walls between the wooden uprights (stiles)	

PERIOD	INTERIOR ARCHITECTURE	FURNITURE	DECORATIVE MOTIFS	FABRICS, COLORS & WOODS	ARTISTS & ARTISANS
William & Mary / The Dutch Influence (1689–1702)	Simpler, more architectural designs In smaller rooms, the ceilings may be unadorned, but in larger areas there may be full, ornamented plaster moldings with painted decorations added Often plaster decorations will imitate Grinling Gibbons' swags and festoons Fireplace becomes a complete architectural unit Dwarfed columns used to support the mantel, which is an architrave, frieze and projecting cornice Marble is used often inlaid with colored marbles Built-in arched niches are designed to house Chinese decoratives and books Rooms are "human sized," more intimate and livable	Veneering becomes more important Straight legs return to favor—square or tapered Highboy is introduced Cabinets, writing tables, dressing tables, bureau mirrors and clocks are in demand Chair stretchers are flat or serpentine and often inlaid Open cabinets are hooded Heavily engraved and/or carved silver furniture is a fad Generally the furniture is lighter, more slender and graceful, highly polished; upholstery appears more frequently	Seaweed marquetry Japanese and Chinese lacquerwork Chinese porcelains and bric-a-brac Pendant catkins carved on chairs and stretchers Grinling Gibbons' trophy panels, swags and festoons Bun feet and mushroom feet appear at the ends of bell or inverted cup turnings of tables, tall chests and state chairs Units are sometimes trimmed with a shell motif on top or crowned with triangular or broken pediment	Velvets Brocades Brocatelles Damasks Crewel embroideries and needlepoint Chintz is introduced for curtain and bed draperies Warm and subdued colors Walnut and mahogany are the major woods used in furniture construction, but pear, lime and sycamore are also used Walls are treated with knotty pine paneling or wallpapers: flocked, Domino (marblelized), paper tapestries (murals)	Grinling Gibbons Daniel Marot, French emigrant designer Samuel Pepys John Dryden

PERIOD	INTERIOR ARCHITECTURE	FURNITURE	DECORATIVE MOTIFS	FABRICS, COLORS & WOODS	ARTISTS & ARTISANS
Queen Anne (1702–1714)	The England of "Good Queen Anne," pious and devout	Curved lines predominate and Chinese motifs appear	Scallop shell appears on cabriole knee	Similar to previous Periods	Sir Christopher Wren, architect
	Foreign influences are "English-ized"	Cabriole leg is foremost choice with knee and ankle carved decorations	Chinese influence in the inturned scrolls at the ends of top rails of wooden chair backs	Mahogany becomes even more popular	William Kent, architect-designer
	Similar to William and Mary	Leg ends in a clubfoot or padfoot	Acanthus leaves adorn splats		Grinling Gibbons
	Mantels are lowered	Sofas and settees with two, three and four chair backs are in fashion	Cross-banding trim on drawers, aprons and case goods panels		Daniel Defoe, writer
	Woodwork is often finished in white	Tilt-top, piecrust and gallerytop small tables appear	Claw and ball foot, Dutch web foot and hoof or paw foot used as support endings		Addison & Steele, writers
	Chinese influence is very strong especially of decoratives and novelties	Tallboys and cardtables introduced	Chair backs are slightly concave at the shoulderline (spoonbacked)		
	Wallpapers are in demand—flockings in damask patterns and murals	Loveseats	Splat (central upright in the chair back) is carved, pierced or silhouetted		
		China closets for side walls or to fit corners and show prized Chinese collections	Seat front and sides are rounded (bell seated)		
		Double chest of drawers			
		Case goods are often designed with double doors finished with a single panel with broken curves on top			

PERIOD	INTERIOR ARCHITECTURE	FURNITURE	DECORATIVE MOTIFS	FABRICS, COLORS & WOODS	ARTISTS & ARTISANS
Early Georgian (1714–1750)	Queen Anne style continues, but with more refinement	Similar to Queen Anne	Carved scrolls	Age of Mahogany	Christopher Wren
	Designs by William Kent show strong Venetian influences and classical details	Mahogany and gilt	Swags of leaves and fruit		William Kent
	Batty Langley, the designer, emphasizes cyma curves for moldings around doors and drawers; also responsible for the later Gothic Revival	More ornate and heavier carved chair rails (yokes) and splats	Eagle heads ending in volutes		Batty Langley
		Windsor chair is a new and light favorite	Lion masks and lion's paws		Thomas Chippendale II
		Wing chairs, commodes, wardrobes	Satyr masks		Abraham Swan
		Thomas Chippendale II (the famous Chippendale) designs in the Queen Anne style with more attention to the intricate carving and the finish	Acanthus leaves and classical elements: pilasters, colonettes		James Gibbs
		Chippendale produces Georgian-styled settees, cupboards, bureaus, dressing tables, secretaries, bookcases and clock cases	Broken, triangular and swan's necks pediments		William Hogarth
		Chippendale uses mahogany with gilt trim and some lacquerwork	Gilt-gesso ornament		Addison & Steele
			Ogee and bracket feet on low case goods		Daniel Defoe
			Around 1735, Chippendale becomes more involved in the French Rococo Style; curleyques, scrolls, twisting foliate, "ribband backs," bombe commodes, French beds, ornate testers, mirrors, mantels and window cornices		Jonathan Swift

PERIOD	HIGHLIGHTS	ARTISTS & ARTISANS
Middle Georgian (1750–1770)	THOMAS CHIPPENDALE II/CHINESE AND GOTHIC STYLES: C. 1750 Chippendale turns to the Chinese Style; straight Marlborough legs and clustered bamboo legs appear on chairs, tables and tall case goods	Horace Walpole Joshua Reynolds Thomas Gainsborough Oliver Goldsmith Samuel Johnson James Boswell Richard Wilson Pergolese, Zucchi and Angelica Kauffman worked on Adam designs as did Josiah Wedgewood
	Tracery and latticework make up the wooded chair backs and doors on cabinets, secretaries and bookcases; panda-like roofs replace the classic pediments on top of cabinets and curio pieces	
	Chinoiserie figures appear on exotic and fanciful frames and over mantels	
	C. 1760 Chippendale enters his Gothic Period; The Gothic Revival; straight and pierced squarish legs, pierced latticework reminiscent of perpendicular Gothic tracery	
	Monumental and very architectural cabinets, secretaries and bookcases	
	THE ADAM BROTHERS/INTRODUCTION OF THE NEO-CLASSIC PERIOD (c. 1762–1792):	
	The Adam Brothers (Robert, James, John, William) architects and designers are greatly influenced by the finds at Pompeii and Herculaneum	
	Responsible for furniture and decorations of many buildings of this period	
	Most interiors are very formal and often domes and classic entablatures are used with or without pilasters or columns	
	Rooms are often semi-circular, segmented or octagonal in plan	
	Cut-out niches in walls are filled with Greek or Roman statues or urns	
	Walls are sometimes painted soft gray or light blue with woodwork and details picked out in white like the classic Wedgewood designs they inspired	
	Walls may also be painted with Pompeiian-like designs	
	Furniture designs tended toward a light and elegant look, not unlike the Louis XVI style of France	
	Console table, demilune commode and various uses of the classic urns were the notable contribution of the Adam brothers as well as a wealth of decorative motifs	
	Hepplewhite and Sheraton designed and produced furniture from Adam specifications	
	Among the many Pompeiian motifs that appear in their interiors and on their furniture designs: oval paterae, rosettes, radiating patterns, urns, ram's heads with garlands and festoons entwined through the horns, pearls in swags, honeysuckle and husks in catenary arches.	

(continued)

PERIOD	HIGHLIGHTS	ARTISTS & ARTISANS
Middle Georgian (1750–1770) (continued)	Painters of the period ornamented the Adam style with amorini, sphinxes and arabesques	
	Gesso composition (anaglypta) and Wedgewood plaques are used to decorate rooms and case goods	
	Many Adam furniture designs are executed in satinwood with marquetry and inlay panels	
	Hardwood is also in use	
	George Hepplewhite is the great "chair" designer in the Adam style. He produces fine, lightly scaled and elegant pieces. The legs are straight and slender and tapering down to the foot (spade, thimble or sabot). His major chair-back designs are: shields, camelbacks, hearts, ovals and wheels	
	Hepplewhite also designed and constructed many handsome consoles, sideboards, and four-poster beds with testers. Most are recognized by the serpentine line in the design and his recurring use of: wheat sheaves, oval paterae, radiating demilunes, ribbons, fluting, reeding, vases and urns, festoons, the three ostrich feather plumes of the Prince of Wales and grisaille paintings of classical figures; worked in satinwood	

PERIOD	HIGHLIGHTS	ARTISTS & ARTISANS
Late Georgian (1750–1770)	Adam Brothers continue as the dominant influence in interior design	Johann Zoffany
	THOMAS SHERATON, THE LAST OF THE GREAT 18th-CENTURY ENGLISH FURNITURE DESIGNERS:	Henry Holland
	Influenced by the Louis XVI style than by the Adam tradition	Joshua Reynolds
	Interiors were often paneled in "paper" with ornamental borders	Thomas Gainsborough
	Chinese wallpapers are especially popular	Joseph Turner
	Carpets are in general use	John Nash
	Persian and Turkish rugs are favored; some imitation "aubussons" are also seen	
	Early- and mid-period furniture is essentially elegant, lightly scaled, and graceful—often done in satinwood with inlays	
	Rear chair legs often continue up past the seat to become part of the side braces for the rectangular chair back	
	Between the ornamental top and mid rails, the space may be filled with one or more ornamented splats	
	Lyres, urns and spindles may also be used for chair-back enrichment	
	Designed twin beds (summer beds), Pembroke tables (drop-leaf tables), kidney-shaped desks and tables, and a variety of dual purpose and convertible furniture	
	He preferred the simple concave or convex arc between two straight corners to the serpentine line of Hepplewhite	
	His later work became bizarre: chair backs made of animal parts, saddle seats, heavily carved knees and curving legs. The squat, heavy pieces are akin to the French Empire Style	
	Sheraton motifs: rosettes, urns, festoons, pendant flowers, sunbursts, vases, inlay work with fine ebony lines between the pieces.	
	Motifs in later work: sphinxes and lions and massive Roman and Egyptian designs	

PERIOD	INTERIOR ARCHITECTURE	FURNITURE	DECORATIVE MOTIFS	FABRICS, COLORS & WOODS	ARTISTS & ARTISANS
English Regency (1811–1820) (continued)	George IV is the Regent Period is comparable to the French Empire (see chart)	Thomas Hope's book of furniture designs, *Household Furniture and Interior Decorations,* is the decorator's "bible" of the period	Brass inlay and applied moldings and ornaments on rather flat, veneered surfaces	Silks Chintz Printed calico "Merino Damask"	William Thackery Jane Austen Sir Walter Scott William Blake John Nash John Soanes Thomas Hope
	Thomas Hope and John Soanes are the major designers	Furniture is being produced by machine and craftsmanship is deteriorating	Antique Roman and Egyptian motifs: sphinx, winged lion, Egyptian head, bearded Bacchus, animal supports, stars, lyres, eagles, etc.	Geometric striped patterns Big, bold designs in strong colors	
	Interiors are less livable and more for show	Less carving and more emphasis on the pattern and color of the veneers		Rosewood and Zebrawood are especially selected for their striking patterns and rich color	
	Barrel-vaulted ceilings top the larger areas	Massive, throne-like chairs, Klismos chairs with scimitar-shaped front and back legs	Big, bold and "S" scrolled end pieces and round bolsters		
	Cut-out niches are filled with large statues, painted stucco walls are especially popular with Roman, Greek and Egyptian motifs reinterpreted	Sofa replaces settee in drawing room; sofa tables to stand in front of sofa		Mahogany "Bird's Eye" amboyna and maple are used for their unique patterns	
		"X"-shaped stools, ottomans			
	Chinese and Indian influences (appear in the Pavilion in Brighton and other stately homes	Work tables, large circular pedestal table. Long sectional dining tables, sideboards, dumbwaiters			
		Heavily curtained four-poster beds; tent or field beds			
		Architectural secretaries and cabinets			

THE HISTORIC AMERICAN PERIODS

PERIOD	HIGHLIGHTS
Early American (1608–1720)	In Virginia and New England: crude copies of the English Jacobean, Restoration and William and Mary styles
Georgian Period (1720–1790)	Good copies of "Queen Anne" produced in Newport and Williamsburgh. Early Chippendale and Sheraton designs are produced
Post Colonial or Federal (1790–1820)	Strong Adam Brothers influence; Hepplewhite and Sheraton designs are popular
Greek Revival (1820–1860)	English Regency and French Empire influence
	THE "AMERICAN EMPIRE" STYLE OF DUNCAN PHYFE:
	Phyfe is especially affected by Sheraton and the English Regency
	Works mainly in mahogany and satinwood
	Produces graceful and elegant side chairs often resembling Klismos chair
	Tables and pedestal supports and flaring legs
	The lyre is a special favorite and is used for chair backs, arm supports; pedestals
	Overstuffed "Grecian" sofas with cornicopia legs and scroll sides
	Uses swags, tassels, plumes, rosettes, vases, urns and bow knots for decoration
	Later work becomes heavy and clumsy